The German-Speaking World

'A delightful, interesting and novel addition to textbook materials available to teachers of German at university level. It has been written very much with the student in mind: the explanatory sections are pitched at a level which is easy to follow without being patronising, the subject matter is dealt with in a varied and interesting way, the tasks are stimulating and realistic.'

Charlotte Hoffmann, *Department of Modern Languages, University of Salford*

This accessible textbook offers students the opportunity to explore for themselves a wide range of sociolinguistic issues relating to the German language and its role in European societies. It is written for undergraduate students who have a sound practical knowledge of German but who have little or no knowledge of linguistics or sociolinguistics. It combines text with practical exercises and discussion questions to stimulate readers to think for themselves and to tackle specific problems.

In **Part one** Patrick Stevenson invites readers to investigate and reflect on issues concerning the status and function of the German language in relation to its speakers and to speakers of other languages with which it comes into contact. In **Part two** the focus shifts to the individual features of the language. This involves, for example, identifying regional speech forms, analysing similarities and differences between written and spoken German, and looking at the 'social meaning' underlying different forms of address. **Part three** explores the relationship between the German language and the nature of 'Germanness'. It concentrates on people's attitudes towards the language and the ways in which it is changing, and their views on what it represents for them.

Key features of this book:

* **Informative and comprehensive**: covers a wide range of current issues
* **Practical**: contains a variety of graded exercises and tasks plus an index of terms
* **Topical and contemporary**: deals with current situations and provides up-to-date information
* **Thought-provoking**: encourages students to reflect and research for themselves

Patrick Stevenson is a lecturer in German in the School of Modern Languages at the University of Southampton, where he teaches German sociolinguistics and German language. He is co-author (with Stephen Barbour) of *Variation in German* (1990), a critical study of German sociolinguistics, and editor of *The German Language and the Real World* (1995), a collection of essays on contemporary sociolinguistic issues by leading German and Austrian linguists.

Routledge Language in Society

The **Routledge Language in Society** series provides the basis for a typical one-semester course. It combines a review of current sociolinguistic themes and relevant reading with a range of practical tasks exploring particular topics, and a selection of readings illustrating the socio-political significance of language-related issues. The focus encourages students to engage directly with important linguistic issues in a variety of ways. The outcome of this process is that students have a greater knowledge of, and sensitivity to, sociolinguistic problems and are able to observe and explore these problems when they have the opportunity to experience them at first hand.

EXISTING TITLES:
The French-Speaking World
Rodney Ball, *School of Modern Languages, University of Southampton*

The German-Speaking World
Patrick Stevenson, *School of Modern Languages, University of Southampton*

The Spanish-Speaking World
Clare Mar-Molinero, *School of Modern Languages, University of Southampton*

LONDON AND NEW YORK

The German-Speaking World

A practical introduction to sociolinguistic issues

- Patrick Stevenson

ROUTLEDGE

First published 1997
by Routledge
11 New Fetter Lane, London EC4P 4EE

Simultaneously published in the USA and
Canada
by Routledge
29 West 35th Street, New York, NY 10001

© 1997 Patrick Stevenson

Typeset in Sabon, Futura, Times and Optima
by Keystroke, Jacaranda Lodge,
Wolverhampton
Printed and bound in Great Britain by
TJ International Ltd, Padstow, Cornwall

*British Library Cataloguing in Publication
Data*
A catalogue record for this book is available
from the British Library

*Library of Congress Cataloguing in
Publication Data*
Stevenson, Patrick.
The German-Speaking world:
a practical introduction to
sociolinguistic issues/Patrick Stevenson
(Routledge language in society; 2)
Includes bibliographical references
and index.
1. German language – Social aspects.
2. German language – Europe, German-
speaking.
3. German language – Dialects.
4. Sociolinguistics.
I. Title. II. Series.
PF3073.S773 1997
306.44′0917′531—dc21   96 13953

ISBN 0–415–12984–2 (hbk)
ISBN 0–415–12985–0 (pbk)

Contents

Part two

EXPLORING LINGUISTIC VARIATION

Part three

CURRENT ISSUES:
LANGUAGE AND 'GERMANNESS'

Illustrations

Tables

Figures

Maps

Acknowledgements

I would like to thank Stephen Barbour, Aidan Coveney, Charlotte Hoffmann and Sally Johnson for their helpful comments and constructive criticisms. I am also very grateful to Helmut Glück and Wolfgang Werner Sauer for providing me with a lot of useful material; to Guy Poos for his guidance on the Luxembourg legal system; and to Bill Brooks for his encouragement and support. Finally, I would like to record my thanks to my Southampton colleagues Rodney Ball and Clare Mar-Molinero, who have written the companion volumes on French and Spanish to launch this new series. We had many fruitful discussions, and their ideas and suggestions were invaluable to me.

Thanks are due to the following publishers and individuals for permission to use material (maps, cartoons, and extracts), the full sources of which are recorded either in the bibliography or where the items appear in the text:

Albrecht-Ludwigs-Universität Freiburg, ARD-News, Aufbau Taschenbuchverlag, BBC, *Bild der Wissenschaft*, Bibliographisches Institut & F. A. Brockhaus, Cambridge University Press, Deutscher Taschenbuchverlag, Dörnersche Verlagsbuchhandlung, Fischer Taschenbuchverlag, *Frankfurter Allgemeine Zeitung*, Edition Melodia Hans Gerig Bergisch Gladbach, Walter de Gruyter, *The Guardian*, Haffmans Verlag, Nymphenburger Verlagshandlung in der F. A. Herbig Verlagsbuchhandlung, Institut für deutsche Sprache, Ernst Klett Verlag, Peter Lang, Verlag J. B. Metzler, Multilingual Matters, Gunter Narr Verlag Tübingen, Nebelspalter-Verlag, Max Niemeyer Verlag, Oxford University Press, Hans-Joachim Paul, RTL Television, Sauerländer Verlag, *Der Spiegel*, Bernd Stein, *Süddeutsche Zeitung*, Suhrkamp Verlag, Buchverlag Ullstein Langen Müller, University of California Press, Verlag der Autoren, *Die Welt*, Universität C. Winter, Professor Dr Harald Weydt, *Die Zeit*.

All possible efforts have been made to obtain copyright approval for all material that has been reproduced here.

Introduction

T HE AIM OF THIS BOOK is to offer students the
opportunity to explore for themselves a wide range of
sociolinguistic issues in relation to the German language. It
is intended principally for undergraduate students of
German who have a reasonably advanced knowledge of the
language, but who may have little or no knowledge of
linguistics in general or sociolinguistics in particular. Relevant theoretical concepts are introduced where necessary,
but the emphasis throughout is on encouraging readers to
think for themselves and to tackle specific problems. To this
end, each chapter is punctuated with a series of practical
tasks and discussion questions designed to stimulate readers
to pursue in greater depth issues raised in the text, and
concludes with suggestions for further reading.

The book has been written with a typical semester-
length course in mind, and it could therefore be worked
through as the principal course text. However, although
there is a progression within each chapter and through the
three parts, it is hoped that the structure of the book is
sufficiently flexible to allow it to be used in various ways
to suit particular needs. For example, individual parts or
chapters could be selected to complement other material,

and students or tutors can decide for themselves which tasks to attempt. The tasks are graded in terms of difficulty and the time required to tackle them (see the description of 'How to use this book', p. xix).

Part one takes as its starting point the question of what we mean by 'the German-speaking world'. The three chapters in this first part of the book invite readers to investigate and reflect on fundamental 'macro-sociolinguistic' issues about the status and function of the German language in relation to its speakers and to speakers of other languages with which it comes into contact. The tasks include both small-scale activities, such as working on definitions of important concepts or interpreting data presented in the form of diagrams or figures, and more wide-ranging reflective exercises such as essays, projects or dissertations.

Part two aims to encourage readers to explore social and regional variation in German from a 'micro-sociolinguistic' perspective. In other words, the focus shifts from the role of the language as a whole to the forms and functions of individual features. This involves, for example, looking at ways of identifying distinctive features of regional speech forms, analysing similarities and differences between written and spoken German, investigating the 'social meaning' underlying different forms of address, and exploring the sociolinguistic implications of the gender system in German. There are many practical tasks and exercises involving the analysis of written texts and transcripts of speech, and there are opportunities to carry out small-scale 'empirical' work, such as conducting questionnaires or gathering material for analysis.

Part three returns to the key issue raised in Chapter 1, the relationship between the German language and the nature of 'Germanness', but this time from a different perspective. These final chapters focus on people's attitudes towards the language and the ways in which it is changing, and their views on what it represents for them. As the tasks here are mainly concerned with analysing and evaluating arguments, most of them are based on (sometimes quite lengthy) readings from primary texts, such as newspaper articles or chapters from books.

One final point: this book is not intended as an introduction to sociolinguistics as such. Where concepts and terminology are used that might be new to readers, they are either briefly explained or used as the basis of tasks requiring readers to find out for themselves what the terms mean. The key concepts are given in **bold** the first time they appear in the text, and they are listed in an 'Index of terms' at the end of the book to provide a quick source of reference and act as an *aide-mémoire*. However, the whole purpose of the book is to demonstrate that there are few, if any, hard and fast answers to sociolinguistic questions and to encourage readers to reach their own conclusions. Therefore, the index of terms does no more than list important concepts and offer a brief guide to the way these concepts are used in the book.

The suggestions for further reading at the end of each chapter are usually quite specific and are intended to direct readers to useful material on particular points. However, it might be useful to consult some or all of the following books, which provide a wealth of background reading, useful information and explanations of important points, both in general terms and specifically in relation to German.

Crystal, David . (1987) *The Cambridge Encyclopaedia of Language*, Cambridge: Cambridge University Press.
Crystal, David (1992) *An Encyclopaedic Dictionary of Language and Languages*, Oxford: Blackwell.
(These are excellent general reference books, which should provide answers to any questions on linguistic terminology and concepts used in the description and analysis of language.)

Holmes, Janet (1992) *An Introduction to Sociolinguistics*, London: Longman.
Wardhaugh, Ronald (1992) *An Introduction to Sociolinguistics*, Oxford: Blackwell.
(Among the many introductory textbooks on general sociolinguistics, these two are perhaps the most accessible and they offer a wide range of illustrations and practical activities.)

Clyne, Michael (1995) *The German Language in a Changing Europe*, Cambridge: Cambridge University Press.
Russ, Charles (1994) *The German Language Today*, London: Routledge.
(Between them, these two textbooks offer a comprehensive survey of most of the topics covered in this book.)

Stedje, Astrid (1989) *Deutsche Sprache gestern und heute*, Munich: Wilhelm Fink Verlag.
(This is a very accessible and lavishly illustrated survey of the historical development of German from its origins to the present day.)

Wells, Christopher (1985) *German: A Linguistic History to 1945*, Oxford: Clarendon Press.

(This is the most authoritative linguistic history of German in English, but at the same time is very readable. A companion volume dealing with the post-1945 period is currently in preparation.)

Finally, if you have access to the World Wide Web, you will find many useful sources of information. A good place to start for the most up-to-date developments and information on current research is the Institut für deutsche Sprache (http://www.ids-mannheim.de).

How to use this book

E ACH CHAPTER INCLUDES a series of tasks and discussion questions, which (except in Chapter 4) are interspersed through the text rather than being listed separately at the end. The purpose of this is to encourage readers to pause and reflect on the issues as they go along and to give them the opportunity to pursue particular topics in greater depth. However, it is not necessary to attempt the activities in order to follow the text, so readers can choose which tasks to carry out and when.

It is assumed that readers will have access to an academic library and many of the tasks can be tackled only by making use of the resources normally found there. Readers will get the most out of the book if they actively seek information and ideas from as wide a range of other sources as possible (for example journals, newspapers, maps, television and radio, CD-ROMs, the Internet). A few of the tasks presuppose contact with native speakers of German, and one or two may best be tackled during a period of residence in a German-speaking country.

To help readers decide which tasks to attempt, they have been graded in terms of difficulty and/or the time and resources required:

■   a question or task that invites the reader to give a quick reaction, or to reflect briefly on a particular point before continuing;

■■   a question or task that involves a practical activity (such as writing a list of ideas, or reformulating a text), or requires the reader to do some further reading in order to explore a particular issue in greater depth or to gather necessary information etc.;

■■■ a question or task that gives the reader the opportunity to undertake an extensive study of a particular issue, for example in the form of an empirical project or an essay or dissertation.

The 'Further reading' section at the end of each chapter is intended to direct readers towards suitable material on specific topics raised in the chapter. The books and articles listed in the Introduction are referred to by their author and their date of publication; full details for each reference are given in the bibliography at the end of the book.

•　　•　　•

The position
of German
in the world

Chapter 1

German

Language, people, place

Das Wort *deutsch*

When we say we 'cannot see the wood for the trees', we are expressing a need to establish a general picture of something that is more than the sum of its parts. Categorising and classifying things we encounter in everyday life are therefore important steps in the process of imposing some kind of order on the infinite varieties of human experience: they are part of a general strategy of 'making sense of the world' by artificially reducing variation to manageable proportions. For example, it is both conceptually and communicatively more economical if we can classify tulips, roses and daffodils as members of the general category *flower* or Volkswagens, Rovers and Nissans as belonging to the category *car* (or *automobile*).

Naming languages is a similar process but, as we shall see, allocating individual varieties to a particular language may be more arbitrary and more complicated than is the case with types of flower or car, and there may be other reasons than convenience or communicative efficiency for doing so. Furthermore, the names themselves are more than mere labels and may reveal a great deal about the relationship between the linguistic forms and their speakers. Consider, for example, the names for English, French and German in Table 1.1. A glance from left to right across the table should reveal at least two interesting points in this respect: first, the fact that many different languages use the 'same' name to designate English and French; second, the fact that there is, by contrast, no general agreement on how to designate German. Language names are most commonly based either on the names of tribes or peoples (here, for example, Angles and

TABLE 1.1 Nationality/language adjectives in a range of languages

English	Italian	Russian	German	Hungarian	Turkish
English	inglese	anglijskij	englisch	angol	ingiliz
French	francese	francuzskij	französisch	francia	fransız
German	tedesco	nemeckij	deutsch	német	alman

Source: based on Townson 1992: 78

Franks) or of geographical locations; some of the labels used for German follow these two patterns, but others derive not from people or place but from language itself.

■■ Find out what you can about the **etymology** of the words *German*, *alman*, *deutsch*, *tedesco* and *nemeckij* (i.e. what is the origin of these words? Did they originally refer to a language, a people or a place?).

From a contemporary **synchronic** perspective, the label *deutsch* has linguistic, ethnic and geographical applications: we may talk of *die deutsche Sprache, die Deutschen, Deutschland*. However, if we consider it **diachronically**, we find that its use to designate a language predates its use in reference to people and place. In other words, the constitution of the ethnic or national group derives from the idea of a 'common' language, and this is what makes the German case particularly significant in the European context: any attempt to define the elusive concept of 'Germanness' has to start (and some would say stop) with the language. However, this creates more problems than it resolves:

> Wenn Helmut Kohl im Laufe der Jahre 1989–1991 wohl hundertmal von der Einheit des *deutschen Volkes* gesprochen hat, dann ist klar, daß dies nur Bürger der alten/neuen Bundesrepublik Deutschland betrifft, also *die Deutschen*. Und es ist ebenso klar, daß Schweizer, Liechtensteiner, Österreicher usw. zwar Deutsch sprechen, aber keine Deutschen sind. Die semantische Aufgabenverteilung scheint gelöst zu sein.
>
> Trotzdem ist die Sache so einfach nicht. [...] Was weithin übersehen wird, ist die Tatsache, daß es sich hier in hohem Maße schlichtweg um ein terminologisches Problem handelt, das unlösbar ist. Hieße die Bundesrepublik Deutschland etwa *Preußen*, dann wären Preußen, Österreich, die Schweiz usw. einfach deutsche oder teilweise deutsche Länder. Dem ist nicht so. Die Realität beschert den deutschsprachigen Ländern außerhalb Deutschlands auch auf weitere Sicht den alten Konflikt zwischen Staatsnation und Sprachnation und die Frage nach dem jeweiligen Deutschsein dieser Staaten. Gerade während der letzten Jahre ist diese Frage angesichts der erreichten Einheit Deutschlands wieder aktuell geworden. Sie wird jedoch – bei verschiedenen Ausgangspunkten – in der Schweiz und in Österreich schon seit einigen Jahren verstärkt diskutiert. In

> dieser Diskussion führt kein Weg am Faktum der Staatssprache Deutsch vorbei, die dort eben nicht etwa nur Bildungs- oder Verwaltungssprache ist, sondern Volks- und Muttersprache seit Anbeginn.
>
> (Scheuringer 1992: 218–19)

So just when we thought we had identified a neat relationship between 'the German language' and 'the German people', we find that things are actually rather more complicated. Scheuringer's argument, for example, confronts us with a number of awkward questions:

- ■ If 'the German language' is in some sense the cornerstone of 'the German nation', what does this mean for 'the Austrians' or the 75 per cent of Swiss citizens whose first language is German?

- ■ What does it mean for the millions of citizens of other states all over the world who consider German to be their 'mother tongue'? Conversely, what implications does it have for those living in Germany (or Austria) for whom German is a second or foreign language?

- ■ More generally, what do you think Scheuringer means by 'the conflict between *Staatsnation* and *Sprachnation*'?

Language, state and nation

Even if we restrict our consideration of the word *deutsch* to the relatively recent past (e.g. post-1945), we can see that its multiple uses and connotations provide a key to many of the currents of social and political history in the centre of Europe. For instance:

- ■■ Explore the ambiguities of the terms *westdeutsch, ostdeutsch, mitteldeutsch* (and consider them also in relation to the older terms *großdeutsch, kleindeutsch*).

- ■■ Look up the entries for *deutsch* and *Deutschland* in a number of different dictionaries published at different times (and if possible in different countries) over the last 100 years: what contrasts and changes do you find?

The official names of the two German states that existed between 1949 and 1990 were *Die Deutsche Demokratische Republik* and *Die Bundesrepublik Deutschland*. While the former was often abbreviated to *DDR*, both in the GDR itself and in the Federal Republic, even in official contexts, the abbreviation *BRD* was never officially sanctioned in West Germany and from the late 1970s was actually prohibited; a university professor, who had used the short form in an official letter, received this stern rebuke from the Bund Freiheit der Wissenschaft:

> Wie Ihnen sicherlich bekannt ist, ist der Ausdruck „BRD" ein semantisches Kampfmittel der DDR gegen die freiheitliche Bundesrepublik Deutschland. Dieses Kampfmittel wird mit aller Konsequenz auch von den extremistischen Kräften in der Bundesrepublik angewandt, die mit unserer freiheitlichen Grundordnung nichts anzufangen wissen und sie bekämpfen.
>
> (Glück and Sauer 1990: 20; originally cited in *Die Glottomane* 4/1976: 6)

■　How could an apparently innocuous abbreviation be considered so threatening?

■ ■　Find out what other terms were used (at what times and by whom) to designate the two German states, and try to discover why the publishers of the *Bild-Zeitung* considered it newsworthy to make the solemn proclamation in August 1989 that they had finally decided 'DDR ohne Anführungszeichen zu schreiben' (see Glück 1992b: 144).

■ ■　Shortly after the (re)unification of Germany in 1990 German embassies issued a press release announcing that the official title of the (new) state was (still) *Bundesrepublik Deutschland*, but that it was acceptable to refer to it informally simply as *Deutschland*. Has there ever been a state officially called *Deutschland*?

From 1990, *deutsch* and *Deutschland* rapidly re-established themselves as demonstrative emblems of national unity. For example, a trade magazine for butchers proudly declared: 'Der deutsche Wurstfreund kann seinen Tisch mit über 1500 leckeren Sorten decken. Dafür sorgen Deutschlands gewissenhafte Fleischer. . . . Genießen Sie also die Abwechslung und den Geschmack, die der große deutsche Wurstschatz bietet' (Glück 1992b: 153; originally in *Lukullus Fleischer-Kundenpost* 31/1990: 2). However, during the existence of the two Germanies, West Germans had increasingly come to use *deutsch* and *Deutschland* with reference to themselves and their state (the following examples all date from before unification in 1990):

> Deutschlands Wäsche atmet auf!
>
> (Persil advertisement)

> Noch ist Deutschland nicht verloren!
>
> (Newspaper headline referring to West German football team; this and the previous example from Schlosser 1990: 53; the latter originally in *Bild-Zeitung* 24 June 1974)

> In der „DDR" wurden seit Kriegsende 14 Wölfe erlegt. In Deutschland sind sie seit Ende des vergangenen Jahrhunderts ausgerottet.
>
> (from an article in the *Bild-Zeitung*, cited in Teubert 1992: 236)

Similarly, it was (and is) commonplace for many West German organisations and institutions to include the word *deutsch* in their title (Deutscher Gewerkschaftsbund, Deutsche Welle). However, while some organisations in the GDR did so too (Deutsche Reichsbahn), many either concealed it by the consistent use of an abbreviated form of the title (FDJ for Freie Deutsche Jugend, ADN for Allgemeiner Deutscher Nachrichtendienst) or changed their name (Deutsche Akademie der Wissenschaften became Akademie der Wissenschaften der DDR).

■   In the light of what we have said above, what do you think was the political significance of the gradual disappearance of the word *deutsch* from public discourse in the GDR? Consider, for example, the following extracts from different versions of the GDR constitution:

Preamble

> Von dem Willen erfüllt, die Freiheit und Rechte des Menschen zu verbürgen, . . . hat sich *das deutsche Volk* diese Verfassung gegeben.
>
> (1949 version)

> Erfüllt von dem Willen, seine Geschicke frei zu bestimmen, . . . hat sich *das Volk der Deutschen Demokratischen Republik* diese sozialistische Verfassung gegeben.
>
> (1974 version)

Article 1, Clause 1

Deutschland ist *eine unteilbare demokratische Republik.*

(1949 version)

Die Deutsche Demokratische Republik ist *ein sozialistischer Staat deutscher Nation.*

(1968 version)

Die Deutsche Demokratische Republik ist *ein sozialistischer Staat der Arbeiter und Bauern.*

(1974 version)

Delimiting the language: what exactly is 'German'?

Much of the discussion in the previous section took for granted the existence of a discrete set of linguistic forms that can readily be subsumed under the label 'the German language'. As with many other abstract concepts (goodness, happiness, beauty), the prevailing view of this notion is based on a paradox: we readily accept that there is such a thing, that it is somehow self-evident, and yet cannot find any convincing way of defining it. In other words, we are generally confident of being able to identify whether a stretch of speech is German or not, but we have no watertight and universally agreed criteria for reaching such judgements.

■   Sometimes, it might not be so straightforward to decide what is German and what is not. Try reading the following four sentences aloud (they are represented in 'normal' script rather than in phonetic transcription for ease of reading): do they *look* German, do they *sound* German, *are* they German?[1]

1   Dat Book is so anleggt, dat't för de tokaamen 10 Johr bruukt warden kann.
2   M'r han ken finanzielli Understetzung. D'abonnements allein helfen uns de Zittung ze bezahle.

1 The four sentences are examples of *Niedersächsisch* (Low Saxon), *Elsässisch* (Alsatian), *Pensilfaanisch* (Pennsylvania Dutch – i.e. *Deutsch*) and *Yiddisch*, respectively. They are taken from Kloss (1978: 102, 133, 139, 196).

3   Die erschte settler fon Levnon County, echssept's weschtlich dehl, ware's menscht fon Deitschland.

4   Die yugnt-delegatn af der velt-konferents far yidish un yidisher kultur deklarirn tsu der yidisher yugnt fan der velt az die yidishe shprakh un kultur senen an integraler un neytiker teyl fun undzer lebn vi yidn baym haintiken tog.

However, while the search for an adequate definition may ultimately be hopeless, the quest for a solution is a necessary part of understanding the problem: if we cannot delimit German, we cannot hope to find satisfactory answers to any further questions to do with its status and use, the number of its speakers, its geographical spread, and so on. The nearest thing there is to a consensus on this issue is that it can best be resolved by combining objective and subjective criteria: in particular, the principle of **linguistic relatedness** on the one hand, and individual speakers' perceptions on the other. In other words, two linguistic forms may be considered to be varieties of the same language if they can be shown to be closely related (in grammar, vocabulary, etc.) and are felt by their speakers to belong to the same language. As a means of forging a link between these two criteria, the concept of **Überdachung** has been proposed, according to which two linguistic varieties are accommodated under the 'umbrella' of a single **standard** language form. For instance, this is how one textbook suggests certain Germanic speech forms can be assigned to either Dutch or German:

> [The] Dutch dialects are heteronomous with respect to standard Dutch, and [the] German dialects to standard German. This means, simply, that speakers of the Dutch dialects consider that they are speaking Dutch, that they read and write in Dutch, that any standardising changes in their dialects will be towards Dutch, and that they in general look to Dutch as the standard language which naturally corresponds to their vernacular varieties.
>
> (Chambers and Trudgill 1980: 11)

However, this temptingly simple approach is not without its problems, especially since it appears to gloss over the controversial nature of the concept 'standard German'. One of the problems, which is fairly easily disposed of, is the common misconception that the 'standard' form of any language is its 'original, uncorrupted state', from which all other forms have subsequently deviated. Far from being a naturally occurring primordial phenomenon, it is always the result of relatively recent and deliberate intervention in the 'natural' development of the language. But this still leaves a number of other issues:

■ If you look up the term 'standard' in an English dictionary, you will find a possibly surprising list of different meanings: it is used, for example, in relation to notions of prestige or quality; in the sense of 'normal, usual, accepted'; and with the meanings 'fixed measure, yardstick' and 'flag, emblem'. Which of the various meanings of the term seem to you to be applicable in relation to language?

■■ Why has the term *Hochdeutsch* traditionally been used to mean what we are calling 'standard German', and why is it a potentially mis-leading label? (See Chapter 4, section on 'Identifying German dialects', pp. 65–8.)

■ The earliest serious attempts to standardise German resulted in the publication of dictionaries and grammars in the eighteenth century. These scholarly works were intended to 'fix' the form of the language, to represent a definitive account of what constitutes 'correct German'. However, if you compare what is contained in these reference works with what can be found in current ones, you will immediately notice considerable differences at every linguistic level. What does this suggest about the process of standardisation, and what implications does this have for the way we think about the 'standard' forms of languages? (See also Chapter 10.)

The issues raised by the last question above are another illustration of the importance of diachronic perspectives on language. However, a synchronic study of different dictionaries and grammars (i.e. ones published around the same time) will also reveal another set of problems for the attempt to incorporate the concept of standard language into the project of delimiting the language as a whole. Just as at any historical moment in the last 200 years we can find 'German-speakers' rallying round several different 'national' flags, so we would find competing representations of 'standard German' that differ from each other sufficiently to provoke a debate on whether there is (at the time in question) one single monolithic form of standard German or whether there are in fact two or three, or even four.

■■ On the face of it, the concept of a standard form seems to imply some-thing absolute, so we may well ask how there can be more than one 'standard German'. On the other hand, we have seen that a historical analysis of the concept forces us to see it as a relative rather than an absolute notion; therefore on the synchronic level it may not necessarily be contradictory to talk of several co-existent (and overlapping) standard forms. Find out what is meant by the term **pluricentric** language and compile a brief case study showing how it can be applied to German. Consider, for example, why the following sentences might seem perfectly normal to an Austrian and a Swiss reader, respectively, but strange to a German:

5   Die Niederlassungsfreiheit wird Österreichs Unternehmen schärfer konkurrenzieren.

> (Glück and Sauer 1992: 23; originally in *Der Standard* 23 October 1991)

6   Der im Kanton Zürich immatrikulierte Autocar verweigerte dem Velofahrer den Vortritt und drängte ihn über das Strassenbord hinaus.

> (Haas 1982: 113)

■ ■ ■ The previous task concerned the form or substance of the language; it dealt with pluricentricity from a formal linguistic point of view. However, if we look at it from a sociolinguistic perspective, we can see that the concept of pluricentricity also has implications on the symbolic level: if one of the functions of the standardisation process is to underwrite the existence of a 'nation' or 'people' (i.e. to establish a 'national language'), what consequences would the adoption of the concept of German as a pluricentric language have for the process of nation-building? Consider, for example, these remarks by two Austrian linguists:

Durch die Orientierung der österreichischen Standardsprache an der Standardsprache der Bundesrepublik stellt sich vorerst die Frage, ob Österreich überhaupt über eine eigene Standardsprache verfügt, da [. . .] für Österreich keine kodifizierte Norm existiert. Ungeachtet dessen sind ca 90% aller untersuchten Personen in Österreich der Meinung, daß Österreich über eine Standardsprache verfügt (vgl. Moosmüller 1991). Bei den restlichen 10% handelt es sich um Personen, die aufgrund ihrer politischen Zugehörigkeit bestimmte politische Verhältnisse wiederhergestellt sehen möchten. Daraus wird schon deutlich, daß der Wunsch nach einer von anderen Staaten unabhängigen Standardsprache eng mit der Konstituierung einer Gruppe als Staat oder Nation zusammenhängt. Daraus erklärt sich auch die von Reiffenstein (1983) gemachte Feststellung, daß die verschiedenen hochsprachlichen Standards zunehmend weniger von Dialektgrenzen, sondern vielmehr von politischen Grenzen abhängen. Die nationale Einheit und Eigenständigkeit Österreichs, die ja nicht immer eine Selbstverständlichkeit war und die in der Bevölkerung Österreichs auch heute noch durchgängig als solche gesehen wird, findet auch in dem Wunsch nach sprachlicher Unabhängigkeit ihren Ausdruck. D.h., nationale Identität wird auf die Sprache transferiert und konstituiert sich über Sprache.

(Moosmüller and Vollmann in press)

Identifying 'German-speakers'

Bald nach der Entmachtung des paraguayischen Diktators Alfredo Stroessner war Anfang 1989 in der Zeitung zu lesen, der Pensionär habe möglicherweise Anspruch auf einen deutschen Paß. Es müsse zuvor geprüft werden, ob sein aus Bayern stammender Vater die deutsche Staatsangehörigkeit jemals verloren habe. Könnte es sein, daß jahrzehntelang an der Spitze Paraguays ein Deutscher stand?

(Teubert 1992: 233)

The conundrum of what constitutes the German language is clearly difficult to resolve, but even if we can decide on a working definition it is not a simple matter to establish who to count as German-speakers. By now it should be clear that there is no straightforward equation between language and nationality or language and citizenship, but just how far do you spread the net to capture everyone who arguably belongs in this category? One recent study comes to the conclusion that the total number of German-speakers throughout the world could be anywhere between 136 and 266 million, depending on which criteria you adopt (Ammon 1991a). Even if we take a narrower focus and base our findings entirely on published statistics, a great deal of care needs to be taken in interpreting the results. Consider the figures in Table 1.2, for example. On their own, these figures have no particular value: we cannot begin to evaluate or comment on them unless we know exactly how the individual totals

TABLE 1.2 Speakers of German as a first and second language in the area where German is an official language (in millions)

Area	German speakers
Germany	77.981
Austria	7.605
Liechtenstein	0.028
Switzerland	4.141
Italy (South Tyrol only)	0.280
Eastern Belgium	0.066
Luxembourg	0.372
Total	90.473

Source: Ammon 1991a: 36

were arrived at. We would need to know, for example, what is meant by 'speakers of German as a first or second language', what sources the figures derive from, and what questions were asked in order to determine the figures.

■■ Draw up a list of questions that would need to be answered in order to interpret and assess the value of the figures given in Table 1.2. (This will also be important when considering research on German as an international language, in Chapter 3.) If possible, consult the book from which the table is taken (Ammon 1991a) and see how many of your questions are addressed there.

The German-speaking countries

If the tasks of delimiting the language and counting its speakers (or perhaps we should now say its users) are fraught with difficulty, it would not be surprising to find that the seemingly uncontroversial generic label 'the German-speaking countries' is actually less straightforward than it might appear. The main problem with the term is that it seems to be an 'either–or' category, which does not correspond to the observable reality: for example, Germany and Austria are surely German-speaking countries and yet their resident populations include speakers of many other languages; conversely, there are substantial German-speaking populations in, for example, France, Canada and Brazil and yet no one would seriously suggest calling them German-speaking countries. However, it is not merely a question of which countries to include in the list: what is more important is the status and function of German in different countries. In other words, the interesting sociolinguistic issue is the relative significance of the German language in different parts of the world, the spatial distribution of its influence.

In order to investigate this question it is clearly necessary to establish a framework consisting of specific categories. The terminology in this area is often confusing and the use of certain terms is far from consistent, but there are a number of key concepts which are commonly encountered in the literature and which can be defined reasonably precisely in a way that is useful for our purposes.

Amtssprache. It is sometimes necessary to distinguish between official status and official function, as there are cases where a language may have one but not the other. However, this distinction is not relevant in situations where German is an official language.

Nationale bzw. regionale Amtssprache. A language may have official status and/or function at either national or regional level, and this is an important distinction as far as German is concerned.

Solo-offizielle bzw. ko-offizielle Amtssprache (or, sometimes, *alleindominante bzw. ko-dominante Amtssprache*). On both national and regional levels, an official language may be the only language that is accorded this position or it may share it with one or more other languages.

Nationalsprache. The use of this term tends to be determined ideologically, but in general it can be said to relate to symbolic rather than practical roles that a language can perform. In some cases a particular language may be both a national and an official language but in principle the two categories are independent of each other.

- Map 1.1 shows where German has the status and function of an official language at national and regional levels: using the terminology given above, try to characterise the position of German in each of these countries more precisely.

15

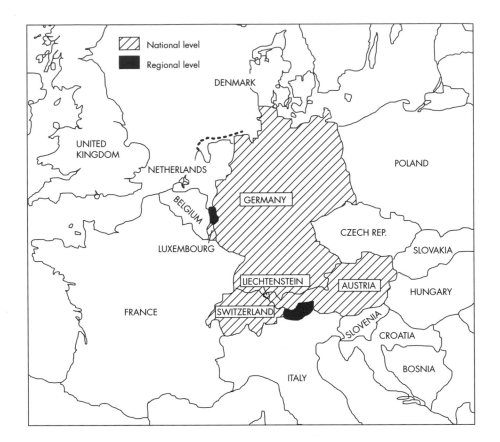

MAP 1.1 Countries with German as an official language
Source: Stevenson 1995a

Conclusions

This opening chapter has raised more questions than it has provided answers. This is partly deliberate, as it is your job to find answers, and partly inevitable, as many of the fundamental questions at issue here defy all attempts to reach a definitive position. However, to make subsequent discussion possible, it is necessary to establish some working generalisations. For example, in spite of our scepticism about the validity and appropriateness of the term we can still use the label 'the German-speaking countries' as a convenient fiction, a shorthand device for referring to Germany, Austria, Switzerland, Liechtenstein and Luxembourg on the basis that German is the, or a, *nationale Amtssprache*.

While all of the questions raised here underlie the themes to be discussed in the rest of the book, there are two particular sets of issues that have been touched on and need to be addressed in more detail: first, the relationships between German and other languages (or, more precisely, between the speakers of the respective languages), especially in the core area of Western Central Europe; second, the position of German in the world, not merely in terms of territorial spread but also in terms of its diffusion through international speech communities and its relative 'value' on the global language market. These two themes will be explored in the remaining chapters of Part one.

Further reading

Ammon (1991a), Chapters 2–6, on the number and distribution of German-speakers.

Ammon (1995b), on the problem of national varieties of German.

Barbour and Stevenson (1990), Chapter 1, on all of the issues raised here.

Clyne (1995), Chapter 2, on German as a pluricentric language.

Coulmas (1995), on the relationship between the German language and national identity.

Fraas (1995), on changes in the use of the terms *deutsch* and *die Deutschen* since 1989.

Glück (1992b), on changes in the use of the word *deutsch* since 1989.

Glück and Sauer (1990), pp. 1–22, on the use of the word *deutsch*, and on alternative ways of referring to institutions in the GDR and the Federal Republic.

Muhr (1993), a collection of essays on various aspects of the German language in Austria.

Russ (1994), Chapters 1 and 3, on the problems of defining German and on German in Austria.

Scheuringer (1992), on the relationship between 'speaking German' and 'being German' in Switzerland and Austria.

Townson (1992), Chapter 3, especially pp. 77–80, on the origins of *deutsch*.

•   •   •

Chapter 2

German in contact
with other languages

Multilingual speech communities:
Switzerland and Luxembourg

Shakespeare's plays have been translated into countless languages, but in the summer of 1989 an experimental production of *Romeo and Juliet* was staged in the Swiss town of Fribourg/Freiburg in which the relationships between languages and between language communities were presented as the central theme: the Montague family spoke German, the Capulets French, and the Prince English, while the monks (in their important function as go-betweens) were bilingual in French and German. The producers denied that the production was intended as an allegory of the Swiss situation, but the audience in this bilingual town, where *die Deutschschweiz* meets *la romandie*, might have been forgiven for thinking otherwise (see pp. 22–34).

Four years later, *A Midsummer Night's Dream* was subjected to an even more radical linguistic experiment in Luxembourg. Following consecutive performances in three different languages (Luxembourgish, French and German), a single multilingual version was devised, using in addition to these three languages the three other languages that complete the repertoire of this small but complex speech community: English, Portuguese and Italian. In this case the audience required not only linguistic versatility but also considerable mental agility, as the different languages were not allocated to individual characters but distributed randomly through the text, with frequent **code-switching** in mid-speech. The script of *Eng Summernight Story*, Claude Mangen's extraordinary adaptation, would therefore make an interesting subject for sociolinguistic study on several different levels.

However, although these events may seem remarkable to some anglophone readers, the (albeit highly stylised) intermingling of languages within a single setting corresponds very closely to the everyday experience of much of the world's population. In most parts of the world (Asia, Africa, Australia, North America, Latin America) **societal multilingualism** is the norm. Even in Europe there are virtually no countries whose populations are linguistically homogeneous.

■■ Which European countries (if any) have no substantial populations of native speakers of a language other than the main language?

■■ In which European countries, other than those that we have called 'the German-speaking countries', are there established communities of German-speakers?

■■ Which communities *within* the German-speaking countries might come under the heading of 'linguistic minorities'?

■■ Which of the communities you have identified in response to the previous two questions would be classified as **autochthonous** groups? Which of them are concentrated in specific geographical locations?

■■ Apart from relative numerical strength, which other factors characterise the relationship between minority and majority linguistic groups within a given society?

■ Now consider the following population figures for Luxembourg shown in Table 2.1.

TABLE 2.1   Population figures for Luxembourg in 1981 and 1993

	1981		1993	
	Number*	%	Number*	%
Total population	364.6	100	395.2	100
Luxembourgers	268.8	73.7	275.5	69.7
Foreigners	95.8	26.3	119.7	30.3
Germany	8.9	2.4	8.8	2.2
United States	0.7	0.2	?	?
Belgium	7.9	2.2	10.0	2.5
Spain	2.1	0.6	?	?
France	11.9	3.3	13.3	3.4
Italy	22.3	6.1	19.9	5.0
Netherlands	2.9	0.8	?	?
Portugal	29.3	8.0	42.7	10.8

Source: statec 1993
Note: * = absolute numbers in thousands

■ Which figures in Table 2.1 strike you as particularly significant?

Given its small geographical area and the high proportion of residents originating from other countries, it would not be surprising to find that most of Luxembourg's inhabitants are multilingual. However, to convince yourself that this is not necessarily the case, you only have to think of multilingual communities like York or New York, south Wales or New South Wales: how many members of the anglophone populations of these locations have an active linguistic repertoire extending beyond a single language? Yet all adult Luxembourgers *are* to some degree trilingual: they acquire Luxembourgish as their first language at home, their early schooling is largely conducted in German, and their secondary (or High School) education is mainly in French. Furthermore, these three languages (as well as English) are widely used in many aspects of everyday life (see pp. 35–40).

Although Switzerland is physically larger, it might be supposed that a similar situation obtains there: admittedly, there is no common 'Swiss' language, but linguistic pluralism is one of the most salient features of its national 'image'. However, consider Maps 2.1, 2.2, 2.3 and 2.4 (pp. 24–7).

■ Allowing for the fact that data about language knowledge and language use derived from census returns is often unreliable, what impression do you think these maps give of the relationship between **individual multilingualism** and societal multilingualism in Switzerland?

■ Does much the same thing apply to each of the language groups represented here, or are there significant differences between them in this respect?

■ Against this background, consider the significance of the views represented in Figure 2.1.

Perceptions of ethnolinguistic difference

We have seen that it is difficult to determine an individual's linguistic competence objectively, but in terms of relationships with speakers of other languages personal perceptions are often more significant: perceived differences may help to construct a barrier to communication just as much as a measurable lack of linguistic knowledge. Where such perceptions take root

(continues p. 28)

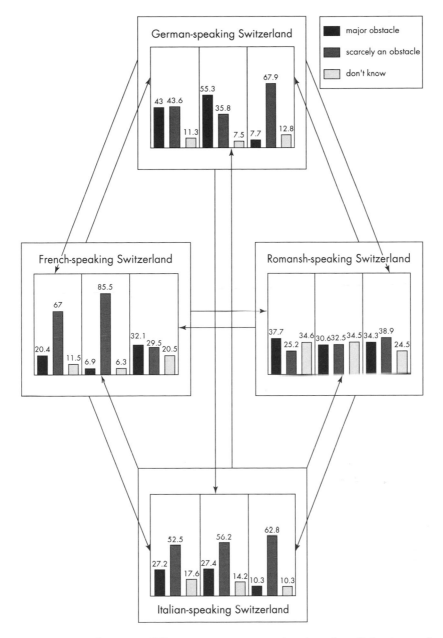

FIGURE 2.1 Do language differences represent a major obstacle to living in another part of Switzerland?

Source: Bickel and Schläpfer 1994

Note: The diagram shows the responses to this question in a survey of young Swiss men about to do their compulsory national service. To read the diagram, follow the arrows: for example, the proportion of francophone respondents who consider that language is 'a major obstacle' to living in German-speaking Switzerland is about the same as the proportion of those that consider it 'scarcely an obstacle' (about 43 per cent), while Italian-speakers overwhelmingly claimed that language was 'scarcely an obstacle' to living in the Frensh-speaking area (85.5 per cent).

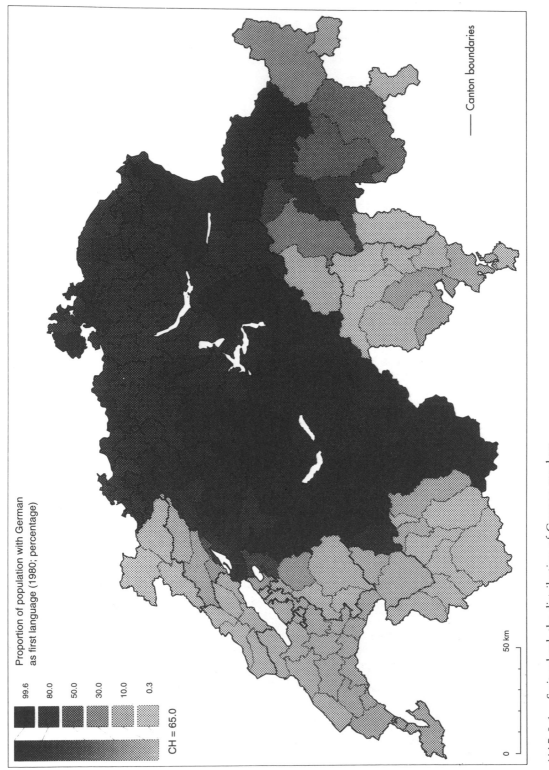

Proportion of population with German
as first language (1980; percentage)

99.6
80.0
50.0
30.0
10.0
0.3

CH = 65.0

Canton boundaries

50 km

0

MAP 2.1 Switzerland: the distribution of German-speakers

Source: Bickel and Schläpfer 1994

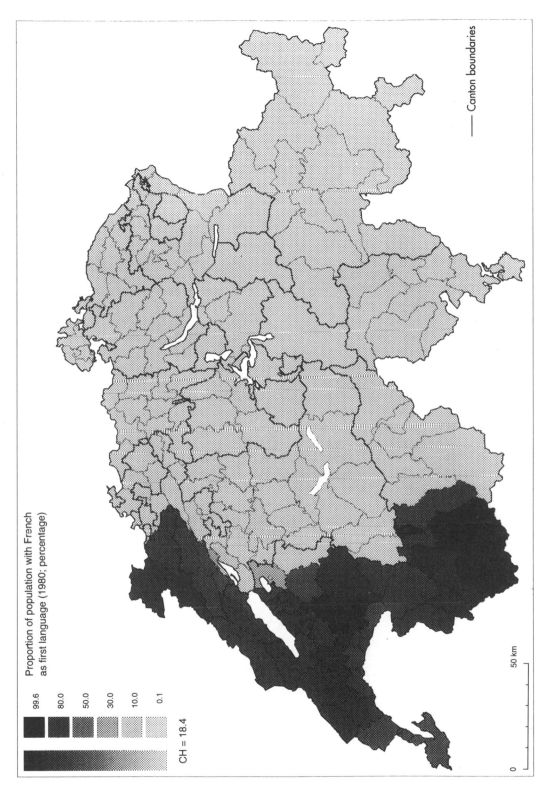

Proportion of population with French
as first language (1980; percentage)

99.6
80.0
50.0
30.0
10.0
0.1

CH = 18.4

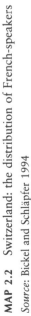
Canton boundaries

0   50 km

MAP 2.2 Switzerland: the distribution of French-speakers
Source: Bickel and Schläpfer 1994

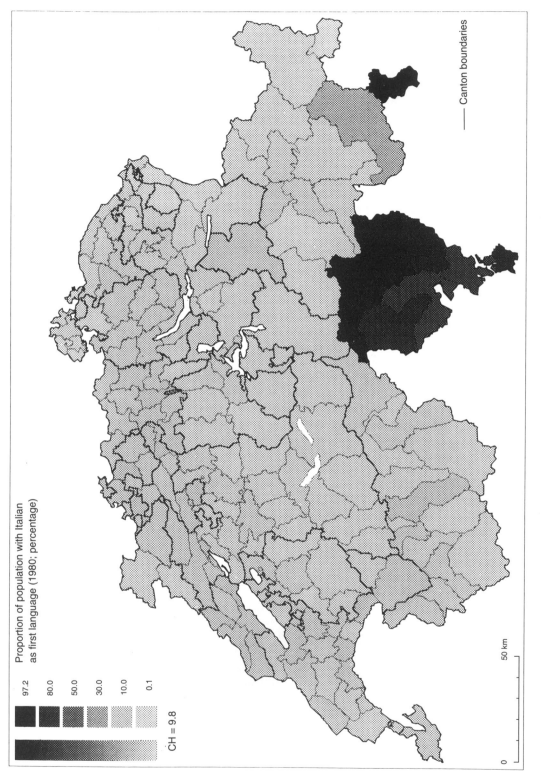

Proportion of population with Italian
as first language (1980; percentage)

97.2
80.0
50.0
30.0
10.0
0.1

CH = 9.8

Canton boundaries

0   50 km

MAP 2.3   Switzerland: the distribution of Italian-speakers

Source: Bickel and Schläpfer 1994

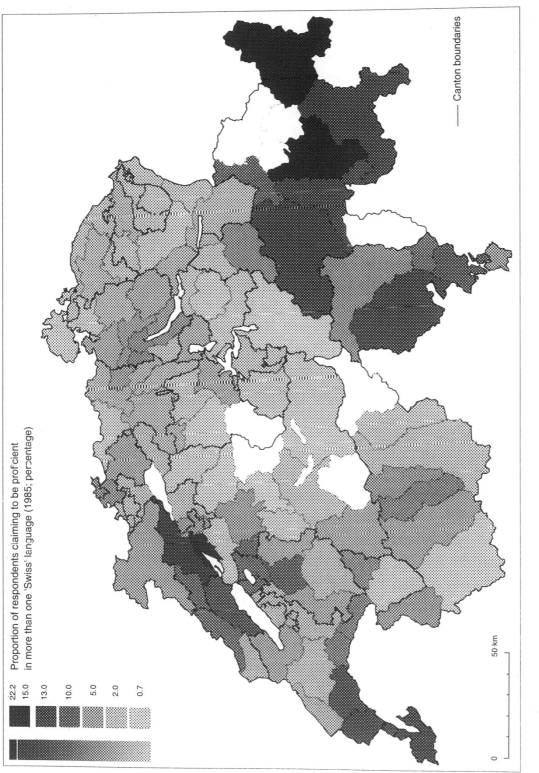

Proportion of respondents claiming to be proficient
in more than one 'Swiss' language (1985; percentage)

22.2
15.0
13.0
10.0
5.0
2.0
0.7

0   50 km

MAP 2.4   Switzerland: extent of individual language knowledge

Source: Bickel and Schläpfer 1994

Note: the map is based on the same survey as Figure 2.1 and represents the distribution of those claiming to be *mehrsprachig*, i.e. to have a good knowledge of at least one other 'Swiss' language in addition to their first language in the consciousness of a social group, they may be taken for granted and become part of what is considered 'common sense' or 'common knowledge'. An example of this process is the formation of 'stereotypes', whereby a kind of identikit image of a 'typical' football fan or burglar or teacher or German is assembled from a collection of 'characteristic' traits, which might include personal habits, physical features, forms of dress, preferred food or drink, speech behaviour, and so on. This image may then serve as a template against which real individuals are matched or may even be substituted for them: in other words, you see what you want to see.

Caricature is, of course, part of the cartoonist's stock in trade, but the success of the cartoon reproduced in Figure 2.2 depends on the readers' willingness to identify the figures portrayed with their own stereotypical images. In this particular case, this would mean that there would have to be widely held perceptions of the 'typical' French-, German- and Italian-Swiss:

FIGURE 2.2   Switzerland: ethnolinguistic stereotypes

Source: Jean François Burgener, *Nebelspalter 25*, 1986

Note: The figure in the middle is saying 'We're all Swiss! Aren't we?' in Swiss German.

that is to say, an important form of social categorisation in Switzerland is in terms of what we might call ethnolinguistic identity. There is a great deal of evidence that this form of identification is indeed widespread and the most profound differences are felt to be between the German-speakers and the rest. The following remarks of a prominent *Romand* (French–Swiss) illustrate this quite graphically:

> Man weiss doch, dass die Romands deutsche Wörter immer in einem pejorativen Sinn gebrauchen. Wenn meine Eltern, die nicht Deutsch sprechen konnten, an Stelle eines französischen Wortes einen deutschen Ausdruck gebrauchten, dann machten sie dies, um etwas geschmackloser, ungehobelter und gröber auszudrücken. Sie empfanden das Deutsche als gröber, schon für das Ohr, mit gröberen Sitten. Meine Mutter sagte beispielsweise *nettoyer*. Wenn sie hingegen *poutzer* sagte, dann bedeutete dies, dass dermassen viel Dreck herumlag, dass ein deutsches Wort gebraucht werden musste.
> (Roland Béguelin, Secretary of the Rassemblement Jurassien, quoted in Bickel and Schläpfer (1994: 135 (original French version on p. 130))

Figure 2.3 shows the extent to which French- and German-Swiss respondents agreed in a study of perceived similarities and dissimilarities between various ethnolinguistic groups (Swiss and non-Swiss).

- What seem to be the most striking (dis)similarities?

- Where do the French- and German-Swiss respondents most strongly disagree?

These figures suggest that not all Swiss share the same view of the relative cultural proximity between different ethnolinguistic groups, and it is not difficult to see that the discrepancies in these perceptions could have a bearing on relationships between the groups concerned. Social psychologists distinguish between 'auto-stereotypes' (how we see ourselves), 'hetero-stereotypes' (how we see others or how others see us) and 'projective hetero-stereotypes' (how we *think* others see us); the most harmonious relations are expected to be found where all three stereotypes match.

- A study based on this approach (Fischer and Trier 1962) comparing French- and German-Swiss found that the French-Swiss are 'liberal and changeable' according to all three stereotypes, while the German-Swiss are 'conservative and constant' except in the auto-

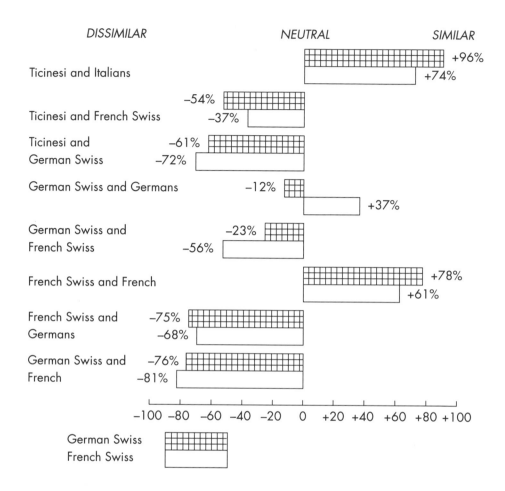

FIGURE 2.3 Perceived similarity between groups in Switzerland
Source: Schmid 1981
Note: The respondents in this survey were either German- or French-speaking Swiss.
The figures represent the percentage discrepancies between those responding that each
of the pairs of groups being compared (e.g. German-speaking Swiss and Germans) are
'very or fairly similar' and those responding that they are 'fairly or very dissimilar'.

stereotype. How would you interpret this finding in terms of image
and self-image? How might it help to explain why French rather than
German is the most used language of communication between
members of the two groups (apart from the fact that French-Swiss
learn standard German rather than *Schwyzertütsch* – a collective
term for Swiss German dialects – which is clearly often a decisive
factor)?

Managing conflict

It seems intuitively obvious that strongly felt ethnolinguistic identities are likely to generate at least the potential for conflict: it is not a matter simply of distinctiveness but of self-worth, which is almost inevitably measured in relation to the perceived worth of an 'other'. However, actual conflict is not inevitable and, even where it arises, its effects can be mitigated in various ways. Most of our discussion so far has been based on two examples (Luxembourg and Switzerland), and these will form the basis of this section too, but this is also an opportunity to bring other contact situations into consideration.

One of the premises of this chapter is that virtually all human societies are multilingual but that they do not all conceive of themselves in the same way. On the one hand, for example, the number of languages used by substantial groups of citizens in Germany, the UK or the USA is very considerable, but none of these countries incorporates this essential fact into its official self-image. On the other hand, Luxembourg and Switzerland not only formally acknowledge the co-existence of several different languages in the public discourse and daily life of the nation, they effectively define themselves in their constitutions as multilingual states.

■■ How is the relationship between Luxembourgish, French and German determined in the Luxembourg constitution (see Newton 1996)?

Until recently, Article 116 of the Swiss constitution stated:

1   Das Deutsche, Französische, Italienische und Rätoromanische sind die Nationalsprachen der Schweiz.
2   Als Amtssprachen des Bundes werden das Deutsche, Französische und Italienische erklärt.

■   What is the significance of the distinction between 'official languages' and 'national languages' in this context?

In a referendum in March 1996, 76 per cent of those who voted were in favour of the following revised version of Article 116:

1   Deutsch, Französisch, Italienisch und Rätoromanisch sind die Landessprachen der Schweiz.

2   Bund und Kantone fördern die Verständigung und den Austausch unter den Sprachgemeinschaften.

3   Der Bund unterstützt Massnahmen der Kantone Graubünden und Tessin zur Erhaltung und Förderung der rätoromanischen und der italienischen Sprache.

4   Amtssprachen des Bundes sind Deutsch, Französisch und Italienisch. Im Verkehr mit Personen rätoromanischer Sprache ist auch das Rätoromanische Amtssprache des Bundes. Das Gesetz regelt die Einzelheiten.

■   What do you think these constitutional changes were intended to achieve?

At this point, it is the differences rather than the similarities between Luxembourg and Switzerland that become interesting. Two particular contrasts are worth isolating: first, while the language legislation in Switzerland derives directly from the fact that the autochthonous population of the country is composed of four ethnolinguistic communities, the Luxembourgers have imposed trilingualism upon themselves by according official status to two non-indigenous languages; second, while there are no territorial constraints on the status of the three official languages in Luxembourg, twenty-two of the twenty-six cantons and half-cantons in Switzerland are officially monolingual. That is to say, according to the so-called **territorial principle**, each canton has the right to declare which language (or languages) will have official status within its territory. This is what gives rise to the impression that there are discrete 'language areas' in Switzerland, as the cantons in which each language has official status are adjacent to each other and therefore appear to form a territorial entity (see Map 2.5).

■   What effect do you think the 'territorial principle' has on individual mobility and the promotion of linguistic diversity amongst the Swiss population as a whole?

■   In what way do you think the territorial principle is intended to protect the smaller linguistic groups? Can it lead to a false sense of security for them (look again at Map 2.1)?

■■   What is the relationship between the territorial principle and the **personality principle** (or the principle of *Sprachenfreiheit*)?

32

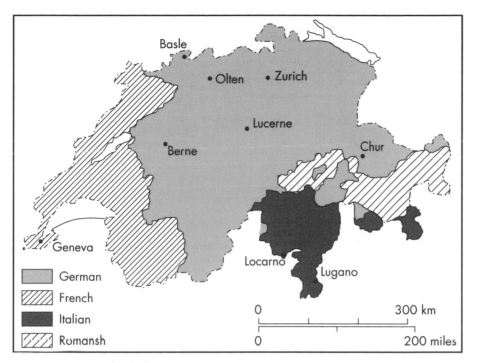

MAP 2.5   Switzerland: 'language areas'
Source: Barbour and Stevenson 1990

The de facto if not de jure division of the country into discrete 'language areas' inevitably highlights both the presence of different ethnolinguistic groups and the considerable differences in their size. However, one of the major arguments that is often advanced as an explanation of the fact that the tensions between these groups does not escalate into open conflict is that the language boundaries do not coincide with any other significant divisions or 'cleavages'. According to this argument, all other cleavages (such as more rich/less rich, Protestant/Catholic, urban/rural) cut across the language divide and therefore reduce its significance.

■ ■   How convincing do you find the 'cross-cutting cleavages' thesis as an *explanation* for the relative lack of conflict in Switzerland? Does it contradict Freud's thesis of the 'narcissism of small differences' (i.e. the view that it is precisely smaller differences that engender fiercer conflict, as the need to demonstrate distinctiveness is greater)?

■ ■ ■ To what extent is the notion of territoriality relevant and useful in other contact situations involving German?

■ ■ ■ What constitutional or other legislative measures exist (a) in relation to German-speaking communities in, for example, Denmark, Belgium, France, Italy, Poland, the Czech Republic, Slovakia, Hungary; (b) in relation to non-German-speaking communities in Germany and Austria?

Outcomes of contact: language maintenance and language shift

Whatever the reasons for languages co-existing within a particular country (historical settlement predating the drawing of political boundaries, migration, colonial/imperial expansion or contraction, expulsion), the very fact of their co-existence raises questions about the consequences of contact. On the face of it, there are only two possible outcomes as far as the **speech community** is concerned: either the multilingual constellation continues in a more or less stable fashion, or one language becomes increasingly dominant to the extent that it ultimately displaces the other(s) altogether. These processes are usually referred to as **language maintenance** and **language shift**, respectively.

However, reducing contact situations to a simple dichotomy begs a number of important questions. For example:

Is it not conceivable that intermediate outcomes arise, whereby the the multilingual repertoire is retained but the relationships between the various languages are reconfigured? (That is to say, both language A and language B survive, but A is now used in some of the situations that had previously been the preserve of B.)

What happens to the languages that are 'de-selected' in language shift: do they, as it were, retreat to another territory (the 'homeland')?

What happens to them if they have no (other) homeland to retreat to (such as Sorbian and North Frisian in Germany)?

What consequences do the processes of maintenance and shift have for the individual members of the speech community?

Furthermore, merely establishing that either maintenance or shift is occurring in a particular setting is one thing, but predicting or explaining these outcomes is quite another: are they, for instance, the result of 'natural' processes of societal development or do they depend on the intervention of political bodies (i.e. governments or official agencies)?

■■ The best-documented contexts in which German is a minority language are in Western Europe (the newly emerging situations in Eastern European countries offer exciting prospects for the researcher but are only really beginning to be studied): North Schleswig (Denmark), Eastern Belgium, Alsace (France) and South Tyrol (Italy). Choose one of these as a case study and compile a brief sociolinguistic profile of it, using the concepts introduced in this chapter.

Language choice: the speech behaviour of individuals

In the theatrical productions described in the first section of this chapter, different practices of individual language use were enacted. In the Swiss example, most of the characters were **monoglots** and the resulting communication problems were the substance of the dramatic conflict. In the Luxembourg example, the fictional speech community was a melting pot of several different languages, which were mixed and blended at will. As 'real' people are not robots or computers, we cannot really expect to be able to predict their behaviour with any great degree of certainty, but neither is their behaviour entirely unpredictable. The central question in the study of individual language choice in multilingual communities is therefore to what extent individual choices are constrained by norms or patterns of language choice that are widely shared throughout the community, or whether they are merely a matter of personal preferences. Consider these two extreme examples:

1 Chaotic choice in a North Frisian family

The father speaks Frisian (F) with his parents, his brother, his brother's wife and their children. He speaks Low German (LG) with his own wife and a form of standard German (SG) with his children.

The mother on the other hand speaks SG with her parents, LG with her husband and SG with her children. She speaks LG with her mother-in-law and F with her father-in-law; SG with her brother but LG with his wife and children. With her husband's brother and his children she speaks F, but with her husband's brother's wife LG. Their children speak SG together, SG with their maternal and paternal grandmothers but F with their paternal grandfather. With their maternal uncle and all his family they speak SG, they speak F with their paternal uncle and his children but SG with his wife.

(adapted from Walker 1980: 23–4; cited in Barbour and Stevenson 1990: 244–5)

■ Can you discern any kind of pattern here? You could try to represent the language choices of the key figures (father, mother, their children) in the form of a diagram.

2 Pre-determined choice in a Luxembourg courtroom

Stages in the proceedings	Language
Presiding judge instructs police officer to summon witness/ defendant	French or Luxembourgish
Police officer summons witness/ defendant	Luxembourgish (or French, if witness is Portuguese)
Personal details of witness/ defendant confirmed	ditto
Prosecutor reads charge	French or Luxembourgish
Presiding judge questions witness/ defendant	Luxembourgish
Other judges and lawyers put questions via presiding judge	French
Presiding judge passes questions on to witness	Luxembourgish
After cross-examination, prosecutor and defending counsel put their case	French

Judges retire to consider verdict:

if verdict returned at once	German or French
if verdict returned later	French
but defendant informed in	Luxembourgish
Transcript of proceedings	German

(information provided by Guy Poos)

■ 'Rules' of language use in such a formal setting are perhaps not surprising, but are there any obvious reasons for the use of the particular prescribed language in each stage of the proceedings outlined here?

It is often claimed that stable societal multilingualism (language maintenance) is most likely to be found where each of the individual languages is assigned to particular functions. In other words, an unwritten social convention determines which language will normally be used in which circumstances: a phenomenon referred to as **diglossia**. According to the original conception, languages (or, more strictly, '**language forms**') that are in a diglossic relationship in a particular speech community are said to be in **complementary distribution**: A is always and only used in one set of **domains** (e.g. classroom, church, workplace), while B is always and only used in another set (e.g. home, bar, club).

■■ The relationship between Swiss standard German and *Schwyzertütsch* is often cited as a classic example of diglossia: how appropriate does this seem to be today?

■■ The related term 'triglossia' is sometimes used to describe the sociolinguistic situation in Luxembourg: what evidence can you find to support or cast doubt on the validity of this description?

■■ Consider how useful the concept of diglossia is for describing other situations in which German is in contact with other languages in a given speech community, and for comparing one such community with another.

In reality, the distribution of functions between languages in multilingual settings tends to be a matter of 'more/less likely' rather than of 'either/or', and individual choice may well be motivated by factors other than the physical or social setting (topic, form of expression, relationship with interlocutor, etc.). Consider the data on language choice in Alsace set out in Table 2.2.

TABLE 2.2 Language choice according to function in Alsace

Context	Alsatian		Alsatian + French		French	
	Students	Adults	Students	Adults	Students	Adults
Telling jokes	8	26	22	26	70	41
Being serious	2	16	7	22	91	57
Giving encouragement	11	16	20	33	69	48
Offering consolation	7	16	14	33	80	44
Complaining	11	11	20	27	68	36
to friends	14	29	32	33	55	31
in a shop	1	1	4	14	95	79
Being angry	20	24	28	22	52	29
with friends	15	31	28	32	57	32
with strangers	6	6	8	9	87	83
Being flattering	8	9	13	25	80	56

Source: based on the results of a questionnaire survey reported in Vassberg 1993: 135
Note: 'Students' means secondary school students aged between 11 and 18. The figures are percentages and have been rounded to facilitate reading.

As Table 2.2 suggests, it is also conceivable that within such a conventional framework language choice can serve to *establish* rather than merely to *acknowledge* the situation. For example, if I know that it is considered normal to use French in a formal or official encounter and Alsatian in an informal or personal exchange, I can show whether I interpret a particular situation as either formal or informal through my choice of language. My interlocutor can then either accept my reading of the situation by responding in the same language or reject it by using the other one. The important point is that this implicit negotiation is only possible where both participants share the same set of norms. Furthermore, the selection of a particular language (or, more generally, a particular 'code' or language variety) in a particular interaction is not necessarily a once-and-for-all decision. Code-switching within an exchange is very common, and more often than not it occurs for a specific reason: for example, to express a change in the formality of the exchange, to mark a particular utterance as humorous or ironic, or to signal the switch to a new topic. **Communicative competence** in a multilingual speech community therefore involves knowing both the norms that condition language choice and the effects that can be achieved by code-switching.

Consider the following brief exchange in a photocopying shop. There are five customers (three university students and two older people). In this conversation both the customer and the proprietor are men in their fifties; the customer addresses the proprietor while he is still dealing with the previous customer. The passages in Alsatian (and their English translations) are given in italics.

CUSTOMER: *Macha ma hundert fufztig.*
               [*Do me a hundred and fifty (copies)*]
PROPRIETOR: Oui, d'accord.
               [OK]
CUSTOMER: (after a moment of reflection) *Nei, mach mir hundert fimfa sevetzig.*
               [*No, do me a hundred and seventy-five*]
PROPRIETOR: Bon.
               [Fine]

(Vassberg 1993: 74)

The obvious question here is: why does the proprietor not **accommodate** to the speech of the customer by speaking in Alsatian? The researcher offers a number of possible explanations:

1   Most customers (including the one here) are students, academics or professionals, so the proprietor prefers not to use Alsatian, as it is still associated with lack of education.
2   The proprietor is using this strategy of 'non-convergence' to indicate his irritation at the customer's pushy manner.
3   He doesn't want to give his other customers the impression that using Alsatian will get you preferential treatment.
4   The other customers might interpret the reciprocal use of Alsatian as an indication that a private (rather than business) exchange was beginning, which might therefore hold things up.

From the available data, there is no way of knowing for sure which (if any) of these interpretations is correct. It is, of course, possible that in certain instances code choice is entirely capricious, but extended observation suggests that in most cases the choice of code fulfils a particular function or purpose.

■   Now study the following two short extracts and attempt to analyse the code-switching behaviour that occurs.

A At a small bakery

The shopkeeper is a woman in her early sixties; the customer, who has not been to the shop before, is in her forties.

BAKER: Madame.
            [Madam?]
CUSTOMER: Donnez-moi deux petits pains aux raisins. *Vu dana runda.*
            [Give me two small raisin rolls. *Those round ones*]
BAKER: (pointing to some rolls in the window) *Die do?*
            [*These here?*]
CUSTOMER: *Nei, die dunda.*
            [*No, those down there*]
BAKER: Oui, voilà, six francs, Madame.
            [OK, there you go, six francs please]
CUSTOMER: (pays and is handed the rolls) Merci, Madame.
            [Thank you]
BAKER: Au revoir, Madame.
            [Goodbye]
CUSTOMER: Au revoir, Madame.
            [Goodbye]

(adapted from Vassberg 1993)

B In a crowded restaurant

As she sits down, customer C1 bumps into the chair of another customer, C2, who is sitting at the next table. Both customers are women in their seventies.

C1:   Oh, pardon, Madame.
      [Oh, I'm sorry]
C2:   Il n'y a pas de quoi, Madame.
      [That's quite all right]
C1:   *Ich ha gmeint ich bin an ehra Stüehl kumma.*
      [*I thought I bumped into your chair*]
C2:   *Ich ha nit gschpiirt.*
      [*I didn't feel anything*]

(adapted from Vassberg 1993)

40

Further reading

On language choice, language maintenance and language shift:
Appel and Muysken (1987), Chapter 4;
Edwards (1994), Chapters 2 and 4;
Fasold (1984), Chapters 1, 7 and 8;
C. Hoffmann (1991), Chapters 8, 9 and 11;
Holmes (1992), Chapters 2 and 3;
Romaine (1994), Chapter 2;
Wardhaugh (1992), Chapter 4.

On diglossia:
Fasold (1984), Chapter 2;
Wardhaugh (1992), Chapter 4.

On code-switching:
Appel and Muysken (1987), Chapter 10;
C. Hoffmann (1991), Chapter 5.5;
Holmes (1992), Chapter 2;
Wardhaugh (1992), Chapter 4.

On language contact involving German:
Barbour and Stevenson (1990), Chapter 8;
Clyne (1995), Chapter 2.

On Alsace:
Barbour and Stevenson (1990), pp. 234–7;
C. Hoffmann (1991), Chapter 12;
Vassberg (1993).

On Luxembourg:
Barbour and Stevenson (1990), pp. 230–4;
Newton (1996).

On Switzerland:
Barbour and Stevenson (1990), pp. 204–17;
Bickel and Schläpfer (1994);
McRae (1983);
Schmid (1981);
Steinberg (1976).

• • •

Chapter 3

German as an
international language

Communicating across languages

Consider this **polyglot** scene in cosmopolitan Prague, a city in the very heart of Europe:

> Ein Pfingsttisch in einem Vorortgasthaus. Zwei Einheimische, zwei Serben, ein Bosnier, ein deutsches Paar, Tamara, eine Ukrainerin aus Kiew. Die Tschechen, sagt die Ukrainerin, wollten mit ihr nicht russisch sprechen. Russisch haben alle gelernt und niemand gemocht und schnell wieder vergessen, so schnell es ging. Also spricht die Ukrainerin mit den Tschechen, die alle Russisch gelernt haben, deutsch. Sie hat Deutsch auf der Schule gelernt, eigenem Bekennen nach nie üben können, spricht es schön und bewundernswert differenziert. Also deutsch mit den Tschechen, deutsch mit den Deutschen. Tamara, die Ukrainerin, spricht russisch mit den Serben und dem Bosnier, die alle Russisch gelernt und es sich gemerkt und keine Berührungsangst haben. Ein Serbe und der Bosnier reden mit den Tschechen und den Deutschen englisch, denn die Tschechen, die alle Russisch gelernt haben, reden kein Russisch. Der Bosnier, der Russisch gelernt hat aber kein Englisch, redet mit den Deutschen italienisch. [. . .] Pfingsten in Prag. Die meisten der hunderttausend Touristen sagen gar nichts mehr: Sie starren beseligt über die Moldau und „The Charles Bridge" hinauf zur Burg.

> (*Süddeutsche Zeitung* 25 May 1994, p. 13)

As another (fictitious) scene in the same location suggests, there are more important life skills than the knowledge of 'foreign' languages:

SCHWEYK: Kennens den: von der Karlsbrücken aus hört ein Tschech ein deitschen Hilfeschrei aus der Moldau. Er hat sich nur iber di Bristung gehengt und hinuntergerufn, „Schrei nicht, hättst schwimmen gelernt statt deitsch!"

> (Bertolt Brecht, *Schweyk im Zweiten Weltkrieg*;
> cited in Eichheim 1993: 272)

Nevertheless, it is obvious that the amount of contact between speakers of different languages, not just in Europe but throughout the world, is greater today than ever before. At the same time, solving the problem of international communication is not merely a practical matter: as the two anecdotes above show, attitudes towards particular languages and their historical associations complicate the issue. So, given the almost limitless number of permutations that could occur in contact situations like the one described above, there is clearly a strong case for a radical, pragmatic solution: use English as a universal **lingua franca**. What could be simpler?

Languages as commodities

English as a Foreign Language (EFL) is the generic name of a 'product' belonging to a branch of the service sector of the British economy which ranks tenth in the league table of contributors to national income. *Deutsch als Fremdsprache (DaF)* plays a less significant part in the national economies of Germany and Austria but it is none the less a major export, and the demand for language 'made in Germany' (and to a lesser extent in Austria) is booming in certain parts of the world. The German government estimates that about 20 million people throughout the world are engaged in learning German at any one time, two-thirds of whom are in Central and Eastern Europe and in the countries of the former Soviet Union. In terms of 'market share' in secondary schools in these areas, German is currently vying with English for the dominant position: for example, depending on school type, both languages are chosen by between 40 per cent and 55 per cent of pupils in Poland, Hungary and the Czech Republic. Demand for German has risen so dramatically since 1989 that a further 10,000 German teachers are needed in Poland, 6,000 in Hungary and 4,000 in the Czech Republic.

For the adult populations of these countries, too, the German language appears to have the kind of appeal that used to be associated with American jeans or American dollars – and this is the point. Competition between languages is often couched in terms of 'cultural prestige' but the bottom line is economic power. As a senior official in the German Foreign Ministry once declared: 'Wer deutsch spricht, kauft auch deutsch.' France has traditionally been the world leader in promoting 'its' language abroad, but other countries also invest heavily in measures that support the export of their languages (for example, the British Council's 'English 2000' project and the Spanish 'Cervantes Plan'). In Germany, there is no one central institution that is responsible for the linguistic export drive: it is backed financially by a number of different ministries and implemented by several so-called 'Mittlerorganisationen' (principally the Goethe-Institut, the Deutscher Akademischer Austauschdienst (DAAD), and the Zentralstelle für Auslandsschulwesen). As a result, overall figures are hard to come by, but some illustrations will serve to show the importance attached to this effort:

- In 1994, the *Auswärtiges Amt* (Foreign Ministry) alone contributed about DM600 million (half of its total 'culture' budget), and in the same year a further DM39 million were added to the initial DM42 million provided for special programmes in Central and Eastern Europe in 1993.
- The Goethe-Institut has an annual budget (1994) of DM300 million and has 157 branches in seventy-seven countries, while the DAAD devotes DM55 million to the promotion of German abroad.

At the same time, critics of the government argue that far too little is being done to support these ventures at what they see as a crucial time: failure to invest on an adequate scale now, they claim, will result in irretrievable losses in the global language market, which in turn will damage Germany's economic prospects. The problem that proponents of the campaign to promote the German language abroad face is that it might provoke associations with earlier (and not just cultural) German expansionism. Consider, for example, the cautious tone of these contributions to a debate on the subject in the Bundestag:

FREIMUT DUVE (SPD): Die Förderung der deutschen Sprache ist kein Mittel irgendwelcher Machtpolitik.... Wir empfinden uns nicht als Teilnehmer einer Sprach- und Kulturolympiade im Wettbewerb mit anderen europäischen Freunden. [...]

DR VOLKMAR KÖHLER (CDU): [Lists criteria determining a language's chances of success in the global arena, then:] Dies alles zusammen macht die Chance einer Sprache aus. Schauen wir auf diese Skala, dann erkennen wir, daß Deutsch in den meisten Punkten gute und wichtige Voraussetzungen erfüllt, Voraussetzungen, die uns die Chance geben – wir wollen ja nicht die Ersten sein, wir machen keine aggressive Sprachpolitik – erstklassig zu sein. ...

DIRK HANSEN (FDP): Ich glaube, wir müssen mit Stichworten wie Ausländerfeindlichkeit, Rassismus, ja sogar Antisemitismus –

Begriffe, von denen wir glaubten, sie seien, auf uns bezogen, eigentlich überwunden – doch wieder umgehen lernen. Insofern, denke ich, ist es richtig, in einer solchen Debatte nachdenklicher zu sein hinsichtlich des Exports von deutscher Sprache, gerade auch in die Staaten Mittel-, Südost- und Osteuropas. [. . .]

(Deutscher Bundestag 1993: 103–6)

■■ Find out as much as you can about the German and/or Austrian government's current policies on promoting the German language abroad. What different means, direct and indirect, can they use to pursue this aim?

■■ Imagine you were given the task of 'selling' the German language abroad: make a list of the positive factors associated with it, that you would therefore want to highlight, and of the negative factors that you would have to try to counteract.

Measuring the value of the German language

What is a language 'worth'? The view of language as a commodity, as a part of international trade, implies that each language has a 'value' relative to that of all the others, but how do you measure this value? In general, the value of a commodity is determined by the laws of supply and demand, but demand is a complex notion. For example, Coulmas (1992: 114–15) points out the need to distinguish between the three terms *Bedarf*, *Bedürfnis* and *Nachfrage* in this context and illustrates this in relation to the market for German in Japan. At Japanese universities, 300,000 students in each year study German (this constitutes the *Nachfrage*). On the one hand, this leads to over-production, as the objective requirement for German language knowledge in industry (the *Bedarf*) is not so high: more German-speaking graduates are produced than the economy can use. On the other hand, the needs of the students (their *Bedürfnisse*) are not met, as what they learn has little bearing on what they will need in the jobs that require German knowledge.

In fact, there is probably no single measure according to which the value of a language can be determined. Furthermore, its *value* only has any meaning in relation to its *users* and the extent to which it is used: the potential value of the German language can only be realised when it is used in concrete situations. So we are left with the search for appropriate criteria for assessing the relative importance of German in the world. Some factors that are clearly significant are rather difficult to quantify: for example, the 'cultural weight' of French in Germany in the seventeenth and eighteenth centuries was considerable, but there is no obvious way of actually measuring its importance in relation to other languages.

To gain some idea of different measures that have been proposed, consider the data in the following tables (taken from Ammon 1991a and 1995a, the most authoritative research published to date):

TABLE 3.1 Number of native speakers of German in comparison to other languages (millions), according to three different sources

Grimes (1984)		Comrie (1987)		Finkenstaedt and Schröder (1990)	
1. Chinese	700	Chinese	1,000	Chinese	770
2. English	391	English	300	English	415
3. Spanish	211	Spanish	280	Hindi	290
4. Hindi–Urdu	194	Russian	215	Spanish	285
5. Russian	154	Hindi–Urdu	200	Arabic	170
6. Portuguese	120	Indonesian	200	Bengali	165
7. **German**	**119**	Arabic	150	Portuguese	160
8. Arabic	117	Portuguese	150	Indonesian	125
9. Japanese	117	Bengali	145	Japanese	120
10. Indonesian	110	Japanese	115	Russian	115
11. Bengali	102	**German**	**103**	**German**	**92**
12. French	63	French	68	French	55

Source: Ammon 1995a

■ How do you think the discrepancies between the three sets of figures in Table 3.1 can be accounted for?

■ Why should any such sets of figures for 'speakers of a given language' be treated with caution?

■ In what respects is the number of native speakers of a language an indicator of its importance?

■ What might figures about the demand for German language learning in Tables 3.1–3.2 reveal?

TABLE 3.2 The 'study strength' of German in relation to other languages

Language	1967	1977	1986	Total	Growth rate
1. English	156,403	283,859	409,920	850,182	2.62
2. French	44,079	111,181	142,480	297,739	3.23
3. **German**	**39,178**	**68,979**	**96,172**	**204,329**	**2.45**
4. Spanish	25,161	22,492	10,821	58,474	0.43
5. Italian	16,957	31,283	34,720	82,960	2.04
6. Russian	16,100	?	?	?	?
7. Japanese	10,086	14,737	14,960	39,783	1.48

Source: Ammon 1995a
Notes: The figures in the table refer to the number of students from countries of other languages studying the seven given languages in countries where these languages are the mother tongue ('mother-tongue countries').
Growth rate = number for 1986: number for 1967.

TABLE 3.3 Number of foreign-language students in schools in the EC countries, according to Eurydice 1989

1. English	18,133,320	(10 countries: all non-mother-tongue countries)
2. French	9,088, 163	(11 countries: all non-mother-tongue countries)
3. **German**	**2,888,011**	(11 countries: all non-mother-tongue countries)
4. Spanish	1,385,801	(9 countries: all non-mother-tongue countries except Greece, Portugal)
5. Italian	215,840	(8 countries: all non-mother-tongue countries except Greece, Netherlands, Portugal)
6. Dutch	212,214	(4 countries: Belgium, France, Germany, Luxembourg)
7. Portuguese	13,708	(3 countries: France, Germany, Spain)
8. Modern Greek	80	(1 country: France)
9. Danish	0	

Source: Ammon 1995a
Note: 'Non-mother-tongue country' means a country whose population does not include a substantial proportion of native speakers of the language concerned

- What do the figures in these two tables appear to show about German in relation to other 'major' languages in this respect?

- What do these tables *not* tell us? In other words, what further information might you want in order to gain a fuller picture?

TABLE 3.4   Foreign-language requirements in job advertisements in newspapers in six European countries, according to Glück 1992 (percentage per language)

	German	*English*	*French*	*Spanish*
Hungary	40	37	3	<1
Poland	26	46	7	<1
France	11	71	–	5
Britain	7	–	15	6
Spain	7	60	21	–
Italy	6	69	9	<1

Source: Ammon 1995a

■   The information given in Table 3.4 is based on a preliminary survey of job advertisements in six European countries (France, Hungary, Spain, Italy, Poland and Great Britain). What bearing do they have on the data given in Tables 3.2 and 3.3?

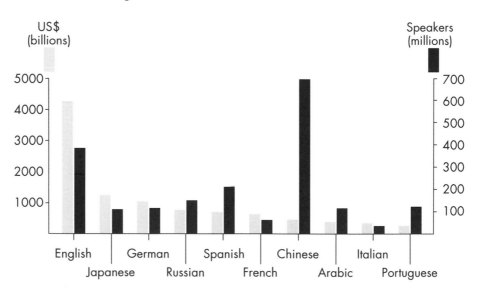

FIGURE 3.1   Economic strength in relation to numerical strength of the ten numerically strongest languages in the world

Source: Ammon 1991a

Note: first column for each language = GNP (US$ billion), second column = number of speakers (millions)

TABLE 3.5 Economic strength of German in comparison to other languages, after Grimes 1984 and Haefs 1989 (in billions of US dollars)

1.	English	4,271
2.	Japanese	1,277
3.	**German**	**1,090**
4.	Russian	801
5.	Spanish	738
6.	French	669
7.	Chinese	448
8.	Arabic	359
9.	Italian	302
10.	Portuguese	234
11.	Dutch	203
12.	Hindu–Urdu	102
13.	Indonesian	65
14.	Danish	60
15.	Greek	49

Source: Ammon 1995a

■ Consider the data in Table 3.5 and Figure 3.1 in relation to Table 3.1: what conclusions can you draw about the interdependency of different measures?

The term 'international language' is rather vague and it has been defined in a number of ways, but it should be clear from our considerations so far that German has an important role to play on the world stage. However, what is also clear is that its international status cannot be derived directly from the kind of data we have looked at so far in this section: it varies in different parts of the world, at different historical moments, and in different domains of use. To illustrate this, we can examine two important domains involving international communication in which the significance of the German language does not always correspond to the significance of German-speaking participants (whether individuals or organisations): trade (or commerce) and science.

■ Tables 3.6 and 3.7 are based on information provided by German chambers of commerce to act as a guide for German companies intending to sell their products in other countries. Put yourself in the position of the sales director of such a company and consider what seem to be the significant facts that emerge.

TABLE 3.6   Number of countries for which particular languages are recommended for German trade, according to Handelskammer Hamburg 1989

	Total	Sole language	Co-language
1. English	122	64	58
2. French	57	25	32
3. Spanish	26	17	9
4. **German**	**26**	**1**	**25**
5. Arabic	12	–	12
6. Portuguese	8	–	8
7. Italian	4	–	4
8. Dutch	4	–	4
9. Indonesian	1	–	1
Czech			
Danish			
Finnish			
Norwegian			
Polish			
Russian			
Slovene			
Swedish			

Source: Ammon 1995a

TABLE 3.7   Countries for which German is recommended for German trade, according to Handelskammer Hamburg 1989

Western and northern Europe	Eastern and southern Europe	Other regions
Austria	Albania	Afghanistan
Belgium	Bulgaria	Chile
Denmark	Czechoslovakia	Israel
Finland	Greece	Mongolia
Iceland	Hungary	Namibia
Luxembourg	Italy	
Netherlands	Poland	
Norway	Romania	
Sweden	Soviet Union	
Switzerland	Turkey	
	Yugoslavia	

Source: Ammon 1995a

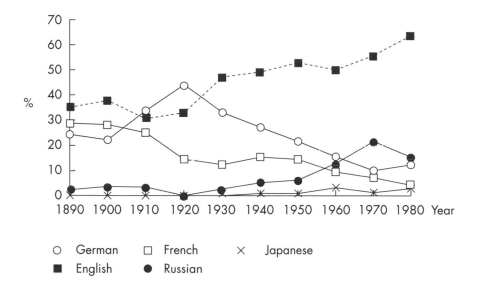

FIGURE 3.2a Languages of publication in the natural sciences between 1890 and 1980 (percentages): averages from French, German, Russian and US bibliographies and data bases
Source: Ammon 1995a

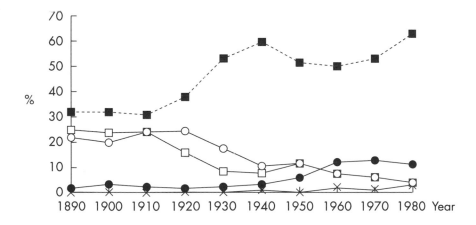

FIGURE 3.2b Languages of publication in the natural sciences between 1890 and 1980 (percentages): according to US bibliographies and data bases
Source: Ammon 1995a

■   In the past, German was often thought of as *the* language of science but this dominant position has long since been taken over by English. One potential indicator of the relative importance of languages in this domain is the number of publications in which each is used. Look at the data presented in the two graphs in Figure 3.2 and try to explain (a) the discrepancies between them, and (b) the progress of English at the expense of the other languages in relation to the historical context.

The German language in Europe

One way of looking at the major changes that have taken place in Europe in recent years is to describe them as a kind of role reversal between East and West. On the one hand, the collapse of the highly centralised, closed, controlled world of Eastern Europe has led very rapidly to the opening up of a highly competitive and diverse new marketplace there. On the other hand, the increasing integration of the European Union (EU) and the European Economic Region has created a more centralised, closed and regulated world in Western Europe. As we saw in the second section of this chapter (p. 45), one of the consequences of the first of these developments is that German is locked in a cultural battle with English in Eastern Europe, aiming to capitalise on the presence of a vast 'learner potential' and on its historical standing as a lingua franca in many parts of this area. However, the market free-for-all in the new east is very different from the bureaucratic democracy of the increasingly powerful institutions of the EU, where the 'free market' in languages is constrained by tradition and vested interests. The article from which the following extract is taken was published before the European Community (Europäische Gemeinschaft – EG) became the European Union in 1993, and before Finland and Sweden became members, thereby adding two further languages to the official repertoire, but this only reinforces the point the author is making.

An jedem Werktag, mittags Punkt zwölf, versammeln sich im ersten Stock der Brüsseler Berlaymont [the offices of the European Commission] die Journalisten zur Pressekonferenz. Dann informiert EG-Sprecher Bruno Dethomas, meist begleitet von mehreren Sprecherkollegen, über das Neueste aus Europa. Der ehemalige Redakteur von *Le Monde* [i.e. Dethomas] nennt die Veranstaltung übrigens *point de presse*. Schließlich ist er Franzose, und neugierige Journalisten sind gehalten, ihre Fragen auf französisch zu stellen. Andere Sprachen sind nicht zugelassen.

Tritt allerdings beim Pressetreff ein EG-Kommissar oder ein hoher europäischer Beamter auf, dann bricht unvermittelt die Vielsprachigkeit aus. Die Dolmetscherkabinen sind besetzt, fast jeder hat seinen Kopfhörer auf den Ohren, und plötzlich sind Fragen und Antworten in allen neun Amtssprachen der Gemeinschaft zugelassen. Dann ist der Idealzustand erreicht, der ein Normalzustand sein sollte: das absolut gleichberechtigte Nebeneinander von Französisch, Englisch, Deutsch, Italienisch, Spanisch, Portugiesisch, Niederländisch, Griechisch und Dänisch.

Daß dies nicht die Regel ist, weiß jeder, der einmal mit den Brüsseler Institutionen zu tun hatte. [...] Arbeitsunterlagen gibt es meist nur auf französisch und englisch. Und Deutsch, die im gesamten EG-Raum am häufigsten gesprochene Sprache? Sie spielt eine ziemlich bescheidene Rolle, und das stört vor allem die deutsche Wirtschaft in zunehmendem Maße.

(Klaus Peter Schmid, 'Chauvi spitzt seine Zunge', *Die Zeit*)

In many international organisations, an important distinction is made between official languages (*Amtssprachen*) and working languages (*Arbeitssprachen*). In such cases, the status of official language on its own is of a more symbolic nature, while the status of working language is more important, as it means that the language is actually used in the business of the organisation. In the EU the distinction is rather more subtle. While the original regulations (agreed in 1958) governing the status of languages in what was then the EEC (European Economic Community) used both terms, in principle the distinction was redundant as all official languages were also working languages. This apparent anomaly was removed in the Maastricht Treaty, which transformed the EC (European Community) into the EU in 1993; Article 217 simply states: 'Amtssprachen sind: Dänisch, Deutsch, Englisch, Französisch, Griechisch, Italienisch, Niederländisch, Portugiesisch und Spanisch.' As all the other regulations remain in place, the implication is that these nine languages (to which Finnish and Swedish should now be added) all enjoy equal status, in that all may be used both internally and externally, and both by individual citizens in dealings with institutions and by representative bodies. However, actual practice is very different from the agreed principle. In reality, English and French are the languages most heard in the offices and committee rooms in Brussels,

Strasbourg and Luxembourg, and the ones most often used in written documents: they are the de facto working languages of the EU. All member states have the right to have documents translated into 'their' official EU language, but the sheer volume of work often results in long delays, which in turn can lead to serious political and economic disadvantages for those concerned.

On the other hand, the German government may be fighting a losing battle in seeking to enhance the status of German within the institutions of the EU, as it cannot necessarily bank on the support of German-speaking officials:

> Deutsche Beschäftigte europäischer Institutionen in Straßburg, Brüssel *and elsewhere* parlieren wie selbstverständlich in der ersten, allenfalls in der zweiten Arbeitssprache. Wen kann es da wundern, daß Deutsch in der Europäischen Union quasi den Status einer 'Untergrundsprache' angenommen hat, zumal höchste politische Autoritäten gelegentlich öffentlich demonstrieren, daß es eigentlich nicht wichtig ist, Deutsch zu sprechen und zu verstehen?
> (Reinhart Olt, 'Sprachexport ist nötig', *Frankfurter Allgemeine Zeitung*, 2 April 1994: 1)

■ ■ Write a short account of the differences between the principle and the practice of language use in the institutions of the EU.

■ ■ Put yourself in the position of the German government and write a concise statement, putting forward your arguments for giving German equal status with English and French as a de facto working language of the EU.

■ ■ ■ Investigate the relative international political importance of the German language by finding out its status and function in different international organisations (e.g. the United Nations and its various divisions such as UNESCO, the World Bank, the World Health Organisation).

■ ■ ■ On the basis of the available evidence, attempt an assessment of the current position of German either as a world/international language or within Europe.

Further reading

Ammon (1991a), the most comprehensive and authoritative study on the subject to date.

Ammon (1991b), focuses on the position of German in the EU.

Ammon (1995a), a concise account in English of the main findings of Ammon 1991a.

Born and Stickel (1993), a collection of papers on the position of German in Europe.

Burkert (1993), contains arguments for enhancing the status of German in the EU.

Clyne (1995), Chapter 1 gives a concise overview of the status of German in contemporary Europe.

Coulmas (1991a), contains a number of useful articles on general and specific issues relating to language policy in Europe.

Coulmas (1991b), on EU language policy.

Coulmas (1992), on the economic value of languages and the idea of languages as commodities.

Coulmas (1993), on the 'value' of the German language.

Eichheim (1993), on the role of the Goethe-Institut in promoting the German language.

Mohr and Schneider (1994), a good summary of the current situation of German in international organisations.

●   ●   ●

Part two

Exploring linguistic variation

Chapter 4

Regional variation
in spoken German

The nature of regional variation in German

One of the most striking characteristics of Germany and Austria is the enduring strength of their regional traditions. Although both modern states are centralised to the extent that they have national governments, located in Bonn (moving to Berlin by the year 2000) and Vienna, respectively, their federal structure means that many powers are devolved to the individual *Länder*, and many people still identify more closely with their *Land* than with their country. Similarly, many Swiss locate themselves socially more in relation to their home canton than to either the nation as a whole or to their ethnolinguistic group (see Chapter 2).

These traditions manifest themselves in many ways: architecture, dress, customs, food and language. English-speakers from, say, the UK or the USA are familiar with the phenomenon of regional variation in spoken forms of English, but even those who have quite an advanced knowledge of German are often taken aback by the sheer extent of the diversity in spoken German. This is a very complex issue, but the main reason for this contrast between English and German is that regional forms of German typically have distinctive features on all linguistic levels (phonological, syntactic, morphological, lexical), while regional forms of English are distinguished from each other (at least in people's perceptions of them) overwhelmingly in terms of phonetic/phonological differences.

The different forms of regional speech in German are not completely distinct from each other, but, as we shall see in the next section ('Identifying German dialects', pp. 65–8), there are ways of looking at the similarities and differences between them that allow us to classify them into groups on linguistic and geographical criteria. For the sake of simplicity, we can say that they form a continuum, ranging from the highly localised rural **dialects** (*Dialekte* or *Mundarten*) to the more widely spoken varieties of **colloquial speech** (*Umgangssprache*). The speech forms nearest to the dialect end of the continuum are linguistically furthest removed from standard German, and can be baffling to the outsider. Indeed, many German-speakers have difficulty identifying and understanding dialects from areas geographically remote from their own. This need not pose insurmountable problems: for example, urban speech forms generally differ less markedly from standard German than rural ones, and regional characteristics persist much more in the south (southern Germany and all of Austria and Switzerland) than in the north. However, even the more 'homogenised' urban speech forms retain many of the features of traditional dialects spoken in the surrounding areas, and speech differences are still considered an important aspect of regional identity.

There is a high level of public awareness of the distinctive characteristics of local and regional speech forms, and in recent years the general resurgence of 'local values' has led to an increase in the prestige, and consequently in the visibility, of these forms in public contexts: many local and regional newspapers carry regular columns in dialect; there are radio and television broadcasts in dialect; and even public notices are sometimes in dialect to create a sense of informality or even humour. For example, Gloy (1977: 77) refers to a notice in a government department in Baden-Württemberg proclaiming 'Do kannsch au alemannisch schwätze' (Du kannst auch Alemannisch sprechen) and to an apologetic notice from the Bremen Senate outside a building site (written in a Low Saxon dialect): 'Dat duert nich lang, wie makt dat ok för ju, un wenn ji nix to doon hebbt, denn kiek man een beten to' (Das dauert nicht lange, wir machen das auch für dich, und wenn du nichts zu tun hast, dann guck' mal ein bißchen zu). The pleasure that some people have in their local speech form is evident in texts such as this tongue-in-cheek notice displayed in an office in Frankfurt am Main, where a Rhenish Franconian speech form is spoken:

ACHTUNG

GOMBJUDER-RAUM

Dieser Raum is voll bis unner die Degg midd de dollsde elekdrische un vollelekdrohnische Anlaache. Staune un gugge därf jeder, awwer rummworschdele un Gnöbbscher drigge uff de Gombjuder, dörffe nur mir, die Exberde.

[Standard German equivalent: Achtung. Computer-Raum. Dieser Raum ist voll bis unter der Decke mit den tollsten elektrischen und vollelektronischen Anlagen. Staunen und gucken darf jeder, aber herumwursteln und Knöpfchen drücken auf dem Computer dürfen nur wir, die Experten.]

Furthermore, interregional rivalry is often manifested in the evaluation of dialects: for example, Figure 4.1 shows the relative popularity and

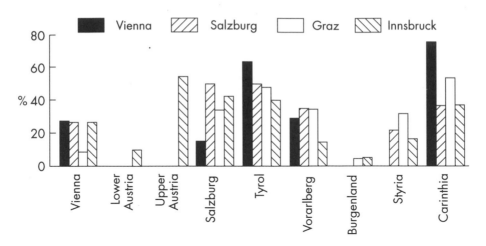

FIGURE 4.1a   Relative popularity of Austrian dialects
Source: Moosmüller 1995

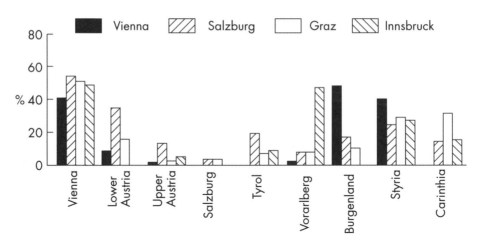

FIGURE 4.1b   Relative unpopularity of Austrian dialects
Source: Moosmüller 1995

unpopularity of Austrian dialects amongst inhabitants of the four cities of Vienna, Salzburg, Innsbruck and Graz.

■ ■   To see for yourself whether you have clear views on variation in your own language, try to draw up your personal 'league table' of ten regional varieties of English (number 1 is your favourite, number 10 is your least well liked). What do you think your preferences are based on? Compare your list with fellow students' versions and discuss with them how they arrived at their ranking orders.

■■ If you have access to native speakers of German, devise a brief questionnaire asking them to evaluate ten regional varieties of German (or the speech forms they associate with ten cities or regions). Ask them to explain their judgements.

The expression of such attitudes is not only an entirely subjective matter, but is also generally more a reflection of (stereotypical) images of the inhabitants of particular places than a response to the speech forms themselves. In the next section we shall attempt to identify the salient observable differences between German dialects. The object of this exercise is neither to perpetuate stereotypes nor to make you into a dialect expert, but simply to establish some basic patterns of similarity and contrast that should give you some idea of what to look out for when trying to determine where a particular speaker comes from. The practical tasks that follow are designed to give some initial practice in 'dialect spotting'.

Identifying German dialects

The most accessible way to approach regional differences is to begin with relatively large contrasts that correspond to the general perceptions of native speakers. The fundamental contrast that German-speakers make, whether they are thinking of language or of virtually any other aspect of social behaviour, is between north and south. 'The north' is, very roughly, understood to be the relatively low-lying, flatter areas of northern Germany, while 'the south' incorporates the higher, more mountainous region of southern Germany, Austria and the German-speaking parts of Switzerland.

These geographical characteristics are worth mentioning here, as they may help to reinforce in your mind the basic linguistic division between Low German (i.e. northern) and High German (i.e. southern) dialects; a line dividing Low from High German dialects would run east–west from just south of Berlin to just north of Cologne (see Map 4.1). Since 'the south' is such a vast area, and since there are important linguistic contrasts between what we might call the 'deep south' and the more northerly part of the area, High German is normally further divided into Central (or Middle) German and Upper German. These basic divisions are represented in Figure 4.2. It is also important to note here that 'High German' is ambiguous, as it is also the popular term for 'standard German'.

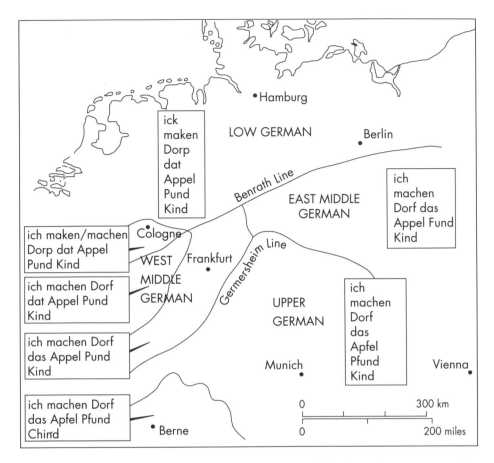

MAP 4.1 The variable extent to which the second sound shift (High German sound shift) affected regional speech forms

Source: Barbour and Stevenson 1990; adapted from König 1978
Note: common words are given as examples

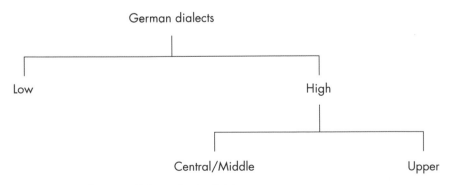

FIGURE 4.2 German dialects: basic divisions

There are many contrasts between Low and High German dialects, but the most prominent feature that distinguishes them is the so-called 'second sound shift' (*die zweite Lautverschiebung*, hereafter LV2 for short). This phonological change began in the southeast of the German-speaking area of Europe and gradually spread north and west roughly between the fifth and eighth centuries AD, but did not progress beyond what dialectologists refer to as the Benrath line (see Map 4.1). In those dialects in which the shift has taken place, the **stop** or **plosive** consonants /p, t, k/ have been replaced by **affricates** /pf, ts/ or **fricatives** /s, x/. For example, while Low German dialects have the older forms /apəl/, /va:tər/ and /ma:kən/ for *Apfel*, *Wasser* and *machen*, most High German dialects have /apfəl/, /vasər/ and /maxən/.

A number of other distinctive features are worth mentioning here, partly as they provide further 'markers' for identifying Low and High forms, and partly as they are also useful in distinguishing between dialects *within* each of the main groups.

Phonology

In addition to LV2, there are three further **phonological** features that are quite distinctive:

1   *Diphthongisation of the vowels* /i:, u:, y:/. In the Middle Ages, most dialects had **monophthongs** (or 'single vowels') in words such as *zît*, *hûs* and *hiute*, corresponding to modern standard German *Zeit*, *Haus* and *heute*. Since then, these single vowels have been replaced in many High German dialects by the **diphthongs** found in the modern standard forms: /ai, au, ɔi/. Virtually all Low German dialects, on the other hand, have retained the monophthongs.

2   *Unrounding of front rounded vowels* /y:, Y, ø:, œ/. In modern standard German, words such as *fühle*, *Fülle*, *Söhne* and *Götter* have front rounded vowels (see **front vowel; rounded vowel**), and these are also to be found in the equivalent forms in most Low German dialects. However, in many High German dialects they are replaced by the corresponding unrounded vowels /i:, ɪ, e:, ɛ/.

3   *Lenition*. **Lenition** is a phonological process in which certain consonants become less strongly articulated. Its most noticeable effect is that it removes the audible distinction between pairs of words such as *Deich* [daiç] and *Teich* [taiç]: both are then pronounced [d̥aiç]

(compare the pronunciation of *writer* and *rider* in American English). The same applies to the contrasts between /b/ and /p/ (e.g. *backen* vs *packen*) and /g/ and /k/ (e.g. *gönnen* vs *können*). The distribution of this feature in the High German area is rather complex, but it is not present in most Low German dialects.

Morphology

Again, there are three **morphological** features that can usefully be singled out:

1   *Case forms.* While High German dialects have two cases corresponding to the accusative and dative forms of standard German, most Low German dialects have a single non-nominative ('oblique') case: for example, *mi* might be used as an equivalent to both *mich* and *mir*.
2   *Plural forms in the present tense.* While High German dialects have two forms, as in standard German, most Low German dialects have a single plural form in the present tense of verbs: e.g. *wir/ihr/Sie/sie spielen*.
3   *Past tenses.* While Low German dialects have both an imperfect (or 'preterite') and a perfect tense, Upper German dialects have only a perfect tense.

Lexis

Apart from pronunciation, differences in **lexis** are probably the most striking features of any dialect. Map 4.2, which shows regional variants for 'to speak', gives an impression of how varied dialect vocabulary still is in German.

Distinctive features of German dialects

Having identified a small number of key features to look out for, we can now give a slightly more detailed outline of the relationships between the various dialects that are conventionally grouped together under the general headings of Upper, Middle and Low German. The notes that

MAP 4.2 Different words for 'speak' in traditional German dialects
Source: Barbour and Stevenson 1990; adapted from König 1978

follow focus mainly on the features mentioned above, but a few additional points of interest are given where appropriate. We shall start in the south and work our way northwards.

Upper German

To some extent, the tree diagram and the labels used in Figure 4.3 are misleading, as they give a false impression of the existence of discrete entities: the reality is much more fluid. However, the labels will be found in any reference work on the subject, and the divisions will enable us to make some useful general observations.

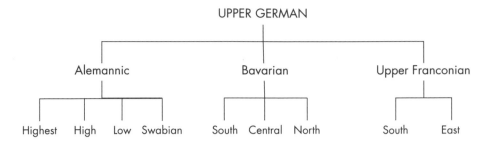

FIGURE 4.3 Upper German dialects

The reason for grouping these various southern forms together, on linguistic as well as geographical grounds, is that they share certain significant structural features.

Phonology The most fundamental distinguishing feature of Upper German forms is that the second sound shift has consistently affected the relevant sounds in all positions (i.e. at the beginning, in the middle and at the end of words). Other common and identifiable characteristics are that front rounded vowels are typically unrounded and that lenition is widespread.

LV2 present throughout:	*Pfeffer, Apfel, Dampf*
unrounding present:	*müde* pronounced [miəd], *König* pronounced [kenɪç]
lenition widespread:	*Teich* and *Deich* both pronounced [d̥aiç]

Morphology In terms of the features mentioned in the previous section, these dialects are similar to standard German in that they have identifiable accusative and dative forms, and (with some exceptions, such as Swabian) have two plural forms in the present tense of verbs (one for the subject *ihr* and one for the subjects *wir/Sie/sie*). An important difference from standard German, as well as from northern speech forms, is that they have no preterite tense. Another common feature is the reduction of certain verbs forms: for example, through the deletion of the unstressed short central vowel ('schwa') in the past participle prefix *ge-* and of the final *-n* in past participles and infinitives.

dual case pattern: accusative + dative
dual plural forms in present tense of verbs
no preterite
reduction of past participle prefix and deletion of final -n
  in participles and infinitives: *gesehen* → *g'sehe* [gze: ə]

Lexis Common lexical features are too numerous to mention here (see Further reading, p. 81), but one very distinctive characteristic is that diminutive forms are of the *-lein* type (as opposed to the *-chen* type found in the north): *-lein/-li/-le/-la*.

While all of these southern forms have certain features in common, there are a number of features that are less widespread and that therefore justify the subdivisions in Figure 4.3. For example, here are some distinctive phonological features that are not uniform across all Upper German dialects:

-   In some Alemannic dialects, the diphthongs /ai, ɔi, aʊ/ may occur in some contexts but not in others, e.g. *frei* may be pronounced [frai], but *Haus* may be [hu:s] and *Schweizerdeutsch* [ʃvi:tsərd̥y:tʃ] (which is correspondingly spelled *Schwyzertütsch* in Swiss German).
-   In High Alemannic and South Bavarian forms, LV2 has affected relevant sounds even in initial position: e.g. *Kind* is pronounced [kxɪnt] or even [xɪnt].
-   All Alemannic dialects have /ʃt, ʃp/ for /st, sp/, even in final position: *ist* = [ɪʃt].
-   Low Alemannic dialects have uvular [ʀ], which is otherwise rarely found in rural areas.
-   In Swabian dialects, certain vowels are nasalised: e.g. *Gans* is pronounced [gãs].
-   In Central Bavarian dialects, /l/ is 'vocalised' (i.e. realised as a vowel): e.g. *Salz* is pronounced [zɔits], just as in some forms of British English *milk* is pronounced [mi:ʊk].

Central/Middle German

Of all the dialect areas, West Central/Middle German is by far the most diverse (see Map 4.1), and there are actually further important sub-

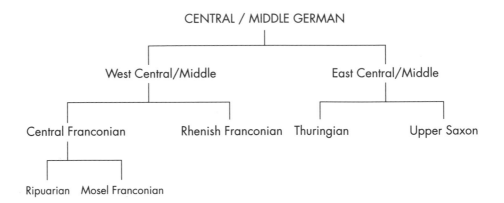

FIGURE 4.4 Central/Middle German dialects

divisions which have not been included in Figure 4.4 in order to avoid excessive detail. One of the reasons for this diversity is that many of the innovations that spread (generally speaking) from the southeast of the German-speaking area gradually petered out the further north and west they progressed.

UNIFORM FEATURES

There are in fact very few uniform features. Apart from the *-chen* type diminutive forms, the only uniform features are morphological.

Dual case pattern: they have distinct accusative and dative forms.
Dual plural forms in the present tense of verbs.
They have both perfect and imperfect (preterite) tense forms.

MAIN DIFFERENCES

Phonology As this is a transition area between south (High) and north (Low), the phonological patterns are highly complex. The famous shape of the **isoglosses** shown in Map 4.1 (*der Rheinische Fächer*, the Rhenish fan) can best be understood by analogy with an electrical flex without a plug: what appears to be a single isogloss running from east to west across the map is revealed to be a 'bundle' of isoglosses that more or less coincide until they reach the Western end of their extent, when they spread out like individual wires emerging from their insulating cover. What this represents is the variable progress of LV2. For example, while all Middle German dialects have the changes

medial /p/ → /f/	*schlafen* [ʃlaːfən]
medial /k/ → /x/	*machen* [maxən]
medial /t/ → /s, ts/	*essen* [ɛsən], *Katze* [katsə]

none have

medial /p/ → /pf/	*Appel* [apəl]

and none have

initial /p/ → /pf/	*Pund* [pʊnt] (but East Middle German has [fʊnt]).

In most forms, /p/ is replaced by /f/ after **liquid** sounds like /l/ and /r/, as in *helfen* or *Dorf*. However, Ripuarian dialects (spoken in the area around Cologne) retain the older forms: [dɔːrp], [hɛlpən]. In some relic forms in Ripuarian and Mosel Franconian dialects, the change /t/ → /s/ has also not occurred: for example, *das* and *was* remain [dat] and [vat].

Low German

Here too, there are more subdivisions than Fig. 4.5 suggests, but they are not significant for our purposes. Furthermore, the differences between West and East Low German are less important than the features that they share and which mark the contrast between Low German and High German.

FIGURE 4.5 Low German dialects

All Low German dialects lack the 'classic' phonological innovations that spread from the south:

No LV2: *Wasser, Pfeffer, ich* remain [vatər], [pɛpər], [ɪk]
No diphthongisation: *Haus* remains [hu:s]
No unrounding of front rounded vowels: *müde* remains [my:də]

and /st, sp/ generally remain /st, sp/, as opposed to /ʃt, ʃp/, in all positions: *Stein* [stain], *bist* [bɪst].

They all have a single 'oblique' (i.e. non-nominative) case: in most dialects, it is a form similar to the standard dative ([mi, di]), but in some it resembles the standard accusative ([mɪk, dɪk]). The encounter with the distinction between accusative and dative in standard German has resulted in the so-called *Akkudativ* in some dialects (notably the urban speech forms of Berlin), which is a kind of confusion of the two: *Ik liebe dir.*

Finally, virtually all Low German dialects have a single plural form for verbs in the present tense (either *-et* or *-en*, but not both), regardless of subject; both perfect and imperfect (preterite) tense forms; and *-ken* type diminutives.

Practical tasks

In this final section of this chapter, a number of practical tasks are offered to give you an opportunity to apply what you have learned about the distinctive features of German dialects. Just as the aim of the descriptive section was not to make you an expert on dialectology but to give you an overview of possible ways of distinguishing regional forms, so here the object is not to try to develop a profile of particular dialects, but rather to give you some practice in observing forms of regional variation by identifying specific features.[1]

---

1 The examples have been chosen more or less at random and have been selected on the basis that they give a sense of the range of variation across the geographical spectrum from south to north. They are taken to be 'representative' only in the sense that they are fairly readily identifiable to native speakers of German (i.e. the original spoken versions of the texts reproduced here in written from). Apart from in the first example, the transcripts of speech are given in 'normal' orthography rather than in phonetic script. This is a crude and imprecise form of representation,

Sample 1: Zurich

Ueli, a 35-year-old native speaker of *Züritüütsch*, was asked to tell the story depicted in a cartoon by Sempé (Figure 4.6). The first part of his account is given below in a broad phonetic transcription, followed by an equivalent version in standard German. Can you isolate phonological and lexical features in his speech that would help you to identify him as a speaker of a Swiss (High Alemannic) dialect?

[alzo: das ıʃ ə gʃıxt fɔn sãpe:, ə bıldŗgʃıxt. dʌ zıtst ə gzɛlʃaft bi:m abıgɛssə, ıʃ luʃtıg, wa:tət ʊfs ɛssə ʊnt fŗtri: bt̩ zıx tsi:t, mıt gʃıxtə. aınə fŗtsɛlt fɔ glati:s ʊnt nəm u:sgang, ʊnt rʊms! dʌ li:gt ŗ. alə amy:zi:rən zıx kœʃtlıx ʊnt naty:rlıx vɛkt di: gʃıxt ɛ:nlıxə ərlabnıs bi: alən ɔndərə. dŗ ɛrʃtə fŗtsɛlt vi: ŗ baim aŋl̩n fɔr lu:tər i:fər n̩ haŋ hınab̥rʊtʃt ʊnt ım vasər landət. d̥ frœlıxkait ʃti:gt]

Also, das ist eine Geschichte von Sempé, eine Bildergeschichte. Da sitzt eine Gesellschaft beim Abendessen, ist lustig, wartet aufs Essen und vertreibt die Zeit mit Geschichten. Einer erzählt vom Glattcis und einem Ausgang und rums! da liegt er. Alle amüsieren sich köstlich und natürlich weckt die Geschichte ähnliche Erlebnisse bei allen anderen. Der erste erzählt wie er beim Angeln vor lauter Eifer einen Hand hinabrutscht und im Wasser landet. Die Fröhlichkeit steigt.

Sample 2: Frankfurt

Frankfurt speech has many of the features typical of Central/Middle German dialects, particularly those known as Rhenish Franconian (*Rheinfränkisch*). The following text is taken from the transcript of an interview with a Frankfurt taxi driver. Comment on the words in italics (some, but not all, of which contain features described under Central/

but it is used here to enable those less practised in phonetic transcription to attempt the tasks, and because the exercises are concerned with the recognition of a relatively few, broadly defined features, as opposed to the close reading of whole passages and fine-grained phonetic analysis; Sample 3 actually appeared in this form. Where it is impossible to represent a particular sound in this way, a phonetic transcription of the word concerned is added in brackets. Most good dictionaries include a section on phonetic symbols.

FIGURE 4.6 Dinner party anecdotes

Source: Sempé 1962

Middle German dialects in the previous section pp. 71–3). You could also compare this authentic text with the pastiche of Frankfurt speech in the office notice shown earlier (p. 63).

INTERVIEWER: Warum haben Sie gerade diesen Beruf gewählt?

TAXI DRIVER: *Da Vada* [faːd̥ə] hat *a Taxiunternehma* gehabt, da *lach* [laɣ] nichts näher, wie der Sohn auch wieder das Taxi zu *übernehme*.

INTERVIEWER: Erzählen Sie mir ein bißchen übers Leben in Frankfurt.

TAXI DRIVER: Öh, ich bin hier ja groß *geworde* in Frankfurt, beziehungsweise *drübbe* in *Saksehause* (Sachsenhausen, die Frankfurter Altstadt), ja, und man gewöhnt sich da natürlich an seine Heimatstadt, und *isch* behaupte, Frankfurt is' *a* schöne Stadt, *gell*. Gibt natürlich *aach* negative *Anzeiche* [antsaiʒə], und Frankfurt is' ja rein geographisch, öhm, *liecht* sie im Zentrum von Deutschland, mir *habe* 'n *große* Bahnhof, da *komme* viele Gäste aus aller Welt, *Geschäftsleude* [lɔid̥ə], und mir *habe* den große Flughafen.

INTERVIEWER: Was müßte ein Gast in Frankfurt unbedingt gesehen haben?

TAXI DRIVER: Ja, vor *alle Dinge* mal *da* Römer, *da Römerberch* (Römerberg), *du* Paulskirche, und das *Goedehaus* [gø̈d̥ə] is' natürlich sehr *wichtich*, und öh unsere neue *alde* [ald̥ə] Oper, die is' aufgebaut *worde*, *hädde* [hɛd̥ə] schon *a* paar Jahr früher aufgebaut werden können. Was haben *mer* noch, *mer* haben *da* Palmegarde [gaːd̥ə] (Palmengarten), man müßte *sisch* den *besischtisch* (besichtigen). Und dann *Saksehause*, und da müßte man also auch *amal* den *Ebbelwei* [ɛb̥əlvai] (Apfelwein) *koste* und *da Ribbsche* [rɪb̥ʃə](Rippchen) mit Kraut *esse*.

Sample 3: Cologne

The popular Cologne-based rock band BAP was one of the first German bands to reject the orthodoxy of the 1960s and 1970s that to be taken seriously you had to sing in English. They were in the vanguard of a movement to compose lyrics not simply in German but in their local dialect, a practice previously associated with traditional folk music and the like. BAP's lyrics are in a stylised form of *Kölsch*, an urban speech variety that derives from Ripuarian (*Ripuarisch*). The text in this exercise is one of their songs; the list of common *Kölsch* features below might help you to understand the lyrics:

/t/ not	→ [s] in some relic forms	*dat, wat, et*
/p/ not	→ [f]	*auf = op*
/p/ not	→ [pf]	*klopft = klopp, Kopf = Kopp*
		Apfelsaft = Appelsapp
/ai/	→ [iː]	*weiß = wieß, bleib = bliev*
/au/	→ [ʊ]	*aus = uss*
/g/	→ [j]	*gestern = jestern*
/b/	→ [v]	*ab und zu = avv und zu*
lenition		*später = späder*
final 'consonant clusters' simplified		*fest = fess*
definite article = *dä* (all genders)		

Miscellaneous lexical items

Zeit	*= Zick*
seit	*= sick*
dein	*= ding*
heute	*= hück*
Ende	*= Eng*
er	*= hä*
wir	*= mer*
weiter	*= wigger*

Read the lyrics and attempt to 'translate' them into standard German (a version is given at the end of the chapter). Then consider which version you find more successful as a rock lyric. NB Tip 1: It is a song about 'lost love'. Tip 2: Don't expect the lyrics to be particularly meaningful!

Jraaduss

1 Manchmohl setz ich he römm un ich frooch mich, woröm
et su kumme moot, wie et kohm, wie et jetz ess
un ich saach mer, dat et irgendwo wiggerjonn muss,
jraaduss
Noch häng ding Bild ahn der Wand un mäht mich rejeläsch krank
ich hann ding Stemm noch em Ohr un ich froore mich nur
ob dat alles nix woor, en dä letzte paar Johr, met dir.

Refrain

Bliev do, wo de bess, halt dich irgendwo fess,
un bliev su, wie du woors, jraaduss.

2 Avv und zo merk ich dann, wie joot et dunn kann,
wemmer Luftschlösser baut un op Zufäll vertraut,
janix mieh plant, op janix mieh waat, nur su.
Dann weet alles verdräng, weil sons nix mieh jet bring,
weil sons himmelblau grau weet und mir alles zovill weet
weil em jeden Jedanke e Bild vun dir steck, jank weg.

Refrain

3 Et woor schön, et woor joot, ahm Eng e bessje ze koot,
dausend un ein Naach, wo Donner un Blitz kraach,
'ne Film ohne Schluß, wo nix ess wie et muß, jraaduss.
Denk ens aff un zo dran, ahn dat wat mer noch hann,
wat uns keiner mieh nemp, weil et wohr ess un stemp,
ahn dat Stöck 'Ich' vun dir und dat Stock 'Do' von mir,
jraaduss.

Refrain

Sample 4: Berlin

Rather like the speech varieties associated with London or New York,
Berlinisch is a speech form that is particularly readily identified by
German-speakers wherever they come from. While there are relatively few
morphological features peculiar to *Berlinisch* (most such non-standard
features are common throughout North Germany), there are a large
number of lexical items typically associated with Berlin (e.g. *Schrippe*
for *Brötchen*, *dufte* for *chic*). However, it is pronunciation features that
are particularly distinctive. The six most common **variables**, with their
standard and non-standard realisations (**variants**), are:

Variable		Standard variant	Berlinisch variant
(g)	*gemacht*	[g]	[J]
(ai)	*einmal*	[ai]	[e:]
(au)1	*auch*	[au]	[o:]

(au)2	*auf*	[au]	[ʊ]
(ç)	*ich*	[ç]	[k]
(s)	*das*	[s]	[t]

(See Schlobinski 1987: 60–7)

It is important to realise that the way these variants are used differs from one speaker to another: few speakers will use the non-standard variant of any of the features on every possible occasion, but most of the *Berlinisch* forms are likely to be found at least some of the time in the speech of a typical Berliner (and this is true of variation in all regional speech forms). A number of factors influence the relative frequency of non-standard realisations, some of which are difficult to account for precisely (e.g. social context, social class or the speaker's mood), but some of the features are subject to identifiable linguistic constraints. For instance, the (au)1 variable is 'lexically restricted', that is to say, it is confined to a small handful of words and is most frequently observed in *auch*. The realisation of the (g) variable, on the other hand, varies according to the phonological context: the non-standard [J] variant tends to be used far more in the affix *ge-* than in any other context (e.g. you are more likely to hear *jerufen* than *jrün* or *eijentlich*).

Some of these features are illustrated clearly in this extract from an interview with an 80-year-old *Berlinerin* (recorded in the late 1980s): how consistent is she in her use of non-standard variants? (Note also other features that are common to many non-standard (Northern) varieties: e.g. *denn* for *dann*; *nich'* as the normal form of **tag question**; **elision** and **assimilation,** as in *hammer* for *haben wir*, *anne Mauer* for *an der Mauer*).

INTERVIEWER: Hat sich in Berlin seit dem Krieg sehr viel verändert?

FRAU S.: Sehr viel, is' ja überhaupt nicht wiederzuerkennen. Wenn ich dran denke, wie wir früher die Friedrichstraße und die Leipzijerstraße 'lang jejang' sind, und der der Potsdamer Platz, det sieht ja heute furchtbar aus. Ik kann mir det ooch gar nicht angucken. Da anne Mauer. Na ja, und der Alexanderplatz, der is' ja auch, hat sich ooch vollkommen jeändert.

INTERVIEWER: Wie haben Sie die Nachkriegsjahre persönlich erlebt?

FRAU S.: [...] Ja, zweiundfuffzich hat denn wohl meine Tochter jeheiratet, und denn kam Peter vierundfuffzig uff da Welt. Na ja, denn ging et eigentlich denn, kam paar bessre Jahre, denn mußte mein Mann uff Rente gehn, weil er schwere Arteriosklerose hatte, nich', der hat 'n Beipaß jekriegt, denn sind wir acht Jahre nach Westdeutschland jezogen, da war ich immer krank. Na ja, denn hatten wir in Berlin wieder eine Wohnung gesucht, sind wir nach Hause jezogen. Inzwischen war denn ooch meine zweite Enkelin jeboren, und nun hab' ich noch zwei Urenkel.

■■■ As we are dealing with spoken varieties of German, there is obviously no substitute for listening to actual speech. Collect your own data in the form of recordings of television or radio programmes, film soundtracks or popular music, and use this for practice in transcription and as the basis for the kind of analysis suggested in the tasks above.

Further reading

Barbour and Stevenson (1990), Chapters 3, 4 and 5, on the form and study of regional variation in German.

Clyne (1995), Chapter 4, on the use and function of dialects and on language in education in Germany and Austria.

Dittmar, Schlobinski and Wachs (1986), on variation in and attitudes towards *Berlinisch*.

Durrell (1992), Chapter 1, on general aspects of regional variation, with many useful examples.

König (1978), contains brief, accessible introductions on many aspects of regional variation, illustrated with a large number of maps and figures.

Mattheier (1980), on how, where and why German dialects are used, and on language use in education.

Moosmüller (1995), on attitudes towards regional variation in Austria, especially in the speech of politicians.

Müller and Wertenschlag (1985), a listening comprehension course on Swiss German, intended mainly to help 'other' Swiss citizens overcome comprehension problems.

Russ (1990), detailed but accessible linguistic descriptions of individual dialects.

Russ (1994), on various aspects of regional variation in German.

Schlobinski (1984), a popularised historical account of research into the form and use of *Berlinisch*.

Schönfeld and Schlobinski (1995), on sociolinguistic changes in Berlin speech since unification.

Appendix

'Standard German' version of BAP song Jraaduss

1 Manchmal sitz' ich herum und ich frag' mich, warum
es so kommen mußte, wie es kam, wie es jetzt ist
und ich sag' mir, daß es irgendwie weitergehen muß,
geradeaus.
Noch hängt dein Bild an der Wand und macht mich regelrecht krank,
ich hab' deine Stimme im Ohr und ich frage mich nur
ob das alles nichts war, in den letzten paar Jahren, mit dir.

Refrain

Bleib da, wo du bist, halt dich irgendwie fest,
und bleib so, wie du warst, geradeaus.

2 Ab und zu merk' ich dann, wie gut es tun kann,
wenn man Luftschlösser baut und auf Zufall vertraut,
gar nichts mehr plant, auf gar nichts mehr wartet, nur so.
Dann wird alles verdrängt, weil sonst nichts mehr etwas bringt,
weil sonst himmelblau grau wird und alles zu viel wird,
weil in jedem Gedanken ein Bild von dir steckt, ganz weg.

Refrain

3 Es war schön, es war gut, am Ende ein bißchen zu kurz,
tausend und eine Nacht, wo Donner und Blitz kracht,
ein Film ohne Schluß, wo nichts ist, wie es sein muß,
geradeaus.
Denken wir ab und zu dran, an das, was wir noch haben,
was uns keiner mehr nimmt, weil es wahr ist und stimmt,
an das Stück 'ich' von dir und das Stück 'du' von mir,
geradeaus.

Refrain

• • •

Chapter 5

Written German,
spoken German

Classifying texts

Die Fete hat in der Aula von der *High School* stattgefunden, und wie wir drin waren, hab ich mit 'n paar von den andern das Klo gesucht. Aber wie ich den Reißverschluß aufmachen will, geht der nich runter, weil da is 'n Hemdzipfel eingeklemmt. Wie ich 'ne Zeitlang dran rumprobiert hab, geht 'n netter kleiner Kerl von 'ner gegnerischen Schule den Trainer suchen, und der kommt mit den zwei Gorillas, und sie probieren, ob sie meine Hose nich aufkriegen. [. . .]

Fast alle haben ihren Preis schon abgeholt und „danke" gesagt, und jetzt bin ich dran. [. . .] Alle fangen sie an zu klatschen und rufen Bravo und stehen sogar auf. [. . .] Ich bin aber so was von verblüfft, daß ich absolut nich mehr weiß, was ich machen soll, und einfach stehen bleib. Dann wird's ganz still, und der Mann am Mikro beugt sich vor und fragt mich, ob ich noch was sagen möcht. Da sag ich bloß: „Ich muß pinkeln." [. . .]

Für den Rest vom Abend hat mich der Trainer böse angefunkt, aber wie das Bankett vorbei war, isser dann doch mit mir und den Gorillas aufs Klo gegangen und hat meine Hose aufgerissen. Ich hab die ganze Schüssel vollgepißt!

„Gump," hat der Trainer gesagt, wie ich fertig war, „du hast vielleicht 'ne Art, dich auszudrücken."

(Groom 1986/1994: 20–2)

The novel *Forrest Gump* is written in the form of a fictitious monologue, a 'first-person narrative', and this short extract (from the German translation) illustrates how the author has tried to represent spontaneous colloquial speech.

■   Read the extract carefully and try to identify features that you would consider characteristic of *spoken* German. Group them under the following headings:

- phonology (e.g. elision: *'n paar* for *ein paar*);
- morphology (e.g. *von* instead of genitive: *für den Rest vom Abend*);
- syntax (e.g. non-standard word order after *weil*: *weil da is 'n Hemdzipfel eingeklemmt* – see also pp. 98–102);
- lexis (e.g. colloquial vocabulary: *aufkriegen*).

Are there any features that do not seem to fit into any of these categories? For example, the text is a narrative: which tenses are used; which connecting words are used to indicate the sequence of events; how is other people's speech represented?

■ ■ Translate the text into English, concentrating on reproducing the colloquial style of the German version. If possible, compare your translation with the original English version.

Like a figure from an H. M. Bateman cartoon ('The boy who said "I need a pee" at the prize-giving ceremony!'), Forrest Gump says the right thing in the wrong place at the wrong time. His solecism is a classic example of communicative incompetence: whether through ignorance or temporary distraction, he fails to observe the 'norms' of communicative behaviour, which can be just as important as the grammatical 'rules' that determine how a sentence can be formed. Full sociolinguistic competence requires knowledge of the possibilities and limitations both of the forms of the language and of their use (we shall discuss this in more detail in Chapter 7).

We all know that we use language differently in different contexts (reflect, for example, on your own practice in telephone conversations, seminars or chats over lunch, in brief written messages, formal letters or essays), but how can we capture the ways in which our usage varies? How should we categorise or classify our usage? Two sets of oppositions that are commonly used for this purpose are written vs spoken and formal vs informal, but they are different in nature: the former at least appears to be an 'either/or' category, while the latter is clearly a continuum. Furthermore, they are interdependent as both written and spoken texts may be more or less formal. Which should we therefore take as primary when it comes to describing and classifying the language of particular texts? Finally, even if we can find satisfactory ways of analysing language use, how should the results of our analysis be presented in grammars and dictionaries? As the title of this chapter suggests, we shall start from the assumption that there are significant differences between written and spoken German, but it should become clear that in practice these contrasts are becoming increasingly blurred.

Constraints on the production of written and spoken texts

Neither written nor spoken texts are produced in a vacuum. For any individual text you can specify certain aspects of the circumstances under which it was produced, and its interpretation will depend, at least to some extent, on this information. Consider the following sets of contrasts that have been proposed for the conditions under which spoken and written texts, respectively, are produced:

Spoken language	*Written language*
1 Face-to-face interaction between participants.	1 Written texts are independent of particular situations.
2 The product of the interaction is the result of a joint effort of the participants.	2 Written texts are produced by individuals in isolation, not as a joint venture.
3 Each utterance is addressed to a particular person and is affected by the speaker's knowledge of/relationship with that person.	3 Written texts are not addressed to specific individuals but are constructed in such a way that they can be understood by a general group of readers.
4 Utterances are spontaneous and are subject to time constraints, e.g. the ability of addressees to maintain concentration, to absorb, process and memorise what is being said to them.	4 Neither writing nor reading a written text is subject to tight time constraints.
5 Speakers can use both linguistic and **paralinguistic** means of communication.	5 Communication can be achieved solely by linguistic means.

6 Speakers can point at objects under discussion.	6 Objects can be referred to only by explicit linguistic means.
7 Utterances may serve a range of functions, e.g. not only conveying a 'message' in terms of their content, but keeping the conversation going or expressing a reaction to another utterance.	7 Written texts are impersonal and do not necessarily convey any information about the author.
8 Spoken texts are 'dynamic': they can be corrected, revised, negotiated as you go along.	8 Written texts are 'static': they are fixed, definitive and unchangeable.

(based on Coulmas 1985: 104)

- Do you agree with the contrasts that are presented here? Would you omit any of the factors or add any new ones?

- Where you find them acceptable, do you think they apply generally to all spoken texts and all written texts? Think of specific examples: e.g. casual conversation, dialogue in a railway booking office, business meeting, telephone call, personal letter, newspaper article, essay, fax and e-mail messages.

- ■ Draw up a list of what you consider to be the crucial differences between the ways in which spoken and written texts are produced in terms of the impact they may have on the language used. Keep these in mind as you work through the following sections.

Some fundamental contrasts in the forms of written and spoken German

Your analysis of the passage from *Forrest Gump* in the previous section was a first attempt to describe the distinctive features of texts in a systematic way. In this section we shall explore the possibilities of this kind of analysis a bit further. First, consider the following extract from a discussion between the writer Günter Grass and a group of (high school) students:

Version A   Unedited transcript of tape recording

Speakers:

A = Chair of discussion group
B = Student
C = Günter Grass

(*Note*: A highly simplified form of transcription conventions is used here: as phonetic details are not significant, ordinary script is used, but there are no capital letters and no punctuation; and dots are used to indicate pauses.)

A: meine damen und herrn .. wer .. möchte das gespräch eröffnen? bitte ..
B: herr grass sie lasen eben aus katz und maus vor .. unter anderem haben sie in diesem stück .. wirliebendiestürme und mehrere andere worte zusammengeschrieben hat das einen
C: mhm
B: besonderen zweck .. soll darauf besonders hingewiesen werden oder
C: ja das sind äh das ist also als stilmittel mein ich damit das sind so begriffe ..
B: ja
C: sind ja eigentlich schlagworte klischees
B: mhm ..
C: äh die ich .. äh die auch so gespielt es wurde gesagt wir singen jetzt wirliebendiestürme .. und das is phonetisch auch übernommen .. und dazu kommt daß dieses wirliebendiestürme .. ein zeitkolorit ist .. s wurde zu einer bestimmten zu bestimmten anlässen gesungen .. deswegen läßt es sich so zusammenfassen ..

(adapted from Schank and Schoenthal 1983: 8)

- Identify features (including at the level of interaction between speakers) that you would consider characteristic of spoken language; compare what you find here with what you said about the *Forrest Gump* passage.

- Now consider the following two versions of the same extract: in what specific ways do they differ from version A?

Version B   Edited version prepared for publication

STUDENT: Herr Grass, Sie lasen eben aus Katz und Maus vor. Unter anderem haben Sie in diesem Stück „Wirliebendiestürme" und

mehrere andere Worte zusammengeschrieben. Hat das einen besonderen Zweck? Soll darauf besonders hingewiesen werden?

GRASS: Ja das sind so Begriffe. Es sind eigentlich Schlagworte, Klischees.
Es wurde gesagt: „Wir singen jetzt wirliebendiestürme", und das ist
phonetisch übernommen. Hinzu kommt, daß dieses „Wirliebendiestürme" ein Zeitkolorit ist, es wurde immer zu einer bestimmten
Zeit zu bestimmten Anlässen gesungen. Deswegen läßt sich das so
zusammenfassen.

Version C   Written version intended as a summary or report

Grass verteidigte am 10.12.1963 in einem Gespräch mit Schülern das
in seiner Erzählung Katz und Maus wiederholt zu beobachtende
Zusammenschreiben von Liedtiteln („Wirliebendiestürme") mit dem
Hinweis darauf, daß dies früher immer auch so gesungen worden sei
und daß er mit dieser Schreibung ein Zeitkolorit andeuten wolle.

Now consider the two texts below, both of which relate to the same event
(an accident in a factory; both texts are taken from Berg et al. 1978: 47).
The first is the transcript of an eye-witness account and the second is the
official report of the investigation into the accident.

Version A   Augenzeugenaussage

Das war so: Ich und der Meister haben in Halle 6 – es war so um 3
Uhr am Nachmittag – 'ne Wasserleitung repariert. Da hinten, wo die
vielen Rohre laufen. Ich kenn mich da nicht aus. Wir warn aufm
Gerüst, so fast 4 Meter hoch. Da is mir schlecht geworden, und ich
hab's dem Meister gesagt. „Hau ab," sagte er, „sonst hagelst du noch
runter. Ich mach das hier alleine." Ich bin also runter und hab mich
auf 'ne Materialkiste gesetzt. Dann hab ich zum Meister
raufgeschaut. Er war grad fertig und hat das Werkzeug in die Kiste
getan. Ich dachte, jetzt nimmt er die Kiste und kommt. Da hat er sich
aufgerichtet und langte nach 'ner Stange vom Gerüst. Aber dann is er
zusammengeklappt und rutschte vom Gerüst runter. Zum Glück is er
auf die Abdeckmatten gefallen. Ich bin gleich hin. Er hat sich nicht
gerührt. Da hab ich laut geschrien. Und dann gings auf einmal zu.
Der Doktor kam und Kollegen und der Hallenmeister, dann der
Krankenwagen und die Polizei. Ich glaub, dem Meister is schlecht
geworden wie mir.

■■ Look again at the *Forrest Gump* passage (p. 84) and your analysis of it, then identify which features of this text you would characterise as typical of (colloquial) spoken German.

■■ In what ways would you change the text if you were to write a formal account of what happened? (You could try writing such an account.)

Version B   Untersuchungsbericht über die Unfallursache

Betr.: Unfall des Karl Troger, Spenglermeister, im Hause, geb. 24.8.41, wohnhaft: Katharinenstraße 12, z.Zt. Städt. Krankenhaus, Abt. 3B. Tag des Unfalls: 10.2.93

Die Untersuchungen zur Unfallursache sind abgeschlossen. Das ständige Gerüst in Halle 6 an der Südwand war zur Zeit des Unfalls in einwandfreiem Zustand. Ein Fehler am Gerüst kann als Unfallursache ausgeschlossen werden.

Die Untersuchung der Rohre hat ergeben, daß aus der undichten Verschraubung eines Gasrohres, das sich unmittelbar neben dem vom Unfallverletzten reparierten Wasserrohr befindet, Gas ausströmte. Nachdem es dem Lehrling Georg Müller schlecht geworden war und T. ihn weggeschickt hatte, muß auch den Unfallverletzten ein Unwohlsein befallen haben, das auf das Ausströmen des Gases zurückgeführt werden kann. Die undichte Verschraubung wurde inzwischen repariert. Außerdem wurde eine Untersuchung sämtlicher Gasrohre in allen Werkshallen eingeleitet, um in Zukunft weitere Unfälle dieser Art zu vermeiden.

■ Which features of this text would you characterise as typical of formal written German?

■■ In what ways would you change this text in order to produce a less formal written account?

■■ Ask a native speaker of German to give an oral account in German of an exciting or dangerous event they have experienced or witnessed. Record their account on tape and then transcribe it. Ask them to give you a written version of the same story, then compare this with the transcript of the spoken version. What differences can you identify in the language and the structure of the two versions?

■■ Finally, before moving on to the next section, try to summarise the kinds of feature you would now expect to find in written and spoken texts, respectively. Consider also to what extent the written and spoken 'codes' of German seem to be distinct from each other.

Blurring the boundaries in modern German

Your conclusions from the previous section should have given you some (albeit very rough and ready) criteria to use as a yardstick for studying spoken and written texts. One way of testing your assumptions about spoken language is to compare 'real' speech with fictional representations of speech. For example, read the following extract from an actual interview:

VERENA D.: Zum Beispiel ham wir einen Club gebildet, vor circa 3/4 Jahren, Inter-Club, ein paar Freunde und ich. Wir wollten mal etwas anderes machen als immer tanzen. Und wir hatten über den Ostermarsch, hatten wir Bekanntschaft mit anderen Jugend-Clubs, und da haben wir uns zusammengesetzt und han beraten und ham beschlossen, da auch so einen Club zu bilden. Und das hat auch dann geklappt. IC [Inter-Club] hat schon inzwischen 15 Mitglieder, feste Mitglieder, is' zwar nicht viel, aber immerhin. Und es macht riesig Spaß, da in dem Club zu arbeiten. Meine Eltern verstehen nun nicht, daß ich mich dafür interessiere, für unsern Club und allgemein für Politik. [...] Mein Vater hat viel Verständnis dafür, aber meine Mutter und meine Großmutter, die auch bei uns lebt, die sind ziemlich ängstlich und verstehen es eben nich mehr so. Das kam eigentlich von meinem Opa, mein Opa, der war lange Zeit im KZ [Konzentrationslager], war verfolgt wegen seiner politischen Ansicht, er war Kommunist, und er hatte viel durchzumachen und dadurch ja auch die ganze Familie.

(Runge 1968: 109–10)

■ Compare this genuine monologue with the passage from *Forrest Gump* on p. 84: which features do they have in common and in which respects do they differ from each other?

Analysing language use in dialogue is often more complex than in monologues, as the interaction between speakers also has to be taken into account (look again at Version A of the Grass interview, p. 88). The following extract from a television interview with Dresden secondary school students (about changes in the school system following unification in 1990) may serve as an illustration:

QUESTION: Was ist für dich jetzt nach der Wende in der Schule anders?

ANSWER: Na, daß es jetzt eben Gymnasium und so was gibt.

QUESTION: Gefällt dir die Schule jetzt besser als damals?

ANSWER: Allerdings ja.

QUESTION: Warum?

ANSWER: Nicht mehr so streng alles.

QUESTION: Was hat sich für dich nach der Wende in der Schule geändert?

ANSWER: Also, es ist ziemlich kompliziert geworden – alles Chaos. Also, es gab keine Lehrbücher dieses Jahr, ziemlich also, es war, wie soll ich sagen, alles Chaos eben.

QUESTION: Hat sich auch in der Unterrichtsform etwas geändert?

ANSWER: Die Unterrichtsform kaum. Sie hat sich nur angeglichen an die westliche Unterrichtsform.

(BBC 1992–4: Series 1, Programme 3)

■   Which features of this text strike you as typical of a spontaneous, informal dialogue?

■   Using this dialogue as your guide, attempt a critical assessment of the following extracts from coursebooks in German as a Foreign Language:

Extract A

MUTTER: In Zwei Monaten gehst du auf die Universität nach Heidelberg, Werner. Wir müssen überlegen, ob du alles hast, was du zum Anziehen brauchst. Komm, wir wollen in deiner Kommode und in deinem Kleiderschrank nachsehen.

SOHN: Gut, Mutter, fangen wir gleich an. Hier sind meine Hemden – ein ganz stattlicher Stoß! Damit komme ich doch sicher aus!

MUTTER: Laß sehen, Werner. Drei weiße Hemden zum guten Anzug, drei einfarbige Hemden und vier gemusterte Sporthemden – ja, das ist eigentlich genug. Und hier sind die Unterhemden – vier Netzhemden für den Sommer und vier Unterhemden mit kurzen

Ärmeln für den Winter. Vergiß nur ja nicht, die Unterhemden bei kaltem Wetter auch wirklich anzuziehen. Ich glaube, daß man sich dadurch manche Erkältung erspart.

(Barsch 1966: 34, cited in Schank and Schoenthal 1983: 34)

Extract B

HANS MÜLLER: Holla, Kinder, das ist fein! Heute ist Schluß; was machst du in den Ferien, Fischer?

ERICH FISCHER: Was ich mache? Wir gehen in den Schwarzwald; wir wollen große Wanderungen durch die Tannenwälder und über die Berge machen. Und du?

HANS MÜLLER: Wir fahren mit dem Auto an die Ostsee, nach Warnemünde; ich will viel baden und schwimmen. Oh, es ist herrlich an der See, und ich schwimme so furchtbar gern. Wir wollen auch einen Ausflug nach Dänemark machen. Von Warnemünde fährt, wißt ihr, eine Fähre, ein großer Dampfer, worauf die Eisenbahnwagen fahren können; die Leute in dem Zug steigen nicht um.

JOHANN SCHNEIDER: Oh, das ist knorke! Hast du das Ding gesehen?

HANS MÜLLER: Ja, es ist riesengroß.

(Gottfried Schulz und Heinz Schlosser kommen heran.)

JOHANN SCHNEIDER: He da! Was macht ihr in den Ferien?

GOTTFRIED SCHULZ: Wir? Wir reisen nach England.

ALLE ZUSAMMEN: Nach England!! Oh, habt ihr Glück!

(Macpherson 1931: 169)

Extract C

ARZT: Na, was fehlt Ihnen denn?

PATIENT: Mein Hals tut weh.

ARZT: Aha, der Hals; zeigen Sie bitte mal! Ja, Ihr Hals ist rot. Sagen Sie mal „A"!

PATIENT: AAAAAA!!!

ARZT: Tut die Brust auch weh? Hier vorne?

PATIENT: Ja.

ARZT: Haben Sie Husten?

PATIENT: Etwas.

ARZT: Das ist eine Angina lacunaris.

PATIENT: Wie bitte?

ARZT: Das ist eine Entzündung. Tun die Ohren auch weh?

PATIENT: Ja, das Ohr links.

ARZT: Haben Sie die Schmerzen schon lange?
PATIENT: Nein, erst zwei Tage.

(Neuner et al. 1986: 52)

■ Why do you think texts A and B are written the way they are? What is the student supposed to learn from them?

■ Obviously, text C is much more 'authentic' than texts A and B, but exactly what is it about the three texts that makes this clear? Is there anything about text C that makes it less than completely convincing?

■ Compare all of these texts with the cartoon in Figure 5.1.

What all of these texts, at least theoretically, have in common is that they are examples of spontaneous colloquial speech produced in informal or semi-formal settings and are intended only for the immediate audience. Whatever degree of authenticity we may attribute to them, they all contain at least some features that enable us to categorise them as 'spoken texts': in other words, they conform to a greater or lesser extent to the *norms* of spoken German. In Chapter 6 we shall see some examples of ways in which spoken texts produced in more formal settings for public consumption are often more readily describable in terms of the norms of written German. As a result, they cast doubt on the validity of this basic distinction between spoken and written German. If we shift our attention here to written texts, however, we can see that the same process frequently operates in reverse: it is increasingly common to find language that we might consider characteristic of spoken German used in written (and printed) texts. This is particularly conspicuous in much modern journalism and in advertising, but is becoming commonplace in many different **text types**, which seems to demonstrate the growing importance of **orality** in modern life: even written texts often appear to 'speak' to us.

If we take the following short passage as a benchmark text, a text that can unequivocally be classified as being constructed in accordance with the norms of written German, we can then look at ways in which a variety of other written texts adopt spoken norms and thereby blur the distinction between what we have taken as fundamentally different categories of text.

■ Read this text carefully and identify features that seem to place the text as a whole firmly in the category of 'written German':

FIGURE 5.1 Representations of colloquial speech

Source: Stein 1995

Für die meisten Menschen ist das Haus oder die Wohnung nicht nur der Ort, an dem sie schlafen, essen, lieben und streiten. Die sprichwörtliche Tür, die sie hinter sich schließen, signalisiert den Rückzug in einen Bereich, der Sicherheit und Schutz gewährt. Geborgenheit und Gemütlichkeit, familiäre Traulichkeit und Selbstverwirklichung, Geselligkeit und Fernsehabend – all das bietet der häusliche Rahmen. Wenn die private Wohnumwelt durchschnittlich alle fünf Jahre neu gestaltet wird, wenn über 50% der Deutschen nahezu jeden Abend zu Hause verbringen, wenn der Wunsch nach einer größeren und schöneren Wohnung in den Ranglisten der Bundesbürger auf den vorderen Platz zu finden ist, wenn fast nirgends – außerhalb des Beruflebens – so viel Energie, Zeitaufwand und Eigenleistung aufgebracht wird wie bei der Verschönerung der eigenen vier Wände, dann steckt hierin nicht nur das Streben nach Brauchbarkeit, Gemütlichkeit und Schönheit. Je größer die Erfahrung von Sachzwang und Ohnmacht in Beruf und Politik und je geringer die Chance des einzelnen, seine Bedürfnisse einzubringen oder gar berücksichtigt zu sehen, um so mehr verlagert sich offenbar der Wunsch nach selbstbestimmtem Handeln in den Freizeit- und da vor allem in den Wohnbereich.

(Brunhöber 1983: 183)

■ Now read the following passages, all of which were published as written texts. In which respects do they seem to contain language more characteristic of spoken texts?

1 Fraunhofer Schoppenstube (review of a Munich wine bar)

Man hat kein Geld fürs Taxi. Man ist eh' in der Nähe. Man hat das Gefühl, einer geht grade noch. Und man hat Sehnsucht nach etwas Warmem, wie Frau Guhls Fleischpflanzl oder Mutterliebe. Man biegt ums Eck und schon strahlen sie einen an, das Besitzerehepaar, mit offenen Armen aus den Schaufenstern lächelnd. Allerdings hat uns diese sichtbare einladende Geste die erste Preiserhöhung seit drei Jahren beschert. Was soll's . . .

(Ammer and Link 1989: 54)

2 Digitale Anmache (magazine article on Berlin night life)

Freitagnacht in Berlin. In der Szenedisco „Tresor" flirtet Tom mit Martina. Eigentlich nichts Ungewöhnliches. Nur: Martina tanzt an diesem Abend im „Cu-Club", einige Kilometer entfernt. Sie turteln via Computer. Dank dem neuesten Trend im Berliner Nachtleben: Computerterminals in Discos und Bars. Für 300 Mark Monatsmiete bekommt jeder Club einen Computer und die passende Software, die Gäste können das Gerät zum Nulltarif benutzen. [...] Vorsichtig sollten Tom und Martina deshalb mit intimen Geständnissen sein – auch im „Boogaloo", „WMF", und „Friseur" stehen bereits Computer. [...] Sollte Martina bereits einen surfenden Freund haben und der so alles mitbekommen, was sie Tom an diesem Abend geschrieben hat, steht ihr ein ganz besonders kommunikatives Treffen bevor.

(Birgit Krans, *Tango* 18, 27 April 1995: 89)

3 Reaktionärer Stinker (reader's letter in student magazine)

Hallo,
wie kommt ihr eigentlich dazu, so einen 'reaktionären Stinker' wie Marcel Reich-Ranicki zu interviewen? Der hat ja richtig Geist. Glaubt ihr nicht, daß ihr eure Leser damit überfordert? Seid ihr nicht zeitgeistig genug, ein Weichei wie Stefan Raab oder sonstige Hohlköpfe zu interviewen, deren blanke Albernheiten auch wirklich jeder verstehen kann – weil sie nichts beinhalten.

(*Audimax*, April/May 1995. 4)

■■ Do the same with the following text, then collect other advertisements from a variety of sources and compare them with each other from this particular perspective (i.e. are they composed more in a written or more in a spoken mode?).

4 Die Dose auf Tour

Die Getränkedosenhersteller tun was! Das werden Aufklärungsaktionen und Pilotprojekte beweisen. Hohe Recyclingsaktionen sind keine Utopie – wenn alle mitmachen und Dosen nicht mehr in der Landschaft oder auf der Straße „entsorgt" werden.

Das Programm reicht von Aktivitäten bei großen Sport-Events über Aktionen an Autobahnen, auf Bahnhöfen und in Urlaubsgebieten bis hin zum Projekt „Saubere Stadt '95". Hier dreht sich einen ganzen Sommer lang alles um Getränkedosen, um den Wertstoffkreislauf, das Sammeln und das Recyceln. Doch nicht nur Information ist angesagt. Zusätzlich gibt es Sammelwettbewerbe und Mitmachaktionen.

> Nicht vergessen: Wer mitmacht, hilft aktiv beim Umweltschutz.
> Gemeinsam schaffen wir's.
>
> (from a publicity leaflet published by Die Getränkedose Hersteller GmbH
> Düsseldorf: *Genießen. Sammeln. Recyceln.*)

What do we mean by 'right' and 'wrong'?

> Ein Gast will in einer Kneipe zahlen. „Sieben Bier", sagt der Wirt,
> „das macht 14 Mark." „Sechs Bier", hält der gelegentliche Besucher
> des Lokals dagegen. „Sieben", beharrt der Wirt. Was erwidert
> der Gast? „Wegen eines Bieres streite ich mich doch nicht!" Oder:
> „Wegen einem Bier wollen wir doch keinen Ärger haben." Dritte
> Möglichkeit: „Wegen 'nem Bier kein Theater." [. . .] Wegen dem
> Wörtchen „wegen" herrscht weitverbreitete Verwirrung. Darf man es
> so gebrauchen oder darf man nicht? Ist der Dativ falsch? Oder muß
> wegen des korrekten Umganges mit der Grammatik immer ein
> Genitiv auf „wegen" folgen? [. . .] Meinetwegen oder wegen meiner
> – letzteres ist laut Wörterbuch „süddeutsch" und auch „selten". Mag
> sein, trotzdessen kann meinetwegen – dem Wörterbuch trotz – beim
> Schreiben, Sprechen und des Stiles wegen mal so oder mal so
> verfahren werden. Statt dem Philologen alles recht machen zu
> wollen, sollten wir stattdessen nachdenken, wann wir wem zuliebe
> uns welcher Fälle bedienen.
>
> (Wolfgang Sauer, 'Von Fall zu Fall', *Die Welt*)

We started this chapter by suggesting that there is an important difference
between what is *possible* in a language regardless of context (described by
rules) and what is considered *appropriate* in a given context (described by
conventions or *norms*). This distinction has a number of consequences for
the way in which we view language in use, and we shall devote the final
section of this chapter to exploring some of them.

It is often argued that what defines a native speaker of a language is
the ability to judge whether a particular 'piece of language' (a sentence or
an utterance) is either possible or appropriate: in other words, he or she
has internalised both the linguistic rules and the sociolinguistic norms, and
can apply both rules and norms when making judgements about actual
language use. In many instances, this is quite unproblematic: for example,
we can expect unanimous rejection of a sentence like 'In Freiburg keine
Vampire wir haben gesehen' as 'ungrammatical', or 'not possible', or

simply 'incorrect, wrong'. Equally, it is likely that virtually all native speakers would acknowledge that an utterance like 'Der ist doch total bescheuert' would generally be considered appropriate or acceptable only in certain contexts (although there may not be general agreement on what these contexts are). However, there are some aspects of language use that are more controversial, as the discussion of *wegen* at the beginning of this section suggests.

■■ Ask a native speaker of German to attempt the following tasks:

1 **Please indicate whether in your view each of the following sentences is**
'correct' (✔),
'not strictly correct but acceptable' (?),
'acceptable in speaking but not in writing' (S), or
'incorrect' (x):

  (i) Maria geht selten ins Kino, weil sie eine Dissertation schreibt. ( )

  (ii) Ich trinke Jägermeister, weil auf dem Etikett hat er die Fauna und innen drin die Flora. ( )

  (iii) Ich glaub schon, obwohl ich kenn mich da nicht so gut aus. ( )

  (iv) Maria arbeitet zu hause, während Gisela muß früh in die Uni. ( )

  (v) Ich konnte nicht anrufen, weil ich war nicht so gut drauf. ( )

  (vi) Maria kann nicht mit uns ins Kino, weil sie muß ein Kapitel fertigschreiben. ( )

  (vii) Weil sie muß ein Kapitel fertigschreiben, kann Maria nicht mit uns ins Kino. ( )

  (viii) Maria kann, weil sie muß ein Kapitel fertigschreiben, nicht mit uns ins Kino. ( )

  (ix) Der Text ist jetzt bald getippt, während mit der Literaturliste ist es noch nicht so weit. ( )

  (x) Trotzdem Maria nicht mit uns kommen will, gehen wir ins Kino. ( )

(based on Glück and Sauer 1990: 44–50)

2 **Please indicate whether in your view there is anything wrong with each of the following sentences, and if so, what the error is:**

(i) Kein Schutt abladen! (Verbotsschild in Berlin)
(ii) Greift Euer Vorteil! (Gaststättenwerbung in Hannover)
(iii) Nur zwei kreative Kräfte können solche zarte und kleine Klangwunder hervorbringen. (Werbeanzeige für Lautsprecher)
(iv) Mach kein Scheiß, laß die Fragebogen weiß. (Volkszählung-Boykott-Parole)
(v) Schickt uns unsere 6 Millionen Gefangene zurück. (*diese woche*)
(vi) Borussias Generalprobe am Sonntag gegen Zweitligist Rot-Weiß Essen war trotz des 6:1 nicht gerade „das gelbe vom Ei." (*Kicker*)
(vii) Ein 27-jähriges Mädel ruft nach Dir. Antwort und kein Vertreterbesuch sichere ich Dir zu. (Heiratsannonce)
(viii) Durchfahrt verboten. Außer Bewohner und Versorgungsfahrzeuge. (Verkehrsschild in Erfurt)
(ix) Weil der Atom dem Demonstrant bekanntlich am allerwenigsten schmeckt? (*Titanic*)
(x) Und dabei hat doch die Wirklichkeit nur die Stadtverwaltung mal kurz den Arsch aufgerissen. (*Titanic*)

(based on Glück and Sauer 1990: 58–60)

■■ If possible, compare the responses of 'your' native speaker with those of other native speakers:

Task 1 How much agreement is there between the various 'judges'? Which sentences receive a common verdict and which ones seem debatable? How would you account for the different judgements in these cases?

Task 2 Have your judges identified an 'error' in each sentence? Do they agree on what the error in each instance is and on how to correct it?

■ Word order and case are two areas of German grammar that typically constitute a challenge to many learners of German: if the responses to these tasks by a number of native speakers are not uniform, what conclusions would you draw from this with respect to the way these features are taught and/or learned?

On the one hand, it could be argued that these tasks are artificial, as very few people apart from teachers have to make such judgements consciously in their everyday lives. On the other hand, one of the primary functions of grammars, dictionaries and other reference works is precisely to provide guidance on just these kinds of linguistic problem. This therefore raises the fundamental question of how such reference works should be written (see also Chapters 10 and 11): for example, is it their job to prescribe the 'correct' form of the language, to be the ultimate arbiters of what is 'right' and 'wrong'? If so, what should a grammar tell us, say, about the use of prepositions like *wegen*? Many existing grammars categorically stipulate the use of the genitive case with *wegen*; if we accept this pronouncement we have to regard the usage of many native speakers as wrong. However, if the common practice of perhaps the majority of native speakers differs from what is specified in grammars, this is surely a rather curious state of affairs. After all, where have the linguistic 'rules' come from that are enshrined in grammars?

We may say that reference works define the standard variety or form of a language, and the fact that individual usage frequently differs from

FIGURE 5.2 Word order with *weil* in colloquial speech
Source: Thomas Körner in *Wochenpost* 31, 1995

this is of no consequence. But as we have already seen in Chapter 1, not only does individual usage vary, but the standard form of a language is also constantly evolving. Linguistic change is a complex process, and it is not always easy to determine whether a given feature is actually undergoing a change from A to B, or whether A and B are simply two variants that co-exist on a fairly constant basis. For instance, does the use of two different word-order patterns after *weil* indicate change in progress, or does it signal different functions? Either way, however, if two or more alternatives exist, and especially if there is a recognisable pattern underlying their use, we are entitled to ask whether a grammar or dictionary should take account of this. (Consider, for example, Figure 5.2.)

■■ Consult as many grammars of German as you can and find out what they have to say about the two features we have been discussing here: word order after *weil* and case after *wegen*. Which do you find most helpful?

■■■ In the light of our discussions so far, do you think there should be separate grammars for written and spoken German, or should the different norms for writing and speaking be integrated into a single grammar? Does the distinction between written and spoken German even seem valid, or does it make more sense to distinguish at the level of formality?

■■■ More generally, do you feel it is possible to reconcile the concepts of rules and norms, or do they conflict with each other?

Further reading

Biber (1991), for a general discussion of the relationships between spoken and written language.

Braun (1987), especially Chapters 1.11 and 2, on a variety of trends in modern German.

Durrell (1992), especially Chapter 1, on ways of analysing linguistic differences between texts, but note that the concept of 'register' is used differently from the way it is used here: see Chapter 6 here.

Glück and Sauer (1990), Chapters 2–6, on the concept of 'norms' and on variation and change in contemporary German.

Glück and Sauer (1995), a very readable account in English of variation and change in contemporary German, illustrated with many examples.

Halliday (1989), for a general discussion of the relationships between spoken and written language.

Schank and Schoenthal (1983), a practical textbook on ways of analysing speech, with many examples.

Wardhaugh (1985), on the structure of spoken language and patterns of conversational interaction.

● ● ●

Chapter 6

Public language

Textual patterns

What is going to happen next in each of the following texts?

1   Good evening. A ridge of high pressure has been building up over
     the east of the country, but there are already signs that it won't
     last. . . .
2   British Airways announces the departure of flight 999 to Vancouver.
     . . .
3   Once upon a time, . . .
4   I, Anna Griselda Jackson, hereby declare this to be my last will. . . .

The answer in each case is simple, but what is it about these openings
that makes the remainder of the text more or less predictable? Part of the
answer obviously lies in the mention of certain key words, e.g. high
pressure, flight, will. However, there is more to it than that. If you asked
someone to write a fictitious weather forecast, airport announcement, fairy
tale, or will, it is more than likely that their text will begin in much the
same way as the relevant example here. Furthermore, we know that flight
departure announcements, for example, have not merely conventional
beginnings but a fairly uniform internal structure (e.g. 'All passengers
holding boarding cards should now proceed to Gate 11'). The point is that
what enables us to speak of particular 'text types' (see Chapter 5) is the fact
that texts performing a common function typically share specific structural
characteristics: for example, jokes need a punch line, and letters need
opening and closing formulas. In other words, individual texts may be
unique in their precise form, but they almost always fit a given pattern or
'template'.

   A template is a pattern cut out in wood, card, plastic or metal, used
to help reproduce a shape accurately in woodwork, cloth design and so
on. However, the word is also used in word-processing terminology to
refer to a file that provides a model for creating a particular type of text
according to a standard pattern (for example, a letter or a CV). In both
cases, the pattern that is predetermined is the outline shape or layout. But
many texts, both spoken and written, and especially those intended for

public consumption, seem to be fashioned on the basis of a more detailed template, which preselects aspects of internal structure: syntax, vocabulary, sequence, and, in the case of spoken texts, even intonation. In this chapter we shall consider three main questions: how and why much public communication is organised; why a knowledge of textual patterns or templates is an important aspect of sociolinguistic competence; and what concrete form these patterns take in German.

Styles and registers

It seems reasonable to assume that most texts directed at a reader or listener are intended to be understood. What we then need to explain is why particular texts have different but predictable patterns: why are they not all the same? One way of exploring this question is by extending the concept of norms or conventions, which we introduced in Chapter 5 to account for regularities in written and spoken German. This entails the recognition that in addition to the overriding purpose of being understood, individual texts normally have a specific *function*: they describe, define, report, inform, instruct, warn, praise, criticise, etc.

■   What are the following texts 'doing'?

1 §211. Mord

(1) Der Mörder wird mit lebenslanger Freiheitsstrafe bestraft.
(2) Mörder ist, wer
aus Mordlust, zur Befriedigung des Geschlechtstriebs, aus Habgier oder sonst aus niedrigen Beweggründen,
heimtückisch oder grausam oder mit gemeingefährlichen Mitteln oder um eine andere Straftat zu ermöglichen oder zu verdecken,
einen Menschen tötet.
(*Strafgesetzbuch*; cited in Möhn and Pelka 1984: 69)

2 §23. Hausordnung

Anerkennung der Hausordnung

Der Mieter erkennt die Hausordnung als für ihn verbindlich an. Ein Verstoß gegen die Hausordnung ist ein vertragswidriger Gebrauch des Mietgegenstandes. Bei schwerwiegenden Fällen kann der Vermieter nach erfolgloser Abmahnung das Vertragsverhältnis ohne Einhaltung einer Kündigungsfrist kündigen. Für alle Schäden, die dem Vermieter durch Verletzung oder Nichtbeachtung der Hausordnung und durch Nichterfüllung der Meldepflichten entstehen, ist der Mieter ersatzpflichtig. [. . .]

Allgemeine Ordnungsbestimmungen

Der Mieter hat von den Mieträumen nur vertragsgemäß Gebrauch zu machen und sie regelmäßig zu reinigen.
Jede Ruhestörung ist zu vermeiden, besonders durch lautes Musizieren. . . .
Teppiche dürfen nur während der zugelassenen Zeit geklopft werden.

(extract from standard Mietvertrag)

3 Weiße Gischt

Pro Person etwa 150g weißen Fisch, ½ l Fischfond oder Gemüsebrühe, Saft von einer Zitrone, 6 Schalotten, 1 Becher flüssige saure Sahne, 50g eiskalte Butterflöckchen, Pfeffer und Selleriesalz.
Schalotten ganz fein würfeln und in einer großen Pfanne mit dem Fond oder der Brühe klar dünsten. Mit der sauren Sahne aufgießen, würzen und etwas einkochen. Dann die kalte Butter einrühren. 4 Fischportionen vorsichtig einlegen, mit dem Zitronensaft begießen und bei geschlossenem Deckel und geringer Hitze gardünsten.

(Semestertip, a student magazine, April 1995: 12)

4 Reißverschluß

Dic beiden Hauptbestandteile eines Reißverschlusses sind die Zahnketten, die an einem Streifen aus Stoff befestigt sind, und dcr Schieber, der den Öffnungs- bzw. Schließvorgang besorgt.
Die Zahnkette besteht meist aus Metallzähnen, die auf ihrer Oberseite kleine buckelartige Erhöhungen und auf ihrer Unterseite entsprechend geformte Vertiefungen tragen. [. . .] Die beiden Zahnketten, die in geöffnetem Zustand einander gegenüberliegen, sind gegeneinander versetzt. Um den Verschluß zu schließen, müssen nur die beiden Zahnketten so aufeinander zugeführt werden, daß sich jeweils die beiden gegenüberliegenden Zähne ineinander verzahnen können.

(Wie funktioniert das? 1978: 582)

■■ Each of these passages is both a representative example of a certain text type and a specific text in its own right. For instance, Text 3 is an example of the text type 'recipe' and at the same time a particular recipe (for *Weiße Gischt*). One consequence of this at the lexical level is that it is often possible to distinguish between vocabulary that you would expect to find in any text belonging to a certain type and vocabulary that necessarily occurs in a particular text. For instance, many recipes will contain words like *würfeln* and *würzen*, but *Fischfond* will only appear in recipes for fish dishes. Try to identify further examples of these two sorts of vocabulary in these texts.

■■ Very often, a single label is not enough to characterise a text. For example, Text 4 above is 'descriptive', but it has two functions: first, to describe what the zip is made of and, second, to describe how it works. In what ways are Texts 1 and 2 and Texts 3 and 4 similar to each other, and in what ways are they different? How are particular functions (e.g. instructions) represented grammatically in these texts?

There are many ways of categorising texts according to type or function, but the essential point underlying any approach is that there is a 'conventional' relationship between form and content in texts belonging to a particular type. In other words, the aim is to identify a range of functions that texts may perform, to analyse how these functions are represented (or 'realised') linguistically, and to study the extent to which form is predictable from content and vice versa. For example, even if we delete the names of the ingredients from Text 3 above we still know that it is a recipe, and if we consult a recipe for *Weiße Gischt* we expect it to have the 'shape' of Text 3. It is precisely this conventional nature of the relationship between form and content that makes parodies like the *Märchen* below possible.

„Rotkäppchen" auf Juristendeutsch

Als in unserer Stadt *wohnhaft* ist eine *Minderjährige* aktenkundig, welche infolge ihrer hierorts üblichen Kopfbedeckung *gewohnheitsrechtlich* Rotkäppchen genannt zu werden pflegt . . .

Vor ihrer Inmarschsetzung wurde die R. seitens ihrer Mutter über das Verbot *betreffs Verlassens der Waldwege* auf Kreisebene belehrt. Sie machte sich *infolge Nichtbeachtung dieser Vorschrift* straffällig und begegnete beim Überschreiten des diesbezüglichen Blumenpflückverbotes einem polizeilich nicht gemeldeten Wolf ohne festen

Wohnsitz. Dieser verlangte in unberechtigter Amtsanmaßung *Einsichtnahme* in den zum Transport von Konsumgütern dienenden Korb und *traf* zwecks Tötungsabsicht die *Feststellung*, daß die R. zu ihrer verwandten und verschwägerten Großmutter eilends war.

Da bei dem Wolfe Verknappungen auf dem Ernährungssektor vorherrschend waren, beschloß er, bei der Großmutter der R. unter Vorlage falscher Papiere vorsprachig zu werden. Da dieselbe wegen Augenleidens krank geschrieben war, gelang dem Wolf die diesfällige Täuschungsabsicht, worauf er unter Verschlingung der Bettlägrigen einen strafbaren *Mundraub* ausführte.

Bei der später eintreffenden R. täuschte er seine Identität mit der Großmutter vor, stellte der R. nach und durch Zweitverschlingung *derselben* seinen Tötungsvorsatz unter Beweis. *Der sich auf einem Dienstgang befindliche Förster* B. vernahm verdächtige Schnarchgeräusche und stellte deren Urheberschaft seitens des Wolfsmaules fest. Er reichte bei seiner vorgesetzten Dienststelle ein Tötungsgesuch ein, welches zuschlägig beschieden wurde. Daraufhin gab er einen Schuß ab auf den Wolf. Dieser wurde nach Infangnahme der Kugel ablebig.

Die Beinhaltung des Getöteten weckte in dem Schußabgeber die Vermutung, daß der Leichnam Personen beinhalte. Zwecks diesbezüglicher Feststellung öffnete er unter Zuhilfenahme eines Messers den Kadaver zur Einsichtnahme und stieß hierbei auf die noch lebende R. nebst Großmutter.

Durch die unverhoffte Wiederbelebung bemächtigte sich der beiden Personen ein gesteigertes, amtlich nicht erfaßbares Lebensgefühl. Der Vorfall wurde von den Gebrüdern Grimm zu Protokoll gegeben.

(*Zeitschrift für Strafvollzug*; cited in Eggerer and Rötzer 1978)

■ Like any caricature, this text exaggerates characteristic features of its 'target'. It contains a number of lexical and syntactic features that are either more or less restricted to 'legal German' (*Mundraub, infolge Nichtbeachtung dieser Vorschrift*) or only likely to occur in similarly formal contexts (*Verknappung, eine Feststellung treffen*). Look at the other words and phrases in italics and try to decide which of these two categories each of them belongs to (i.e. 'legal German' or 'formal language').

The kinds of textual differences we have touched on in this section are variously described as examples of different **registers** or different **styles**.

■ ■ Read the discussions of these terms in Durrell (1992: 3–8), Holmes (1992: 276–82), Hudson (1996: 48–53) and Wardhaugh (1992: 48–53), and try to decide for yourself what is the most useful way of understanding them. Which features of the texts above would be covered by each of these terms, respectively?

As with many terminological disputes in linguistics there is clearly no 'correct' definition of these terms. The important point is to be explicit and consistent in your own usage. For our purposes here, style is taken to refer to attributes of a text over which the producer of the text can exercise considerable control and with which s/he seeks to achieve a particular effect or create a particular impression: understood in this way, style has various dimensions, such as formal/informal, personal/ impersonal or serious/humorous. Register is restricted here to features of a text over which the producer has relatively little control and which are to a large extent determined by the topic and the function of the text (for example, there is no alternative to *Kündigungsfrist* for 'period of notice' in a tenancy agreement). This distinction is as arbitrary as any other that has been proposed, but it is reasonably clear and enables us to analyse individual texts on two levels simultaneously. For instance, virtually all legal documents are both dominated by features of a register we could call 'legal German' and composed in a formal, serious style. However, it is quite common for other registers to be associated with a range of different styles. Consider, for example, the mixture of (pseudo-)scientific register with both serious and jocular styles in these passages from a magazine article about car drivers:

DER SHOWMAN: Die mit Hilfe eines potenten Autos erfahrbare Steigerung des Selbstwertgefühls ist für ihn nicht unbedingt von der Realisierung des theoretisch gegebenen Fahrleistungspotentials abhängig. Es genügt, sich in Tagträumen auszumalen, was sein könnte, wenn der Fahrer nur wollte. Der Träumer betrachtet sich dabei gleichsam von außen. Er wird zu seinem eigenen Publikum. Narziß im Blechschmuck. [. . .]

DER RIVALE: [. . .] Die Trabis auf unseren Autobahnen verschaffen dem Rivalen ein besonderes Vergnügen: Wenn er einen dieser Stinker überholt hat – etwas enger, als es vielleicht nötig gewesen wäre – und ihn im Rückspiegel zusammenschrumpfen sieht, dann malt er sich genüßlich aus, was die Beifahrerin im Trabi jetzt wohl zu ihrem Partner sagt. Das tut gut. Jetzt fühlt er sich mal wieder stark und frei.

(Horst Nowak, 'Spielzeug für Männer', *Esquire* 8/1990: 48–51)

■■ Using any sources available to you (advertisements, instruction leaflets, degree regulations, chemistry textbook, etc.), collect a number of texts and analyse them in terms of style and/or register (be sure first to specify how you understand the terms you use in your analysis).

Addressing the public

Although we are not always conscious of the fact, we are constantly bombarded with messages in everyday life. They come from a variety of sources and have different purposes. The most general category is perhaps the public notice or announcement issued by some form of authority to the public at large or to a particular group. These texts are usually brief and have an informative or directive function:

Hier entsteht eine neue Filiale der Commerzbank (informative)

Unbefugten ist der Zutritt verboten (directive)

although sometimes these functions may be combined:

Vorsicht auf Gleis 3 (directive), es fährt ein der InterRegio-Zug Mannheim nach Frankfurt (informative).

Directive texts are perhaps the most common and they are characteristically composed in a formal, impersonal style. The following notices

Der Aufenthalt auf der Treppe und die Mitnahme von Hunden zum Oberdeck sind nicht gestattet (sign in Berlin bus)

Das freie Umherlaufenlassen von Hunden ist untersagt (notice in Berlin park)

are more frequently encountered than ones such as this one, a remnant from the GDR past in a Cottbus park:

Bürger! Schont die Grünflächen!

Or are they? Some direct forms of public address, such as the universal 'Zurückbleiben!' warning latecomers on the underground (subway) that the train is about to leave, have been commonplace for a long time, but there is a growing tendency to talk directly to the public in both written and spoken announcements.

■ Consider the following public notices from the perspective of their relative formality and directness; what effects are achieved by the more impersonal/indirect texts and how might you account for the trend towards more personal/direct notices?

1 Bewahren Sie Ihren Fahrausweis nach beendeter Fahrt bis zum Durchschreiten der Sperrenanlage bzw. bis zum Verlassen der Busse oder Schiffe auf. (sign on public transport in Hamburg)

2 Durch die Abnahme und Nachprüfung der Einrichtungen übernimmt die Deutsche Bundespost keine Gewähr dafür, daß die privaten Fernmeldeeinrichtungen ordnungsgemäß arbeiten. (notice in telephone kiosk)

3 Liebe Gäste! Bitte prüfen Sie Ihre Rechnung, bevor Sie das Hotel verlassen, und vergessen Sie nicht, Ihren Schlüssel an der Rezeption abzugeben. (notice in hotel)

Beside the texts that aim to inform or instruct the public there is a second important category which consists of texts that openly seek to persuade. They are issued by particular interest groups and are generally directed at specific target audiences. Leaflets promoting a film or play, commercials advertising a product, posters urging us to vote for a politician or political party, banners and leaflets exhorting us to take some form of action: all of these texts are saying 'fly me!' In this sense, all texts in this category are a form of advertisement and the intended recipient is a potential consumer, so it might be interesting to explore the extent to which they share a linguistic shape (or 'textual template').

■■ Gather as many examples as you can of short, 'public' texts that come into the category of 'persuasive' texts and see whether you can identify any common linguistic strategies. For example: how is the potential consumer addressed? How is the 'product' presented? Is reference made to other, competing products? If so, in what way? What kind of appeal is being made to the recipient (factual/informative, emotional, warning, etc.)?

Finally, on a rather different level, there is a range of text types that typically appear in both broadcast and print media, and which constitute an important means of communicating with the public in the form of ostensibly spoken texts. However, these texts are either actually written and then read out (news bulletins, public speeches), or spoken but made public in written form and read as if they were written texts (interviews). Some of these forms of 'public address' will be examined in the next two sections.

Speaking the news

Until relatively recently, many German news bulletins (on radio and television) were anything but audience-friendly: the language was complex, formal and abstract, so that considerable concentration was required just to follow what was being said. Unlike their anglophone counterparts, who for a long time have read their scripts from an autocue and reinforced the illusion of speaking directly to the viewer by apparently maintaining eye contact, German-speaking television newsreaders made no attempt to conceal the fact that they were reading from a script on the desk in front of them. Furthermore, no concessions were made to the fact that viewers did not have this script available to them and were therefore obliged to process the information being delivered to them on the basis of a single hearing. Effectively, there was no difference between the news as written in serious newspapers and the news as read on radio and television.

The explosive growth of satellite and cable channels in the 1980s changed all that. The greatly increased consumer choice meant that there was fierce competition for viewers even amongst news programmes. It could no longer be taken for granted that viewers would routinely switch the television on at 7 p.m. to watch *heute* or at 8 p.m. to watch *Tagesschau* or at 10 p.m. to watch *Zeit im Bild*: the needs and desires of the consumer now had to be taken into account. This led on the one hand to greater differentiation between programmes (they needed to develop a more distinctive 'style'), but on the other hand to a general shift in the direction of 'infotainment' (like all other programmes, even the news had to conform to the pleasure principle).

One important aspect of this trend is something we noted in Chapter 5: the increasing dominance of 'orality' in public life. Weighing machines speak our weight, cash dispensers welcome us to the bank, signs in public car parks demand to know 'have you paid and displayed?', word processors ask us 'do you really want to delete this file?': whichever medium is used to convey such messages, in each case we have the sense of being spoken to. In the age of interactive media, we can now go a step further and engage in a constructive dialogue with all sorts of computer-driven devices. In this context, it is not surprising that the spoken word (whether or not it is transmitted through the medium of speech) has become the norm in so many forms of public communication.

The extent to which this principle has influenced the presentation of the news, especially on television, can be seen in the changes in the structure of the news programmes, in the 'performance' of the newscasters, and in the composition of the news texts themselves. With the exception of short 'updates' and some local bulletins, most television news broadcasts no longer merely feature a single reader, a talking head in the studio, nor do modern newscasters belong to the school of venerable and revered oracles. Today the news is a show with a cast of characters headed by a newscaster or an 'anchorperson' (on the commercial channels usually a team of two), who introduces us to, and occasionally converses with, a whole network of reporters and correspondents. As a result, an individual news programme may consist of a range of different speech events: presenter greets audience, presenter chats to co-presenter, presenter reads news item, reporter interviews 'significant person' (politician, footballer, film star, witness, victim, lottery winner), correspondent gives on-the-spot account of recent event, presenter asks reporter/correspondent for further details on viewers' behalf, and so on.

■■ Although the linguistic construction of television news and current affairs broadcasts on German-language channels has changed significantly in recent years, there are still considerable differences between programmes in terms of the relative formality and complexity of the texts. Where would you place the following extracts on the scales formal ↔ informal and complex ↔ simple? Which features of the texts are your judgements based on?

Text 1

MODERATOR IM STUDIO: Wie Frankreich ist auch Deutschland von einem Blutskandal erschüttert worden. So ist eine große Zahl von Patienten in der Vergangenheit bei Bluttransfusionen mit kontaminiertem Plasma, mit dem HIV-Virus, infiziert worden. Seitdem dieser Tatbestand bekannt ist, ist von vielen Seiten der Ruf nach einer strengeren Kontrolle der Privatfirmen laut geworden, die Krankenhäuser mit dem Plasma beliefern und deren Überwachung der Blutspender. Auch wird heftig darüber diskutiert, ob die Patienten den HIV-Test wirklich anonym machen können sollten, wie es derzeit der Fall ist. Nach Ansicht einiger sollten sich alle HIV-Träger als solche den Behörden zu erkennen geben. Diese Kritiker der gegenwärtigen Praxis streiten für die sogenannte Meldepflicht. Nur wenn alle Virusträger bekannt sind, so lautet ihr Argument, könne die Gesellschaft wirkungsvolle Schritte zur Verminderung des Risikos einleiten. Diese Aussicht sei wichtiger als der Schutz der Privatsphäre.

(BBC 1992–4 Series 3, Programme 3)

Text 2

MODERATOR IM STUDIO: Schlechte Nachrichten aus Deutschland Ost sind an der Tagesordnung. Die von dieser Woche heißt: Nur jeder zweite Jugendliche hat Aussicht auf einen Ausbildungsplatz, so die Bundesanstalt für Arbeit am Montag. In Finsterwalde, einer kleinen Kreisstadt zwischen Berlin und Dresden, sind fast 60 Prozent arbeitslos. Das ist ein Rekord, selbst für die neuen Bundesländer. Vor der Wende galt das Städtchen in der ehemaligen DDR als bedeutender Industriestandort. Das ist vorbei. Am meisten betroffen sind die Frauen; sie stellen rund zwei Drittel der Arbeitslosen.

REPORTERIN IN FINSTERWALDE: Finsterwalde, ein Name wie aus dem Märchenbuch. Doch märchenhaft ist hier nur die Vergangenheit, die Zeit vor der Wende. Damals, als alle noch Arbeit hatten, als Finsterwalde noch ein blühendes Städtchen in der Niederlausitz war. Die Gegenwart sieht anders aus. Über 20 Prozent Arbeitslose, 50 Prozent Kurzarbeit. Eine Wirklichkeit – für die Finsterwalder bis vor kurzem noch eine Horrorgeschichte aus einem fernen Land.

(BBC 1992–4 Series 2, Programme 8)

Text 3

MODERATOR IM STUDIO: Seit der Wende ist Leipzig ein ganz gefährliches Kopfsteinpflaster. Kriminelle demolieren da in einer Nacht Läden, die der Sozialismus in 40 Jahren nicht kaputt gekriegt hat. Manche „Tante Emma" müßte jede Nacht die Polizei anrufen – wenn sie nun schon endlich Telefon hätte! Deshalb patrouillieren z.B. im gefährdeten Stadtteil Leutsch jetzt bewaffnete Bürgerwehren. Die Menschen wollen sich selber helfen. Manche Ladenbesitzer müssen sich jetzt um das bemühen, wovon sie früher nun wirklich genug hatten: Ladenhüter nämlich. Denn die Polizei scheint machtlos. Der Sachse singt, heißt es. Aber das tut er eben gerade nicht. Jedenfalls nicht auf der Polizeiwache, wenn die Beamten was herauskriegen wollen! Dieter Weiß versucht trotzdem das Schweigen in der Nacht zu brechen.

REPORTER IN LEUTSCH: Schlechte Beleuchtung, wenig Autos unterwegs. Nach 22.00 Uhr traut sich hier kaum jemand auf der Straße. Der Stadtteil Leutsch in Leipzig – wie ausgestorben.

(BBC 1992–4 Series 1, Programme 2)

■ While the main news programmes on the established terrestrial channels in Germany (ARD's *Tagesschau* and ZDF's *heute*) are now broadly similar linguistically, they still sometimes differ in various respects from the programmes on commercial cable/satellite channels such as Sat 1 and RTL. In what ways do the following two extracts, for example, show the greater shift towards a colloquial, oral mode and a more personal style in the *RTL-Aktuell* broadcast than in the more conventional *Tagesschau* bulletin?

TAGESSCHAU: Die internationalen Aktienbörsen haben heute schwere Kurseinbrüche hinnehmen müssen. In Frankfurt gab es sogar die größten Tagesverluste seit Bestehen der Bundesrepublik.

RTL-AKTUELL: Der schwärzeste Tag seit Jahrzehnten an der Frankfurter Börse. Die Besitzer deutscher Aktien verschleuderten heute ihre Papiere ohne Rücksicht auf Verluste.

(Püschel 1992: 19)

■■ Watch some German news broadcasts on commercial channels and try to identify linguistic features that contribute to what Muckenhaupt (1994) calls the 'Boulevardisierung' ('tabloidisation') of the news, e.g. short, punchy sentences; dramatic style; colourful imagery; simplified, black and white accounts of events.

Another significant aspect of the diversification of television news production is in the composition of different components of individual news broadcasts. Consider the following extracts from *Tagesthemen*, the late-evening news programme on ARD:

MODERATOR: Guten Abend meine Damen und Herren. Ich begrüße Sie zu den Tagesthemen mit folgenden Beiträgen:

OFF-STIMME: Luftschlag: Die Nato zeigt die Zähne.
Diätpillen: Der Tod aus der Kapsel.
Filmfest: Der Kampf um die Löwen.

MODERATOR: Monatelang haben Nato und UNO gezaudert und gezögert, seit vergangener Nacht zwei Uhr haben sie ihre Taktik geändert. Nato-Kampfflugzeuge und die Artillerie der schnellen multinationalen Eingreiftruppe griffen serbische Stellungen vor Sarajevo und den UN-Schutzzonen Gorazde und Tusla an. In mehreren Wellen bombardierten den ganzen Tag über rund 60 Flugzeuge die serbischen Stützpunkte. [...] Über einen Tag, der möglicherweise einen Wendepunkt in diesem gräßlichen Krieg markiert, berichtet Friedhelm Brebeck.

KORRESPONDENT (FILM-BERICHT): Der Nato-Kampfbomber: Einer von 60 und das ist schon die dritte Welle. Sarajevo heute um 9 Uhr. Daueralarm und im Radio warnen sie immer wieder „Geht nicht ’raus“, und fünf Kilometer weiter zertrümmern die Nato-Raketen präzise eine serbische Munitionsfabrik. 11 Uhr: Die UNO-Truppe verlegt ihre tägliche Konferenz in den Keller, Alarmstufe rot. Der politische Sprecher, Ivanko, ist Russe und offensichtlich zufrieden. In Moskau wird er damit keine Freunde haben, aber hier ist er ein loyaler UNO-Mann. Der erste Angriff ist in der Nacht um 2 Uhr gestartet worden, es ist eine Reaktion auf das Massaker vom Montag in Sarajevo.

MODERATOR: In Belgrad begrüße ich jetzt unsere Korrespondentin, Karola Beier. Guten Abend Frau Beier.

KORRESPONDENTIN (IM STUDIO IN BELGRAD): Schönen guten Abend nach Hamburg.

MODERATOR: Frau Beier, die Verhandlungen gehen jetzt weiter, Karadzic und Milosevic an einem gemeinsamen Verhandlungstisch: eine Überraschung, ein Trick oder ein erfreuliches Zeichen?

KORRESPONDENTIN: Also, ich glaube auf jeden Fall, es ist ein erfreuliches Zeichen. Papier ist zwar geduldig, wie man weiß, aber wichtig ist jetzt erst mal, daß die Verhandlungen nicht abgebrochen werden, sondern fortgesetzt werden. Ich glaube, die serbische Seite hat heut' wirklich ein starkes Interesse signalisiert, ein Ende der Luftschläge der Nato herbeizuführen, und sie wissen ganz genau, daß man jetzt in den nächsten Tagen dafür schnell zu einem Waffenstillstand kommen muß, und ich denke, dafür bestehen jetzt in diesem Moment erst mal ganz gute Chancen. [. . .]

MODERATOR: Der Gegenschlag der Nato und mögliche Konsequenzen: Franz Stark vom Bayerischen Rundfunk kommentiert.

REDAKTEUR IM STUDIO: Auch in der Politik, verehrte Zuschauer, gibt es Situationen, in denen die Emotion mehr zählt als ein ursprünglicher Auftrag. Der Auftrag der Vereinten Nationen lautete „Friedenserhaltung, nicht Friedenserzwingung", und natürlich kommt in diesem Auftrag auch der Begriff der Vergeltung nicht vor. Aber der niederträchtige Beschuß Sarajevos am vergangenen Montag, als bereits Verhandlungen sich abzeichneten, brachte das Faß zum Überlaufen. Man braucht kein Bellizist zu sein, um gutzuheißen, was heute geschah. Daß UNO und Nato nach Monaten leerer Drohungen und Demütigungen mit der Ankettung von Blauhelmsoldaten als Geiseln endlich die schweren Waffen der Serben in den Sperrzonen zerstören wollten und die Herren Karadzic und Co an den Verhandlungstisch bomben: Kein gerecht denkender Mensch wird dies also verurteilen wollen. Aber es hilft auch kein Heruminterpretieren: Mit diesen massiven Angriffen sind UNO und Nato in begrenztem Umfang zur Kriegspartei geworden und darin stecken Unwägbarkeiten, auch wenn man jetzt eben gehört hat, daß Milosevic das Heft in die Hand nehmen will und offensichtlich Karadzic unter Kuratel stellt, aber einiges fällt vielleicht den bosnischen Serben doch ein, vielleicht brüten sie neue Methoden der Geiselnahme aus, etwa unter der Zivilbevölkerung. Oder was ist, wenn nicht nur bosnische Moslems sondern auch die kroatische Armee in Ostslawonien die Gunst der Stunde nutzen wollen, wenn es also doch zur weiteren Eskalation auf dem Balkan kommt, und die Nato de facto bereits Kriegspartei ist, und schließlich, wie wird man in Moskau reagieren? Das sind zur Stunde noch offene Fragen, eine Eskalation ist nicht mehr so wahrscheinlich aber nicht ausgeschlossen, doch wenn die bosnischen Serben nicht völlig irrational reagieren, könnten die Bomben von heute den Balkan ein Stück näher an den Frieden herangebracht haben.

(*Tagesthemen*, ARD, 30 August 1995)

■■ Five different text types are used to present the main news item in this bulletin: headline; presenter text; correspondent film report; conversation between presenter and correspondent; and commentary. To what extent does each of these five subtexts have a distinctive pattern? Use the following checklist as a guide:

- syntax (simple vs complex sentences, **hypotactic** vs **paratactic** sentence construction, active vs passive, etc.);
- text structure (random sequence, sequence determined on logical basis according to points in an argument, sequence based on chronological order of events; linguistic means of expressing relationships between elements of text, such as conjunctions);
- vocabulary (abstract vs concrete, descriptive vs emotive, etc.);
- style (formal, colloquial, idiomatic);
- perspective (general vs particular/specific, detached/matter-of-fact vs interpretive, etc.);
- focus (events, people, issues).

Now read the following extract from the *RTL-Aktuell* bulletin broadcast on the same day:

OFF-STIMME: Strafaktion: Die Nato fliegt den ganzen Tag über massive Angriffe gegen bosnische Serben

Rassenhaß: Hauptbelastungszeuge gefährdet mit Beschimpfungen den Simpson-Prozeß

MODERATOR: Guten Abend und herzlich willkommen bei RTL-Aktuell. Mit dei größten militärischen Einsatz in ihrer Geschichte hat die Nato heute Vergeltung für den serbischen Granatenangriff auf Sarajevo geübt. Mehr als 60 Kampfjets bombardieren seit heute früh serbische Stellungen in ganz Bosnien. Ein Nato-Flugzeug wurde dabei abgeschossen. Auch die schnelle Eingreiftruppe war mit schwerer Artillerie an der Aktion beteiligt. Fünf Beobachter der Europäischen Union kamen bei den Angriffen auf serbischem Gebiet ums Leben. Nach Angaben der Serben sollen darüberhinaus weitere sieben Menschen getötet worden sein.

KORRESPONDENT (FILM-BERICHT): Zwei Uhr morgens. Der Himmel über Sarajevo wird von mehreren Explosionen grell erleuchtet. Die Nato-Bomber greifen serbische Stellungen rund um die Stadt an. Eines der Ziele ist ein wichtiges Waffendepot. 4 Uhr: Die Crew des US-Flugzeugträgers Roosevelt bereitet ihre Maschinen für einen zweiten Angriff vor, rüstet sie wieder mit Bomben aus. Von der

Roosevelt und von verschiedenen italienischen Nato-Basen via Aviano steigen die Jets in Richtung Sarajevo auf. Diesmal werden auch Raketenabwehrstellungen der Serben um die UNO-Schutzzonen Gorazde und Tusla beschossen. Im Anschluß daran setzt die schnelle Eingreiftruppe ihre schwere Artillerie ein und feuert mindestens 600 Granaten auf serbische Stellungen am Berg Igman. Im Laufe des Tages fliegen die Nato-Jets weitere Angriffe. Zunächst verfolgen die Einwohner Sarajevos die Vergeltungsschläge mit Genugtuung, doch die Antwort der Serben läßt nicht lang auf sich warten: Granaten schlagen in der Stadt ein.

(RTL-Aktuell, 30 August 1995)

■■ If you apply the analysis based on text type to the three elements of this extract, what similarities and differences do you find between them and the corresponding components of the *Tagesthemen* broadcast?

■■ If you have access to suitable equipment, record a number of news programmes on different channels (television and/or radio) and compare either their presentation of a particular story or the programme as a whole. Use the criteria introduced above, and where appropriate take into account also the following factors:

- how presenters relate to viewers, to each other and to other journalists;
- how the whole bulletin is structured (e.g. headlines, series of items, summary of main points);
- how each item is structured (e.g. presenter-intro/summary followed by reporter/correspondent account, followed by presenter rounding off; presenter-intro followed by film report);
- the linguistic construction of texts (e.g. syntactic complexity, degree of formality/colloquialness, degree of abstractness/concreteness, personality/impersonality, etc.).

Public speaking

The interview with Dresden schoolchildren in Chapter 5 (p. 92) showed in a particularly transparent way the kinds of linguistic and textual feature that we might expect to find in spontaneous speech. It is likely that adults would express themselves rather more coherently, but as the interview with Günter Grass (also in Chapter 5, pp. 87–8) revealed, even those who make their living from constructing texts do not necessarily speak very fluently on every occasion. The same applies to politicians and other public figures who spend much of their lives giving interviews and making speeches. However, there are times when people in the public eye need to give the impression of being completely in control of their subject matter. Consider the following extracts from an interview with Professor Heydemann, the former Environment Minister of Schleswig-Holstein:

FRAGE: Wäre das Land Schleswig-Holstein gerüstet, um die Folgen einer Tankerkatastrophe in Grenzen zu halten?

HEYDEMANN: Mit 100 000 Tonnen Öl, die wenige Kilometer vor der Küste aus einem geborstenen Tanker auslaufen und die der Westwind auf den Strand drückt, kann niemand spontan und ohne jeglichen ökologischen Schaden fertig werden. [. . .]

FRAGE: Welche Einrichtungen stehen Ihnen im Falle einer Katastrophe zur Verfügung?

HEYDEMANN: Wir haben für Großunfälle an der Weser- und Elbemündung drei Spezialschiffe stationiert. *Außerdem* liegen an der deutschen Nord- und Ostseeküste zwei *Mehrzweckschiffe* mit Ausrüstung *zur Bekämpfung von Ölunfällen* und 14 mittlere und kleinere Schiffe, vor allem *für den Einsatz in Küstennähe.* [. . .] *Auf die Dauer* kann es *jedoch* nicht die Lösung sein, daß die Länder *jede Vorsorge treffen* müssen für mögliche Unfälle, verursacht durch den Unsinn unsicherer Großtanker. Man muß *vielmehr* verhindern, daß es überhaupt zu einem großen Tankerunfall kommt.

FRAGE: Wie wollen Sie das verhindern?

HEYDEMANN: *Der erste Schritt muß es sein*, die Tanker kleiner zu machen. [. . .] *Es muß auch bei uns durchgesetzt werden*, daß Tanker künftig nur noch mit einer doppelten Wand *gebaut werden dürfen.* Und wir brauchen bessere Verkehrsleitsysteme für die Schiffahrt an den Küsten.

FRAGE: Weil Häfen, in denen Öl verladen wird, zu nahe beieinander liegen?

HEYDEMANN: Ich denke, es ist ganz wesentlich, die Ölumschlagplätze zu konzentrieren. [. . .] *Je weniger große Umschlagplätze, desto leichter ist die Überwachung und Katastrophenvorsorge.*

(Bild der Wissenschaft)

■ A number of lexical, syntactic and discourse features have been highlighted in italics: comment on them in the light of the fact that this is an authentic, unscripted interview.

Of course, we do not know whether transcripts of interviews that appear in print have been 'sanitised' or tidied up, as is the case, for example, with the official records of parliamentary debates. But even making allowances for this possibility, it is clear that this kind of spoken text is much more consciously and carefully constructed than other forms of spontaneous speech. Consider the following extracts from an interview with Peter Hartz, the Personnel Director of Volkswagen, from this point of view:

FRAGE: Wie sicher sind die Arbeitsplätze bei VW?

HARTZ: Sie sind relativ sicher, wenn wir das von uns vorgelegte Konzept verwirklichen.

FRAGE: Warum wollen Sie dann bis 1998 fast 30 000 Stellen streichen?

HARTZ: [...] Wir haben in unseren westdeutschen Standorten Ende des Jahres etwa 94 000 Beschäftigte, ohne die Vier-Tage-Woche wären es 20 000 weniger. Bei den Produktivitätsfortschritten, die wir machen, werden wir allerdings in der Tat in den nächsten Jahren unsere Belegschaftszahlen weiterhin anpassen müssen.

FRAGE: Ohne Kündigungen?

HARTZ: Keine den Arbeitsmarkt belastenden betriebsbedingten Kündigungen, keine Sozialhärten, kein Kahlschlag, daran halten wir – in einem überschaubaren und beeinflußbaren Zeitraum – fest.

FRAGE: Wollen Sie für geleistete Mehrarbeit tatsächlich Schecks geben, die sie später einlösen können?

HARTZ: Ja. Die Zeit-Schecks sollen eingelöst werden, wenn wir weniger Arbeit haben; die Mitarbeiter können sie verwenden, um später in Teilzeit zu arbeiten oder früher in den Ruhestand zu gehen. Das ist eine Möglichkeit, die den Interessen des einzelnen Rechnung trägt und auch für das Unternehmen Flexibilität bringt.

FRAGE: Die Gewerkschaft hält das für einen PR-Gag.

HARTZ: Wir halsen uns das nicht aus Spaß auf, sondern um die Beschäftigung zu sichern. Mit Hilfe dieser Schecks lassen sich die komplexen Arbeitszeitsysteme jedem Mitarbeiter in drei Sätzen erklären: Sie arbeiten in der Produktion im Durchschnitt 28,8 Stunden pro Woche und erhalten dafür ihr Entgelt. Wenn sie mehr arbeiten, geben wir ihnen dieses Zeit-Wertpapier. Und damit machen sie in Abstimmung mit uns, was sie für richtig halten.

('Ganz schön mütig: Interview mit VW-Personalvorstand Peter Hartz über die Beschäftigungsprobleme und die Pläne des Konzerns', *Der Spiegel*, 30 October 1995: 90–1)

Whether or not the company's idea of offering its workers *Zeit-Schecks* is a 'PR-Gag', the catchy name indicates how important the concept of 'quotability' is in the domain of public communication. Not every interview will be reproduced in its entirety, indeed it is far more common for interviews to be used as the raw material for an article, with only particularly striking passages being quoted, and so practised interviewees know that their key points must be expressed in such a way as to catch the eye of the headline writer or the ear of the television news producer.

■■ Which features of Herr Hartz's responses indicate that he is a practised public speaker?

■■■ Look back over the analyses you have made of the various texts in this chapter. To what extent would you say the features of the textual patterns that you have identified are specific to German (or at least differ from those of comparable texts in English)? In what sense is the ability to recognise and use these patterns an aspect of sociolinguistic competence?

Further reading

Durrell (1992), Chapter 1, on varieties of language, especially register; with illustrative texts and analysis.

Holly (1995), for a clear survey of different aspects of language use in television texts, including the news.

Holmes (1992), Chapter 10, on style and register.

Hudson (1996), Chapter 2.4, on style and register.

Möhn and Pelka (1984), for a detailed discussion of register with many examples and illustrative analyses.

Muckenhaupt (1994), for a thorough exploration of the ways in which the presentation of German television news has developed.

Scharschik (1973), a collection of historically important political speeches.

Wardhaugh (1992), pp. 48–53, on styles and registers.

•   •   •

Chapter 7

Communicative conventions and social relations

Communicative (in)competence

> Of course, it might not have been as serious as for the distracted night heron that Lorenz reports forgot to make his bow of greeting at the nest and was attacked by his own young [...], or an unfortunate female gentoo penguin who neglects to bow in greeting to her mate when he is defending their territory. . . . But it *was* serious.
>
> (Ferguson 1976: 140)

The 'serious' event that the American linguist Charles Ferguson is referring to in these ominous lines is the outcome of an informal experiment he had conducted as a preliminary step in his research into what he calls 'politeness formulas'. Against his normal practice, he deliberately failed to return his secretary's customary 'Good morning' on two successive occasions. While the first omission merely caused surprise, by the time he had greeted her with no more than a silent smile for the second time considerable tension had developed in his office and his colleagues were seriously beginning to wonder what was wrong with him (was he on the verge of a breakdown? Was his marriage collapsing?). Misunderstandings like this are easily repaired with a simple explanation and an apology, but trivial though this isolated episode may be, taken together with Ferguson's zoological parallels it serves to show that even such mundane routines as greetings are both rule-governed and culturally relative activities. In other words, there are particular ways of 'doing' greetings and these may differ from one culture to another, indeed even among subgroups within one culture. For example, in a Chinese workplace, Ferguson's behaviour would have been considered perfectly normal.

■   Greetings constitute one speech event among many that make up a substantial proportion of our everyday encounters with other people. Others include asking for directions, making/accepting/ declining an offer of a drink, making an appointment, telling a joke/story. Can you add to this list? Choose one speech event and analyse in as much detail as possible the 'rules' that apply to its structure (a) in your own cultural environment and (b) in any German-speaking environment with which you are familiar (or consult a native speaker of German). You will need to take into account such variable factors as the following: do the participants know each other? If so, how well and on what basis? Is one older than the other(s)? Are some elements of the structure obligatory and others optional? Is there a particular sequence in which the various elements must occur?

Looking at language from this perspective means treating it as a form of social behaviour: the term **talk** is often used to designate the object of study in this area of sociolinguistics, which itself is generally referred to as the 'ethnography of communication'. What we are concerned to do here is to investigate the 'rules of talk' in a given speech community, starting from the premise that in order to 'belong' in a particular community it is not enough to know how to form linguistically acceptable utterances, rather it is also necessary to know which of the linguistic forms available are considered appropriate in any given situation. This difference between 'saying things right' and 'saying the right things' is what underlies the distinction between 'linguistic competence' and 'communicative competence'.

> [Communicative competence] deals with the social and cultural knowledge speakers are presumed to have to enable them to use and interpret linguistic forms. A child who uses a taboo expression in public and causes embarrassment is said not to 'know better', i.e. not to have acquired certain rules for social conduct in the use of language. [...]
>
> Communicative competence extends to both knowledge and expectation of who may or may not speak in certain settings, when to speak and when to remain silent, whom one may speak to, how one may talk to persons of different statuses and roles, what appropriate nonverbal behaviors are in various contexts, what the routines for turn-taking are in conversation, how to ask for and give information, how to request, how to offer or decline assistance or cooperation, how to give commands, how to enforce discipline, and the like – in short, everything involving the use of language and other communicative dimensions in particular social settings.
>
> (Saville-Troike 1989: 21)

Of course, human beings are not robots, and the mere fact that we have acquired a knowledge of the social and linguistic conventions that constitute communicative competence does not mean that we automatically act in accordance with them. They represent the 'normal' or 'default' patterns of behaviour that we know will be expected in a particular setting, but we are always at liberty to select a different pattern: one aspect of communicative competence is knowing the likely consequences of disregarding the 'rules of talk'. Communicative *in*competence, by contrast, means not knowing what the relevant rules of talk are. Culturally specified differences in sociolinguistic conventions range from particular contrasts (for example, using linguistically similar forms to convey quite different messages – 'see you later' means 'goodbye for now/until the next time we meet', but 'bis später' means 'goodbye until the time we have arranged to meet again later') to whole areas of communicative activity (such as making apologies or complaints, giving explanations, or making requests).

Cultural differences of these kinds can also apply between particular groups within one society or speech community. One striking example of this can be seen in the speech styles of youth subcultures. Being 'young' is not just about age, it's about attitude, and the acquisition of so-called *Jugendsprachen* is an important part of belonging to the subculture. But like most special codes, *Jugendsprachen* have a double function: they are inclusive ('speak like this and you're one of us') and exclusive ('if you can't speak like this, you're not one of us'), and one of the essential features is that they are very elusive. Consider the following passage of allegedly authentic *Jugendsprache*:

BENE: Weißt Du – die echt zombigen Tanten sind nicht so leicht anzugraben. Ich bohr' mich zweimal die Woche in 'ne Disco . . . seh zu, wie die sich da auf der Tanzfläche einen abhotten . . . und bei Gelegenheit laß ich bei 'ner Tussi 'nen Spruch los. Obwohl – eigentlich nervt mich das.

INTERVIEWER: Was stört Dich denn da am meisten?

BENE: Also, da gibt's immer so'n paar Aufreißer-Typen, die sich die echt tollen Bräute keilen. Die schmier'n denen unheimlich was vor, powern voll rein – und die Disco-Torten stehn da auch noch drauf. Das ist doch Fuzzi, sowas.

(Müller-Thurau 1983: 30–1)

There is a degree of authenticity in some of the vocabulary and sentence structures (at the time it was published, that is), but the text is deliberately and self-consciously composed. Attempts to record and decipher *Jugendsprachen* in order to make them accessible and translatable are often doomed to failure as these speech forms change very rapidly, precisely to evade 'capture' by outsiders. As a result, dictionaries and glossaries of *Jugendsprachen* are usually out of date as soon as they are published. And there is more to belonging in youth subcultures than picking up a new vocabulary: it also typically involves developing verbal skills, such as improvising (often obscene) parodies of popular television programmes or acting out quick-fire verbal duels. Consider, for example, the way the speakers in this conversation pick up a reference to James Bond and develop a short sequence making fun of one of their teachers:

A: ich hab den gar nich gesehen auf'm elternabend.
M: der sieht schrecklich aus.
A: ziemlich gammelig kann das sein?
M: ja. der sieht aus wie james bond. [*Lachen*]
I: wie welcher?
J: sag ich doch, ziemlich gammelig.
M: conney, so total schleimig, weiß ich auch nich so total öh . . .
J: wie heißt die lehrerin?
M: frau hinz.
J: mein name ist hinz [*lacht*] hans hinz.
A: hinz und kunz.
M: und ich hab die lizenz zum töten [*lacht*].
A: mit schlechten zensuren! [*Lachen*]

(Wachau 1990: 54; cited in Schlobinski 1995: 332)

In everyday life, much of our energy is devoted to constructing and maintaining social relationships through talk, whether it be in the form of simple routines such as greetings or more complex forms of interaction such as banter and repartee. In the following sections, we shall explore some of the ways in which particular communicative conventions operate in German-speaking contexts by looking in some detail at two important aspects of interaction that affect all social groups and lend themselves to comparisons with the practices in other cultures: politeness routines and patterns of personal address.

Politeness routines

The word politeness is used here not in the evaluative sense of 'etiquette' or 'good manners': rather, it is used in a neutral, semi-technical sense to refer to practices which evolve within a speech community and whose purpose is to maintain the smooth running of social intercourse by maintaining good relations between speakers. It is based on the assumption of mutual respect at a fundamental human level, and to that extent is probably at least in principle a universal feature of human societies. However, the actual practices may be culture-specific and are frequently complex in the way they operate.

For instance, a common stereotype of German-speakers (especially, perhaps, Germans) is that they tend to be more 'direct' than English-speakers in the way they conduct themselves in interaction with other people. It is easy to see how this impression can arise, as some everyday forms of expression in German lack the characteristic modal forms of the English equivalents (or make them less prominent by embedding them within the sentence), which have the effect of reducing the force of the utterance. Compare, for example, the following:

1a Gibst du mir die Kassette?   1b Would you give me the cassette?

2a Ich bekomme den Steak.   2b I'd like the steak (, please).

3a Sagen Sie uns bitte sofort   3b Please let us know at once if . . .
    Bescheid, wenn . . .

- In what specific ways would you say the English sentences above are less 'direct' than the German ones?

However, the 'evidence' for this stereotypical contrast is fragmentary and the claim largely a matter of speculation. It is also based on a sweeping generalisation about the speech behaviour of 'the Germans' and 'the British' (and what about 'the Austrians' or 'the Swiss', 'the Americans' or 'the Australians'?). Nevertheless, the perception remains for many people, and since perceived behaviour has a major part to play in people's attitudes towards others it would be interesting to see whether it is possible to find **empirical** support for this view.

In an attempt to investigate the hypothetical English/German contrast under experimental conditions, two pairs of native speakers (one English and one German) were asked to act out a series of role-plays involving simple everyday situations, all of which fell into one of two categories: complaints or requests (the experiment is described in full in House and Kasper 1981). On the basis of the recorded interactions, eight levels of directness were established; these can be illustrated by the following German utterances, which are in the sequence 'least direct' to 'most direct':

Complaints

1   Seltsam, gestern war meine Bluse doch noch ganz sauber.
2   Da ist ein Fleck auf meiner Bluse.
3   Schrecklich, dieser Fleck wird wohl nie wieder rausgehen.
4   Hast du etwa meine Bluse angehabt?
5   Du hast den Fleck draufgemacht.
6   Du hättest die Bluse nicht ohne meine Erlaubnis nehmen sollen.
     (Du hast meine ganze Bluse ruiniert.)
7   Ich finde es gemein von dir, daß du einfach meine Sachen nimmst.
8   Du bist wirklich unverschämt!

Requests

1   Es ist sehr kalt hier drin.
2   Warum ist das Fenster offen?
3   Kannst du das Fenster zumachen?
4   Du kannst das Fenster zumachen.
5   Mir wärs lieber, wenn du das Fenster zumachen würdest.
6   Du solltest das Fenster zumachen.
7   Ich muß dich bitten, das Fenster zuzumachen.
     (Ich bitte dich, das Fenster zuzumachen.)
8   Mach das Fenster zu!

The study was very much preliminary in nature, and we cannot really draw any firm conclusions from it, but the results are at least suggestive and interesting. The most general finding was that the Germans used more direct utterances overall than the English participants, and that the English ones did not use the two most direct levels at all. However, the study was a little more subtle than this, as a number of so-called 'modality markers' were identified and their use examined. These markers were of two types, which again can be illustrated with German examples:

Downgraders

Ich wollte dich bitten, . . .
Hättest du was dagegen, wenn . . .

Könntest du uns irgendwie 'n paar Platten oder so leihen?
ein kleines bißchen
Du bist ein netter Kerl, Peter, aber . . .
Man tut so etwas einfach nicht, Herr Schmidt.

Upgraders

absolut, furchtbar
wirklich, ausgesprochen
sicherlich, gewiß
(Das ist aber) verdammt (unverschämt von dir!)
Warum hast du das mir nicht vorher gesagt?
Es ist doch ganz klar, daß . . .

The function of these markers is clearly to 'fine tune' the utterances by decreasing or increasing levels of directness. The interesting findings in this respect were that:

–   the Germans used more markers overall and indeed twice as many upgraders, while
–   although the English participants did not use the two most direct levels, they subtly reinforced the strength of their most direct utterances by using more upgraders, for example: (student to fellow-student who is giving a party) *Do you realise* you're making *a hell of* a noise?

■   Allowing for the flimsy nature of the evidence, how would you interpret these findings?

■■   Devise a similar test and recruit some anglophone and German-speaking guinea pigs to take part in it. Think carefully about the kinds of factors you should take into account when selecting your participants, e.g. country/region of origin, age, sex, occupation, personality (e.g. relatively lively and extrovert, or quiet and serious).

The power of the personal pronoun

One of the most crucial ways of establishing and maintaining social relations, part of the daily test of our command of politeness conventions, is in knowing how to address people we are talking or writing to.

However, pronouns of personal address in English are less problematic sociolinguistically than their counterparts in German, where the choice speakers are required to make (*du* or *Sie*) is by no means as straightforward as even advanced textbooks in German as a Foreign Language seem to suggest. The fact that the very act of selecting one form or the other is lexicalised (i.e. it is explicitly recognised in the existence of the verbs *duzen* and *siezen*, as in 'wollen wir uns nicht duzen?') shows that this is a conscious process.

The importance of making the right sociolinguistic choice underlies not one but two epistolary novels by Werner Lansburgh. In the following extracts from the beginning of the first book, the narrator immediately raises the problem of how to address the recipient of his letters:

> Dear Doosie,
> warum ich Sie Doosie nenne, fragen Sie? Well, my dear, don't you understand German – verstehen Sie denn kein Deutsch? I am calling you Doosie, weil ich noch nicht recht weiß, ob ich Du oder Sie zu Ihnen sagen soll. Deshalb. That's why. [. . .]
>
> Sie wissen es sicher schon selber: „Brüderschaft", fraternity, brotherhood, sisterhood etc., das alles ist im Englischen untrinkbar, simply undrinkable. Und wie Sie sicher gleichfalls wissen, as you probably know as well, geht Brüderschaft wie so vieles andere in England sehr diskret vor sich – such things happen quietly, discreetly and informally. Etwa so: Man sagt „you" zueinander, bis plötzlich der eine den anderen ganz lässig, fast unmerklich – casually – mit dem Vornamen anredet, with his or her Christian name – oder auch, vielleicht etwas amerikanischer, aber deshalb keineswegs schlechter: with his or her given name.
>
> (Lansburgh 1977: 7–9)

The narrator's caution is prudent: there have been a number of famous court cases in which the use of *du* was alleged to be not only inappropriate but insulting and even illegal.

■ It is easy to see that knowing whether to say *du* or *Sie* belongs to a speaker's communicative competence, but in the absence of clearly codified rules for selection (for example, in a reference grammar) it is not so easy to see how all speakers might agree on how to make the choice. How did you learn to use *du* and *Sie*? If you were a teacher of German, how would you deal with this?

- Consider the flowchart in Figure 7.1. This is an attempt to represent schematically the decision-making process involved in the selection of the appropriate pronoun in German: do you think it is accurate as far as it goes?

- The flowchart is an idealised representation (obviously no one consciously works their way through such a series of questions), but even allowing for that, what fundamental flaw must there be in any such rigid and 'logical' system? Consider, for example, the following exchange between a German beggar (A) and a Turkish man (B):

B: Haben Sie viel gearbeitet bis jetzt und hier bei Ecke stehen und von Hunger von andere Menschen betteln.
A: *Sie* ham Recht.
B   Es ist nicht gut.
A: Nein, is nicht gut. Türkisch Mann, *Du*?
B: Ja.
A: Ich merk es.
B: Ja, muß man helfen aber . . .
A: *Sie* brauchen mir nicht helfen.

(Hinnenkamp 1982: 68)

- Consider also this one between two colleagues, overheard in the staff room of a school:

ER: Sag mal, Jutta, ich hab' zwei Karten fürs Konzert, kommst du mit?
SIE: Das ist sehr freundlich von Ihnen, Herr Albrecht, aber ich bin schon verabredet.

- What does the use of personal pronouns and other forms of address reveal about the relationships between the various participants in these dialogues?

- However much we might refine a schema like the one in the flowchart, it is difficult to see how it could incorporate rules for changing from the use of one pronoun to the other with a given interlocutor. How and when do speakers change from *Sie* to *du* and vice versa? Is this change automatic at some given point in a relationship? Is it necessarily reciprocal or may it affect only one of the people concerned (i.e. may one person say *du* while the other uses *Sie* in the same conversation)? Is it always permanent or may it be temporary?

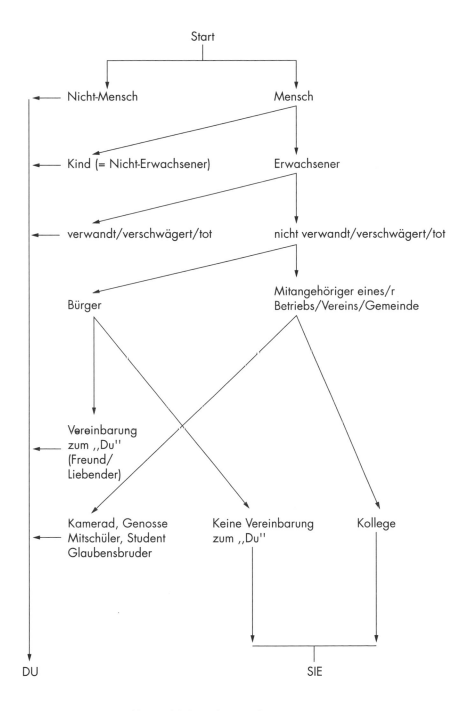

FIGURE 7.1 A possible model for selecting *du* or *Sie*
Source: Augst 1977

At least in modern German the choice (for singular reference) is limited to two options, but this relatively simple situation has been the case only since about the mid-nineteenth century. If you trace the development of personal pronoun usage from Old High German (OHG) times (roughly from the eighth to the eleventh century) to the present, you will find that it can be represented by a kind of anvil shape. At the beginning of this period and at the end usage is relatively 'focused', i.e. in OHG *du* was the universal form of address, today there is a choice between just two terms, *du* or *Sie*. But in the intervening periods it became increasingly 'diffuse', culminating with a choice between five forms at the end of the eighteenth century (in ascending order of formality or respect): *du*, *Er/Sie* (third-person singular), *Ihr*, *Sie* (third-person plural), *Dieselben*.

As an illustration of the more differentiated patterns in the early nineteenth century, consider the ways the characters in these short exchanges from Büchner's play *Woyzeck* (written in the mid-1830s) address each other.

Hauptmann [Army captain] *auf einem Stuhl, Woyzeck* [a common soldier] *rasiert ihn.*

HAUPTMANN: Langsam, Woyzeck, langsam; ein's nach dem andern. Er macht mir ganz schwindlich. Was soll ich dann mit den zehn Minuten anfangen, die Er heut zu früh fertig wird? Woyzeck, bedenk' Er, Er hat noch seine schöne dreißig Jahr zu leben, dreißig Jahr! macht 360 Monate, und Tage, Stunden, Minuten! Was will Er denn mit der ungeheuren Zeit all anfangen? Teil Er sich ein, Woyzeck.

WOYZECK: Jawohl, Herr Hauptmann.

[. . .]

HAUPTMANN: Woyzeck, Er hat keine Tugend, Er ist kein tugendhafter Mensch. [. . .]

WOYZECK: Ja Herr Hauptmann, die Tugend! ich hab's noch nicht so aus. Sehn Sie, wir gemeine Leut, das hat keine Tugend. [. . .] Es muß was schöns sein um die Tugend, Herr Hauptmann. Aber ich bin ein armer Kerl.

HAUPTMANN: Gut Woyzeck. Du bist ein guter Mensch, ein guter Mensch. Aber du denkst zu viel, das zehrt, du siehst immer so verhetzt aus. [. . .]

(Büchner 1971: 92–4)

■ How do you interpret the fact that the Hauptmann and Woyzeck

COMMUNICATIVE CONVENTIONS

use different forms to address each other (i.e. they follow a non-reciprocal pattern)? How would people in a comparable situation today address each other?

■■ Take this analysis further by studying the forms of personal address used between characters in plays from different historical periods in terms of the correlation between address form and social relationship.

■■ The complex pattern that existed at the end of the eighteenth century was called by one contemporary 'ein Barometer der Höflichkeit': find out what the relationship was between these various forms.

■■ Are there now, or were there in the past, differences in patterns of address in Germany, Austria and Switzerland? Why was this one of the aspects of language use that was frequently cited as a source of communication problems between Germans from 'East' and 'West' after unification in 1990?

■■■ How might the changes in personal pronoun usage act as a 'barometer' of changes in the organisation of German society? (Note that the more focused patterns are generally symmetrical or reciprocal – i.e. both interlocutors use the same form to each other – whereas the more diffuse patterns are partially asymmetrical.)

Paradoxically, perhaps, the superficially simpler system in modern German may in some ways be more complicated to implement or manage. Some of the grey areas are rather special cases (for example, how do you address someone in a sauna, or a childhood friend whom you have not seen since your school days?), but the uncertainties have grown with the increased instability in the system since the late 1960s. The social conflict associated with the so-called '1968 generation' was all about challenging conventional social relationships, and for a while the various permutations of personal pronouns and other forms of address (names, titles) became a potent means of attacking the existing order and forcing individuals to align themselves with one side or the other. The most obvious consequence of this was the spread of *du* into areas that had traditionally been considered the preserve of *Sie*: between staff and customers in certain shops and bars, between presenters of radio and television programmes and their audience or participants in phone-in programmes, or between new colleagues if perceived to be of a similar (youngish!) age or political orientation (i.e. of the Left).

In practice, while most situations are relatively straightforward, there are many everyday encounters in which the choice of personal pronoun is far from automatic. In these cases, speakers have to ask themselves: 'If I say *du* (or *Sie*) to you, what am I trying to tell you – and what will you think I am trying to tell you?' Consider this situation:

In der Praxis meiner Zahnärztin [. . .] werden Patienten eines gewissen Schlages oder Alters von den Arzthelferinnen geduzt, von der Zahnärztin aber nicht. Ich nehme an, daß [. . .] die Arzthelferinnen sich als Kollektiv kennzeichnen möchten. Warum dieser Code auf den Patienten ausgeweitet wird, ist mir rätselhaft. Wenn Taxifahrer du sagen, habe ich manchmal den Eindruck, als wollten sie das Gefälle, das durch die Situation des Taxifahrens entsteht, vor sich selbst leugnen: „Ich sitze zwar vorn, aber ich könnte genausogut hinten sitzen."

(Ulf Erdmann Ziegler in *Die Zeit*)

Some situations can give rise to considerable agonising:

Nehmen wir an, Sie seien irgendwo zwischen 25 und 55, trügen statusneutrale Kleidung (Jeans, Parka, Leder-Boots), und um Sie sei jene Aura angepaßter Unangepaßtheit, die es schwer macht, Sie gesellschaftlich einzuordnen. [. . .] Nehmen wir weiter an, Sie gingen in einen „jugendlichen" Plattenladen, etwa um nach dem aller-neuesten von Michael Jackson zu fragen. Während Sie vor dem schnauzbärtigen Verkäufer stehen, der aussieht wie der Camel-Mann nach einer dreiwöchigen Kneipentour, gehen Sie blitzschnell die Möglichkeiten durch: „Haben Sie . . . ?", „Hast du . . . ?", „Habt ihr . . . ?" Das Sie, finden Sie, ist in dieser Umgebung fehl am Platz, wirkt ein wenig steif und lächerlich, hier sind alle per Du. [. . .] Das Du und das Ihr andererseits kommen Ihnen ein wenig unnatürlich vor, und in der Drogerie nebenan hätten Sie sie niemals gebraucht. Schließlich haben Sie gelernt, daß man Fremde siezt. Klänge das Du nicht auch viel zu anbiederisch? Oder käme sich der mit Du titulierte Verkäufer gar als Kind behandelt vor? So entziehen Sie sich dem Dilemma lieber und drücken sich unpersönlich aus: „Gibt es . . . ?" Oder Sie entschließen sich doch zum Du und könnten sich dann gleich die Zunge abbeißen, denn zurück kommt ein Sie und macht Ihnen klar, daß man Sie hier keineswegs als seinesgleichen zu akzeptieren gedenkt. Oder Sie nehmen das Sie und bringen dann kaum das

„Michael Jackson" über die Lippen, denn der Verkäufer könnte ja nun denken, Sie seien so ein Alter, der es auf die Verführung von Minderjährigen abgesehen hat.

(Zimmer 1986: 53)

At the crest of the wave of increased *du*-usage, in the mid-1980s, the satirical magazine *Titanic* declared in a letter to its readers:

Deutsche! Irgend jemand hat neulich herausgefunden, daß 85% von Euch bereit sind, sich duzen zu lassen. Ihr findet das gut. Wir nicht. Merkt Euch das. Titanic.

(*Titanic* 4/1984: 12; cited in Kretzenbacher 1991: 16)

Since then, the situation has stabilised to the extent that *du* is still used much more widely than pre-1968, but it has not displaced *Sie*, and indeed some would argue that the trend is now moving in the other direction.

■■ Draw up a list of twenty everyday situations and decide whether you would use *du* or *Sie* in each case. Then ask a number of German-speakers what they would say. Where do the native speakers disagree with you? Where do they disagree among themselves? Discuss with them what the reasons for the different choices might be (for example, take into account their age, sex, occupation, etc.).

The boundaries between *du* and *Sie* may have shifted, but they have not disappeared. As many other languages, such as English, have dispensed with or never had such a choice, it would seem that there has to be some reason for a speech community to continue to burden itself with an un-economical system of personal address. In other words, the sociolinguistic benefits are still perceived to outweigh the costs. Some of the tasks above may have revealed some clues to what the benefits may be: they can perhaps be summarised as 'providing a surprisingly subtle and flexible means of articulating social relationships'. However, we are still left with a number of unanswered questions.

■ If the scope of *du* has been extended, it follows that the scope of *Sie* has been reduced: is it possible to specify what their respective functions now are?

■■ It has been suggested, for instance, that there are different 'kinds' of *du*, e.g. what the writer Monika Maron calls 'das Boutiquendu',

139

'das therapeutische Alternativdu', 'das Gewerkschaftsdu' and 'das Minderheitendu'. What do you think these terms mean? Ask native speakers whether they agree that *du* be classified in these (or other) ways, and whether the same applies to *Sie*.

■ In modern German there are very few situations in which the non-reciprocal *du* ↔ *Sie* pattern occurs (now virtually only in the context child ↔ adult), but while this pattern marks among other things some form of social inequality, in what sense (if at all) is the converse true? For instance, what does reciprocal *Sie* between employer and employee, or between lecturer and student, represent in terms of their social relationship? What significant aspect of their relationship is concealed by this reciprocal usage? To what extent would their relationship change if the two parties agreed to change to reciprocal *du*?

Underlying these particular questions is the fundamental problem: what is the 'social meaning' of personal pronouns? As regards the structure of the system as a whole, it has been argued that an asymmetrical pattern such as the following can be interpreted in terms of power (or status) and solidarity:

higher social rank   *Sie* ↔ *Sie*

$$\uparrow \quad \uparrow$$
$$\downarrow \quad \downarrow$$

lower social rank   *du* ↔ *du*

Reciprocal usage of either *du* or *Sie* at the horizontal level indicates solidarity within a social rank or class, while non-reciprocal usage at the vertical level indicates the difference in power or status between two ranks or classes. According to this argument, the shift from this pattern to the generally symmetrical pattern that obtains today marks a fundamental change in the structure of society from the dominance of the so-called 'power semantic' to the 'solidarity semantic'. However, this analysis has also been heavily criticised, and other ways of analysing what the two pronouns represent have been proposed, such as 'respect' vs 'lack of respect', 'distance' vs 'intimacy', 'unfamiliarity' vs 'familiarity'.

■■■ From your reading of the relevant literature, draw up a list of arguments for and against the various interpretations of what differences in patterns of address mean. If possible, illustrate your analysis with examples from any available sources: literary texts, letters in newspapers and magazines, films, television or radio programmes (talk shows, game shows, phone-ins, etc.), personal observations. To what extent do the practices you observe conflict with the patterns or norms you have acquired as a learner of German?

Further reading

Ammon (1972), a critical analysis of the social meaning of German personal pronouns.

Augst (1977), Section A, 'Zur Syntax der Höflichkeit', gives a diachronic survey of German address patterns from Old High German to the present, with suggestions for research on particular aspects.

Bayer (1979), with particular emphasis on the post-1968 period.

Beneke (1993), on attitudes and communicative behaviour of young people in East and West Berlin after unification in 1990.

Clyne (1995), Chapter 5.

Glück and Sauer (1990), Chapter 8, on *Jugendsprache*, address forms and other aspects of personal interaction in German.

Holmes (1992), Chapter 11, on politeness and patterns of address in general, not in relation to German.

House and Kasper (1981), for the experiment comparing English and German 'levels' of politeness.

Kretzenbacher (1991), a detailed but entertaining account of recent trends, including East/West differences, with many concrete examples.

Saville-Troike (1989), an excellent introduction to the whole area of communicative competence from a sociolinguistic perspective.

Schlobinski (1995), for a critical account of earlier work on *Jugend-sprachen* and illustrations of analysis based on whole interactions rather than on individual items of vocabulary.

Wardhaugh (1992), Chapter 11, on politeness and patterns of address in general, not in relation to German.

Zimmer (1986), Chapter 3, 'Das brüderliche Du', for a more journalistic but still serious discussion of address forms in German.

• • •

Chapter 8

Language and gender

The problem of reference

The cartoon shown in Figure 8.1 was intended as a graphic illustration of the problem of students who are nominally registered at a university but who do not appear to exist, or at least are not actually attending the course. Coincidentally, however, it illustrates what some see as the 'phantom' existence of women in texts that appear to include them in their scope of reference but are often understood to refer only to men. Presumably not all 'phantom students' are male, but the unambiguously male representation of this phenomenon in the cartoon is characteristic of the stereotypical images of certain categories of person that have been revealed in many empirical studies: asked to draw 'a doctor' or 'a manager' on the one hand,

FIGURE 8.1 The problem of representation: *Der Phantomstudent*

Source: Klaus Karlitzky in *uni-aktuell* (Albrecht-Ludwigs-Universität Freiburg, 17 December 1985, reproduced here from Schoenthal 1989)

Note: the original caption read 'Der Phantomstudent ist an den deutschen Universitäten zu einem handfesten Problem geworden'

or 'a nurse' or 'a secretary' on the other, both male and female test subjects more often than not produce pictures of a man in the first case and a woman in the second. Given the relative distribution of men and women in these occupations, these responses may not be surprising, even if they are disturbing. By contrast, there is on the face of it no particular reason to perceive 'a student' as male.

However, there is a small but significant difference between 'a student' and 'ein Student'. The fact that in English neither articles nor nouns are marked for grammatical gender means that it was possible to write and read the first paragraph of this chapter in very general terms: whatever mental image you or I may have of 'a doctor' or 'a nurse' is not derived in any way from the form of the words in these noun phrases. In German, male and female practitioners of these occupations are distinguished from each other both grammatically and lexically (*ein Arzt* vs *eine Ärztin, eine Krankenschwester* vs *ein Krankenpfleger*). The same applies to 'students' but, according to conventional grammars, while *eine Studentin* can only refer to 'a female student', *ein Student* may be used to refer either to 'a male student' or to 'any student, regardless of sex'. This non-specific use of the masculine form must be intended in the caption of the cartoon (Figure 8.1), but how many people would draw a female student if asked to supply a picture to accompany the caption? (You could find out by asking German-speakers to do this.)

■   The same problem would clearly arise with 'a doctor' in German, but what about 'a nurse'? How many other pairs of occupational titles can you find that do not conform to the *Arzt/Ärztin* pattern (i.e. where the term denoting a female practitioner is derived from the male term by adding the suffix *-in*)? What do such pairs (and the occupations they designate) have in common?

The problem here is one of reference, but it is a sociolinguistic (rather than merely linguistic) issue because many women feel linguistically excluded from texts which do not explicitly include them, in the same way that they feel excluded from certain occupations. It is therefore important to see debates on feminist linguistics in the context of the women's movement that began in the late 1960s (although it was a further ten years before the debates took off in Germany). Our discussion in this chapter will focus on two closely related questions: does the root of the problem lie in the language itself or in the way that it is used, and does the solution therefore lie in changing the language or in changing the speakers?

Concepts of gender

> Das masculinum scheint das frühere, größere, festere, sprödere, raschere, das thätige, bewegliche, zeugende; das femininum das spätere, kleinere, weichere, stillere, das leidende, empfangende; das neutrum das erzeugte, gewirkte, stoffartige, generelle, unentwickelte, kollektive, das stumpfere, leblose.
>
> (Grimm 1870/1976: 357; cited in Hellinger 1990: 62)

Jacob Grimm was many things but he was not one of Germany's first feminist linguists. This passage appears to be part of an attempt to characterise grammatical features in semantic terms: in other words, it suggests that 'genders' are not merely grammatical categories to which nouns are arbitrarily assigned but rather a means of organising the vocabulary of the language according to semantic criteria. Furthermore, the masculine and feminine genders are defined in relation to each other, in a way that appears to propose a connection between 'masculine' and 'male' and between 'feminine' and 'female', in terms not simply of biological characteristics, but also of social roles and norms of social behaviour. The passage therefore implicitly merges three different conceptions of gender: grammatical, semantic (or 'natural') and social.

Grammatical gender is an inherent and (generally) invariant attribute of German nouns, and it is crucial to the operation of the nominal system: for example, you need to know that *Tasse* is feminine in order to select the appropriate form of article, adjective and pronoun in a sentence like 'Ich habe dein*e* blau*e* Tasse gefunden, *sie* ist im Wohnzimmer'. Since the allocation of nouns to each of the three gender classes is generally arbitrary (consider, for example, *der Löffel*, *die Gabel*, *das Messer*), grammatical gender is not sociolinguistically significant except where it conflicts in certain ways with semantic gender.

■■ Some nouns are said to be 'inherently specified for sex of referent'; for example, *Königin* and *Onkel* have the semantic properties (+female) and (+male), respectively. By and large, the grammatical gender of such nouns corresponds to the natural or semantic gender for which they are specified (*Königin* is feminine, *Onkel* is masculine): what exceptions can you find?

■ Other human nouns are not inherently specified for sex of referent (they may refer to either male or female) but are still assigned to a single grammatical gender; for example, *der Mensch, die Person, das Individuum*. Can you think of contexts in which this potential linguistic conflict might lead to social or communicative problems? (We shall examine some examples in the next section, pp. 147–51.)

As the label suggests, social gender is a social rather than a linguistic category, but it has sociolinguistic significance in the impact it has on language use. While biological gender is an objective category determined by purely physiological factors, irrespective of social or cultural environment, social gender is an acquired status that is the result of specific social and cultural processes. In other words, biological gender is an absolute quality that is genetically determined, whereas social gender is a relative quality that is socially constructed. So for example, all human beings are deemed to be male or female on the basis of certain universal physical features, but the kinds of behaviour associated with or considered appropriate for males and females, respectively, vary from one society or culture to another.

■ What kinds of stereotypical assumption about appropriate roles and behaviours of men and women or boys and girls can you think of? To what extent do such assumptions have a bearing on (expected) language use? How does this relate to our earlier discussion of nouns like *Arzt* and *Krankenschwester* in the section on 'The problem of reference' (pp. 144–5)?

Generic forms

In German, there are three ways of specifying the sex of a noun's referent:

lexical:	*Bruder/Schwester; weiblicher/männlicher Passagier*
grammatical gender:	*die Angestellte/der Briefträger*
morphological:	*Präsident/Präsidentin*

Very often two means of specification are combined (*die Präsidentin*). There is therefore generally no difficulty in specifying the sex of a particular referent if we wish to do so. However, the other side of the coin is that this tripartite system makes it difficult to avoid at least appearing to specify the referent's sex, even when you don't want to: for example, when it is unknown or immaterial, or when the referents constitute a mixed-sex group. In English, it is possible to make such general statements as:

1   Any good musician can improvise.
2   All good musicians can improvise.

In such cases the noun, whether singular or plural, cannot be identified as having exclusively male or female referents (how it is perceived may be a different matter, as we have seen). In German, however, there is no way of avoiding the use of a noun phrase marked for grammatical gender, and so the representation of the idea underlying sentences 1 and 2 above is less straightforward. Conventional grammars prescribe the use of the masculine form in such contexts, so that the German equivalents to sentences 1 and 2 would be:

3   Jeder gute Musiker kann improvisieren.
4   Alle guten Musiker können improvisieren.

As there are distinctive feminine forms in both singular and plural (*Musikerin, Musikerinnen*), these sentences are ambiguous: they can be taken to include either all male musicians or all musicians (both male and female). Sentences 5 and 6, by contrast, can only refer to female musicians:

5   Jede gute Musikerin kann improvisieren.
6   Alle guten Musikerinnen können improvisieren.

Nouns and pronouns which are used to refer to all members of a particular class or category (whether animate, such as musician, child or bird, or inanimate, such as furniture or vehicle) are said to be used 'generically'. Some German nouns (e.g. *Kind*) are inherently **generic** with respect to sex, in that they can only be used to specify sex if qualified by an additional element (e.g. *weibliches Kind*). Nouns such as *Musiker* and *Musikerin* can be used generically, in the sense of referring to all male or all female musicians, respectively (and therefore not distinguishing between, say, red-haired and blond members of either category), but according to conventional grammar only the masculine form *Musiker* can be used generically in the sense of non-sex-specific. The use of masculine forms of nouns and pronouns as supposedly 'inclusive' generics in this sense is the central issue in debates on language and gender in German: if masculine forms are given a dual function, does their use as supposed generics actually make women 'invisible'? How can we be sure that women are included in utterances where these forms are used?

Problem 1: Mensch[1]

Unlike *Musiker* or *Bürger*, but like *Kind* or *Individuum*, *Mensch* appears to be both inherently generic and gender-neutral: it denotes the general category 'human being' and can only be used sex-specifically if modified accordingly (see Figure 8.2).

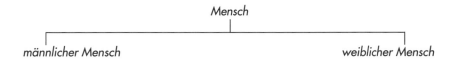

FIGURE 8.2 *Mensch* as a generic noun

Generic nouns are important, as they are an economical means of making general statements that apply to all members of a particular category or class without having to specify all the sub-categories or individual members:

> 7   Die Menschen unterscheiden sich von den Tieren durch ihre Sprachfähigkeit.

But consider the following sentences:

> 8   Mit der Geschlechtsreife wird der Mensch gebärfähig.
> 9   Manche Menschen gebären lebende Junge, andere legen Eier.

■   Clearly, both of these sentences would be considered ungrammatical, but for a different reason in each case: why?

■■   It would be logical for sentence 10 to be considered unacceptable on similar grounds to sentence 8: try asking native speakers whether they find it acceptable or not.

1   The three 'problems' discussed in this and the next section (pp. 152–6) are based on Pusch (1984), and some of the example sentences are also from this source.

10   Jede Sprache entwickelt sich nicht anders als jeder Mensch sich
      vom Kind zum Jüngling, vom Jüngling zum Mann und zum
      Greis entwickelt.

■■   Then ask them whether they find each of the sentences in the
      following pairs equally (un)acceptable:

11a   Im Unglück sind zwanzig Menschen ums Leben gekommen,
      darunter vier Männer.
11b   Im Unglück sind zwanzig Menschen ums Leben gekommen,
      darunter vier Frauen.
12a   Alle Menschen werden Brüder.
12b   Alle Menschen werden Schwestern.

■■   Look through any popular magazine or newspaper and see if you
      can find further examples of 'doubtful' generics.

Problem 2: cats and customers

Consider the following two hypothetical situations:

A woman enters a shop with her (male) cat, and the shop assistant
says:

13   'Sie sind heute schon der dritte Kunde mit einer Katze.'

A man enters a shop with his (female) cat, and the shop assistant
says:

14   'Sie sind heute schon die dritte Kundin mit einem Kater.'

■   It could be argued that only one of these utterances (14) is
      problematic, but it could also be argued that both of them are: what
      do you think?

■   If you accept that there may be problems with both utterances, why
      would they be of a different order?

■   If the second utterance (14) were made in the first situation and vice
      versa, what (if anything) would be implied about the previous two
      customers – and cats – in each case?

While all the relevant nouns in these sentences (*Kunde, Kundin, Katze, Kater*) are marked for grammatical gender, your answer to the first question above will depend on whether you consider all or only some of them to be semantically marked for sex of referent (e.g. does the meaning of *Kunde* necessarily include the property [+male]?). Figure 8.3 summarises the nature of the problem in graphic form. Each part of the diagram represents a **hyponymous** relationship. However, one of the hyponyms in each case is identical to the superordinate term. In other words, both *Kunde* and *Katze* are ambiguous, in that they can be used either as semantically marked, sex-specific terms, or as unmarked, generic terms.

FIGURE 8.3 The ambiguity of *Kunde* and *Katze*

Now consider the representations of further hyponymous relationships shown in Figure 8.4.

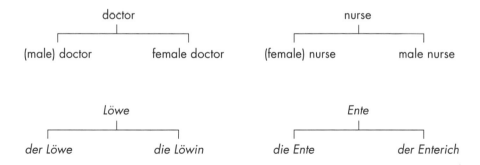

FIGURE 8.4 Hyponymous relationships in English and German

- Why are the words 'male' and 'female' in the English examples in parentheses? What is the difference between the two German examples? Can you see a connection between the two sets of examples? Draw up a list of animal names in German and see whether you can establish any common factor between those that follow the *Löwe* and the *Ente* patterns, respectively.

Neutralisation and *Sprachtherapie*

There are two general strategies that can be adopted to tackle the kinds of problem that have emerged so far: either you can try to exploit the existing resources within the language, or you can try to introduce changes to the structure of the language. Both approaches can be illustrated in the next problem.

Problem 3: students

Figure 8.5 shows that *Student/Studentin* presents the same problem as *Musiker/Musikerin*. The apparently gender-neutral singular and plural forms are actually identical to the respective masculine forms, and although sex of referent is marked grammatically (by means of articles) for both feminine and masculine in the singular, only the feminine forms are also marked morphologically (with the suffix *-in(nen)*). Consider now some possible solutions to the problem of asymmetry shown in Figure 8.5 (the solutions are shown in Figures 8.6, 8.7, 8.8 and 8.9).

'generic singular'	der Student	
feminine singular	*die* Student*in* *der* Student	masculine singular
feminine plural	die Student*innen* die Studenten	masculine plural
'generic' plural	die Studenten	

FIGURE 8.5 'Students': status quo

'generic singular'	der Studierende	
feminine singular	*die* Studierende *der* Studierende	masculine singular
feminine plural	die *weiblichen* Studierenden die *männlichen* Studierenden	masculine plural
'generic' plural	die Studierenden	

FIGURE 8.6 'Students': solution A

'generic singular'	der Student		
feminine singular	*die* Student	*der* Student	masculine singular
feminine plural	die *weibl.* Studenten	die *männl.* Studenten	masculine plural
'generic' plural	die Studenten		

FIGURE 8.7 'Students': solution B

'generic singular'	der Student		
feminine singular	der *weibl.* Student	der *männl.* Student	masculine singular
feminine plural	die *weibl.* Studenten	die *männl.* Studenten	masculine plural
'generic' plural	die Studenten		

FIGURE 8.8 'Students': solution C

'generic singular'	das Student		
feminine singular	*die* Student	*der* Student	masculine singular
feminine plural	die *weibl.* Studenten	die *männl.* Studenten	masculine plural
'generic' plural	die Studenten		

FIGURE 8.9 'Students': solution D

■■ First analyse precisely what each of the four proposed solutions has to offer: to what extent are they 'working within existing resources' or 'introducing changes to the form of the language'? What are their strengths and weaknesses in relation to the status quo? Which of the solutions, if any, do you find the most satisfactory?

For some (especially perhaps people like the city councillors discussed in the next section, see pp. 158–9), this kind of exercise might be no more than a curious linguistic game. However, in at least two particular contexts the importance of ensuring that both men and women are explicitly included, and not merely implicitly *mitgemeint*, should be uncontroversial: legal texts and job advertisements (and of course all other texts referring to people's jobs). For example, in the light of our considerations so far, how would you view this (now superseded) article in the Swiss constitution?

15   Alle Schweizer sind vor dem Gesetz gleich.

The principle of using the 'generic masculine' (i.e. the masculine form to refer to both male and female) in legal texts has a long history. Gerhard Stickel (1988: 330), for example, cites the following sentence from the Corpus Iuris Civilis (a collection of texts on Roman civil law):

16   Pronuntiatio sermonis in sexu masculino ad utrum sexum plerumque porrigatur.
      (If the masculine sex is named in a ruling, this nevertheless generally refers to both sexes.)

The argument is that this is simply a more economical approach than to name both men and women in each instance. Sentences 17 and 18 show how rigorously this principle is (or was) applied in current German legislation and in the former GDR (both examples from Stickel 1988: 343):

17   Der Ehegatte eines Angeklagten ist in der Hauptverhandlung als Beistand zuzulassen.
      (From Paragraph 149 of the *Strafprozeßordnung* (code of criminal procedure))
18   Mieter einer Wohnung sind beide Ehegatten, auch wenn nur ein Ehegatte den Vertrag abgeschlossen hat.
      (From Paragraph 100 (3) of the *Zivilgesetzbuch* (code of civil law) of the GDR)

■   Passages such as these have been referred to as 'Beispiel für die Perversion einer frauenfeindlichen deutschen Rechtssprache' by one commentator, and as 'vorzügliche Belege für geschlechtsneutral verwendete Maskulina' by another: which view would you support?

In accordance with the principle of equal opportunities, paragraph 611b of the *Bürgerliches Gesetzbuch* (civil code) states, with splendid internal inconsistency:

19 Der Arbeitgeber [sic!] soll einen Arbeitsplatz weder öffentlich noch innerhalb des Betriebs nur für Männer oder nur für Frauen ausschreiben.

However, to implement this kind of regulation and to rewrite legal texts without the generic masculine means finding a suitable linguistic pattern. In some cases, overt personal reference (as in 20a) can be avoided by using more abstract formulations referring to the function performed by the person concerned (as in 20b) (these examples are from Gorny 1995: 554):

20a Die Beratungsstelle kann im Bedarfsfall einen Arzt, einen Juristen hinzuziehen.
20b Die Beratungsstelle kann im Bedarfsfall ärztliche, juristische Fachberatung hinzuziehen.

More generally, one obvious possibility that is already available is simply to use the so-called *Paarformel*: *Bewerber und Bewerberinnen, jede Mitarbeiterin und jeder Mitarbeiter*. Other forms of *Splitting*, which are more economical (*Sparformeln*), all entail the use of **orthographical** devices:

brackets: *alle Lehrer(innen)*
oblique stroke: *liebe Wähler/innen*
capital -I: *unsere LeserInnen*

There are obvious advantages in these proposals, as they appear to supply a solution to the problem of inclusive reference while avoiding the cumbersome and long-winded effects of the *Paarformel*. However, they have certain limitations. As they depend on orthographical symbols, it is difficult to see how they could be used in spoken texts, although it is conceivable that *LeserIn*, for example, could be pronounced with a slight pause before the last syllable [le:zɐʔɪn] in order to distinguish it from *Leserin* [le:zərɪn]. But even in written texts problems may arise, especially in the singular in cases other than the nominative, and in texts where repeated reference is required.

■ How would you translate the following sentence using *Sparformeln*?

21 We are looking for a highly qualified engineer.

■ Critics of these proposals often like to ridicule them by inventing highly complex sentences or (more fairly) by quoting clumsy examples from real texts. Can you think of more satisfactory ways of writing sentences 22 and 23 (both from Stickel 1988: 349)?

22 Der/Die Bürgermeister/in ist Vorsitzende/r im Rat. Im Falle seiner/ihrer Verhinderung übernimmt sein/ihr/e Stellvertreter/in den Vorsitz.

23 Der/Die sterbende Patient/Patientin hat im besonderen Maße Anspruch auf eine seiner/ihrer Würde entsprechende Behandlung und Unterbringung. Hierzu gehört auch ihm/ihr auf seinen/ihren Wunsch hin das Sterben zu Hause zu ermöglichen.

■■ Look at job advertisements in a German-language newspaper and see how many actually conform to paragraph 611 of the *Bundesgesetzbuch* (sentence 19). In those that do, which approach do they use?

Totale Feminisierung

The solutions to the problem of generic reference discussed in the previous section collectively offer a number of advantages and disadvantages, but it is clear that considerable imagination, ingenuity and flexibility are required to devise a workable approach that can be applied successfully in a wide range of contexts. Indeed, many working parties in Germany, Austria and Switzerland have been set up to address this general issue, and the results of their deliberations can be found in published guidelines (for example, Hellinger et al. 1985; BRD Report 1991; Swiss Report 1991).

However, not everyone is content with these guidelines: some feminists argue that they are too limited in scope, as they are concerned only with a very specific set of contexts and have no impact on everyday usage. They also contend that all such solutions fail to get to the root of the problem since they ignore what the critics see as the fundamental asymmetry or **androcentricity** of the language itself. They point, for example, to the constraints prescribed in conventional grammars, according to which the following sentences (from Trömel-Plötz 1982) are ungrammatical, even when the referent(s) is/are female:

24 Jeder Passagier möge *ihren* Platz identifizieren.

25 Für die Untersuchung brauchen wir jemanden, *die ihr* Kind noch stillt.

26   Wer hat *ihren* Lippenstift im Bad gelassen?

As an early form of resistance to these 'masculine' norms, as well as adopting the various forms of *Splitting* for gender-neutral reference, many feminists introduced new ways of representing the sex of referents and insisted on flouting conventional rules of grammatical agreement (the examples are from Pusch 1984):

27   In London müßte man einkaufen. Da geht's einem gut. Da geht's sogar *einer* gut.

28   Was kann *frau* [in place of *man* as only women are intended as referents] tun, um nicht Phonotypistin werden zu müssen?

29   Wo käme *Mann* [in place of *man* as only men are intended as referents] auch hin, wenn er nicht mal mehr ungestraft ein bißchen belästigen darf?

30   Was macht *mensch* [in place of *man* as a genuinely gender-neutral pronoun] damit?

31   Denn nicht *jedefrau* kann Abitur haben.

32   Vielleicht rufe ich jemand an, von *der* ich weiß, daß *sie* allein ist.

However, some feminist linguists consider that this even 'partial feminisation' of the language does not go far enough. On the one hand, many of the new proposals (both *Splitting* and the more radical innovations) have not gained wide acceptance, and on the other hand completely gender-neutral language is not possible in German. How, asks leading feminist *Sprachkritikerin* Luise F. Pusch, do you translate a book title like *The Sceptical Feminist* in a way that is acceptable for a feminist work (rules out *Der skeptische Feminist*), does not exclude men, whom the original title intended to include (rules out *Die skeptische Feministin*), is not hopelessly clumsy (rules out *Der/Die skeptische Feminist/in*), and does not change the meaning of the original (rules out *Skeptischer Feminismus*)? Arguing that 'the injustices of patriarchal languages' can only be resolved by political, and not by linguistic, means, she proposes a still more radical strategy:

> Feminisierung ist für den Mann sozusagen die ultimative Bedrohung, das schlechthin Unerträgliche. Um dem zu entgehen bzw. nicht länger ausgesetzt zu sein, wird er möglicherweise zur Kooperation bei der Entwicklung einer für beide Geschlechter gerechten und bequemen Sprache bereit sein.
> (Pusch 1990: 96; in the subsequent four pages, she lists her arguments in favour of *totale Feminisierung*.)

Under the programme of 'total feminisation', the compromises of 'partial feminisation' would be swept away by a complete reversal of the status quo. Some steps in this direction have been taken: for example, the regulations for the award of doctorates in the Faculty of Computer Science at Hamburg University state:

> 33   Der Fachbereich Informatik verleiht den Grad einer Doktorin –
> bei männlichen Kandidaten den Grad eines Doktors – der
> Naturwissenschaften (Dr. rer. nat.).

And all official titles in the city parliament of Rostock are exclusively feminine: the mayor, for example, is *die Bürgermeisterin* regardless of the sex of the incumbent (both examples from Gorny 1995: 552, 556). Whether or not the aim of provoking men into accepting the need for change will be achieved by such a strategy remains to be seen, but the impact it can have was clearly demonstrated by a 'feminised' speech by a city councillor in a committee meeting in a southern German town. Although the feminine forms were recorded in the official transcript using the capital *-I*, as the councillor herself indicated in her speech that they should be, she declared at the start her intention 'eine Rede in rein weiblicher Form zu halten'. Here is an extract from the transcript (the meeting was concerned with the election of members of the Foreigners' Committee):

STADTRÄTIN A.:   [. . .] ich hoffe, daß die heutige Entscheidung auch ein Neuanfang ist, ein Neuanfang, der übrigens von vielen Ausländer-Innen mit viel Hoffnung begleitet wird. Der AusländerInnenrat ist kein beratender Ausschuß . . .

STADTRAT G. (ZWISCHENRUF):   Sie haben *den* Ausländ*er* vergessen!

STADTRÄTIN A.:   Nein, ich rede mit dem großen I, wie ich Ihnen erklärt habe. – Der AusländerInnenrat ist kein beratender Ausschuß, sondern er ist ein Beirat . . .

STADTRAT G. (ZWISCHENRUF):   Was ist mit *den* Ausländ*ern*?

STADTRAT K.:   Lassen Sie sie doch mal ausreden!

STADTRAT G.:   Sie reden doch viel mehr als ich!

STADTRÄTIN A.:   Wenn Sie mich ausreden lassen würden – (Weitere Zwischenrufe, die durcheinandergehen) Sind Sie fertig?

BÜRGERMEISTER (ZU STADTRÄTIN A.):   Machen Sie bitte weiter. (Weitere Zwischenrufe, u.a. „Dürfen Männer nicht wählen?")

STADTRÄTIN A.:   Klingeln Sie doch mal, Herr Bürgermeister.

BÜRGERMEISTER: Ja, ja, wenn der Weihnachtsmann wiederkommt. [. . .]

STADTRÄTIN A.:   [. . .] Insgesamt sind neun Wahlkreise gebildet, die nach den Nationalitäten gebildet sind: Es sind also jeweils einen Wahlkreis für TürkInnen, ItalienerInnen, AsiatInnen, GriechInnen, Jugoslaw-Innen, SpanierInnen und PortugiesInnen, AfrikanerInnen, Ameri-kanerInnen und weitere EuropäerInnen.

(Während dieser Ausführungen gibt es immer wieder Unruhe und Zwischenrufe im Gremium, u.a. „Erscht mol selba deitsch lerne"; „Da kann ja jeder kommen, unmöglich! Des brauche ma uns net biete lasse, net mit mir! Verhunzung! Da wird unsere Sprache verhunzt!")

STADTRÄTIN A.:   [. . .] Ich freue mich über Ihre Reaktion. Das zeigt, daß das ein erfolgreicher Versuch ist.

(Thimm 1993)

■■■ Find out what you can about the various guidelines for gender-neutral language that have been produced in German-speaking (and perhaps also anglophone) countries and try to decide what you think the most appropriate measures are.

■■■ If you were appointed to a commission whose task was to review proposals for changes to the structure of 'standard German' as it is represented in reference grammars and textbooks, how would you view the innovations discussed in this chapter?

Further reading

Hellinger (1990), for a very readable contrastive account of feminist critiques of German and English.

Hellinger (1995), for a clear summary in English of the issues relating to German, with many examples.

Pusch (1984), still probably the best collection of original, very provocative and often humorous essays on the key issues.

Pusch (1990), a more recent collection of essays by Pusch covering similar territory to the earlier volume.

Samel (1995), for a wide-ranging account of feminist linguistics, including topics not dealt with in this chapter, such as sex-typical speech behaviour and conversational styles.

Trömel-Plötz (1982), a rather repetitive and not very recent collection of essays, but still useful for lucid presentation of key arguments, with many illustrations.

Chapter 9

Multicultural society
and
intercultural encounters

Multilingualism in Germany

In 1992 the resident population of Germany included about 6.5 million people from 200 countries ranging in number from one (Vanuatu) to 1.85 million (Turkey). This is equivalent to 8 per cent of the total population. While many of these were temporary residents (students, for example), a substantial proportion consisted of long-term residents who therefore constitute part of the permanent population. The continued insistence of some politicians that 'Deutschland ist kein Einwanderungsland' and their rejection of the characterisation of German society as multicultural therefore fly in the face of the facts: in some major cities (e.g. Frankfurt, Munich, Stuttgart, Berlin) 'foreigners' account for up to a quarter of the population.

It is customary in official terms to classify these 'foreigners' into at least four categories, although this in itself may be controversial: *Arbeitsmigranten* (formerly *Gastarbeiter*, mostly from Mediterranean countries), *Aussiedler* (people from Eastern Europe and the former Soviet Union claiming German descent), *Asylanten* (people seeking asylum to escape persecution in their own country) and a miscellaneous category including, for example, mainly white-collar employees of multinational companies or of international organisations like the EU or UN. This complex mix of nationalities, linguistic backgrounds and social and economic circumstances inevitably ensures that intercultural encounters are an everyday occurrence. However, the fact that German remains the sole officially sanctioned language in the public domain means that the command of German is often a decisive factor in the successful outcome of these encounters. The level of competence in German that incomers have on arrival varies enormously and the provision of tuition outside the state school system is also variable. To a large extent, therefore, people depend on developing a knowledge of the language without tuition, simply in the course of normal day-to-day interaction (in the workplace, at school, in shops, etc.). How far they progress from the so-called **basilect** (rudimentary level) towards the **acrolect** (native-like competence) depends on a range of factors, such as age on arrival, degree of contact with native speakers at work and in leisure time, and motivation in terms of need. But how do people learn German in this unstructured way? How can we account for the fact that people from quite different linguistic backgrounds often develop a remarkably similar form of German (but one that differs from any 'native' form of German)? Can we learn anything about the general processes of language acquisition by studying what happens in the German context? And how do native speakers and non-native speakers 'manage' everyday encounters through the medium of an unequally mastered language?

Forms of non-native German

The speech of all non-native learners of German could be used as a source of raw material for studying the untutored acquisition of the language. However, the most widely studied and documented forms of non-native German are those produced by members of the largest category of foreigners mentioned in the previous section, the *Arbeitsmigranten*. Indeed, since the late 1960s, what for a long time was known as *Gastarbeiterdeutsch* has been one of the most extensively investigated phenomena in German linguistics (some even talk of a special brand of linguistics called *Gastarbeiterlinguistik*; see Hinnenkamp 1989). We shall therefore concentrate on these forms, but before continuing you might reflect on the reasons for the special academic interest in this topic.

■■ Find out what you can about the social and economic background to the large-scale immigration into Germany between the mid-1950s and the mid-1970s.

■ The first study of *Gastarbeiterdeutsch* appeared in 1968: why do you think so much attention was focused on this issue at this particular time?

Now consider the following utterances (sentence 5 is a film title; the others are authentic examples taken from Keim 1984):

1   Der arbeitet mehr mit Kopf.
2   Ich fahre Espania zwei Wochen.
3   Deine Sohn viel dumm.
4   Aber ich nix verstehe, ich nix gut sprechen Doktor.
5   Angst essen seele auf.

6   Wann komme, vielleicht fünf Jahre hierbleibe.

7   Erste Januar, vorgestern nachmittag, viele Schenke.

8   Kind alles in der Türkei geboren.

9   Meine Schwager hatse hier gewese.

10   Du das verkaufen?

11   Im Momento ich möchte bleiben hier.

The one thing that all these utterances have in common is that they are in some way 'deviant': they are clearly not 'standard' German, but they also differ from non-standard German as might be produced by native speakers. For example, it is most unlikely that native speakers would produce utterance 1, although they might well say:

1a   Der arbeitet mehr mit dem Kopf.

In other words, while using the demonstrative article (*der*, *die*, *das*) in place of personal pronouns is perfectly normal in colloquial speech, omitting the definite article in a prepositional phrase is not.

- In what ways are the other ten utterances 'deviant'? You might find it helpful to try to rewrite them in what might be considered 'acceptable' German.

- On the basis of this tiny corpus, draw up a list of features that occur in these forms of German. You can then refer to this list (and add to it) when you examine further passages below.

One way of classifying these features is to say that they are forms of 'simplification': for example, these learner varieties typically have no articles, no adverbs and no **copulas** (verbs like *sein* or *aussehen* that link the subject with a complement). They also contain fewer syntactic structures, there is virtually no inflectional morphology (e.g. verb or adjective endings), and the vocabulary is reduced to a core of key everyday words.

Now consider the following two passages. The first one is a transcript of part of an authentic interview with a Greek man; the second one is an extract from Rainer Werner Fassbinder's film *Angst essen seele auf* (1973).

A Interview with Thanassis

[...] Ich komm von Grieche mit zwei Kinda, meine Frau anrufen Athen, mir gesagt, komm, deine Kinda hier, und dann nix gefunden deine Platz für Arbeit. Ich kommen jetzt zwei Monat später, [. . .] zu mir gesagt, muß deine Kinda wieder zurück nach Griechenland. Ich gesagt, ein Moment, ich kommen nach Deutschland [. . .] zu mir gesagt, ja, aber deine Kinda kommen nach Hause von die Schule nix richtig das gemacht, nix richtig das gemacht, nix richtig das gemacht, nix richtig das gemacht. Ich klopft die Kinda, ich schlagen die Kinda, aber die ander Seite ich schlagen die Kinda, die ander Seite meine Frau anrufen Sozialamt. Du kennen Sozialamt? Kommen Sozialamt gesagt, meine Herr, deine Kinda muß komm mit die Kindergarten. [. . .] Ich keine deutsch Kollege, ich alleine. Warum, die Kollege heute nix gut. Kollegen sind gut wann deine Tasche voll. Gib bißchen Geld deine Tasche, deine Kollegen gesagt, natürlich, komm mit, aber sie kein Geld, keine Kollegen kommen zu dir.

(adapted from Blackshire-Belay 1991: 237–8)

B Dialogue from Angst essen seele auf

(Emmi, a German widow in her fifties, is on her way home from work and on an impulse goes into a bar frequented by foreign workers. She sits by herself until Salem, a Moroccan, is goaded by his friends into inviting her to dance.)

YOUNG WOMAN AT THE BAR. [*zu Salem*] Was ist? Willst du nicht mit der Alten tanzen?

SALEM: Was – ik mit alte Frau tanzen?

WOMAN: Klar, was denn sonst? Deine Beine sind nicht kaputt, oder?

SALEM'S FRIEND: Was ist los?

SALEM: Sie sagt, ik soll mit alte Frau tanzen. OK. [*zu Emmi*] Du tanzen mit mir?

EMMI: Wie bitte? Tanzen?

SALEM: Ja. Du allein sitzen, makt viel traurig. Allein sitzen nikt gut.

EMMI: Warum eigentlich nicht. Obwohl ich hab' mindestens 20 Jahre nicht mehr getanzt. Eher mehr. Vielleicht kann ich gar nicht mehr tanzen.

SALEM: Makt nix. Tanzen ganz langsam. [*Sie gehen auf die Tanzfläche*]

EMMI: Wo kommen Sie denn her?

SALEM: Klein Stadt in Marokko, Tismit.

EMMI: Ach, Marokko.

SALEM: Ja, viel schön. Aber nix Arbeit.

EMMI: Sie sprechen aber gut deutsch. Sind Sie schon lange hier?

165

SALEM: Zwei Jahre. Immer viel arbeiten.

EMMI: Ich habe auch viel Arbeit. Arbeit ist das halbe Leben.

SALEM: Du nix Mann, verheiratet?

EMMI: Mein Mann ist tot. Schon lange. Was arbeiten Sie denn?

SALEM: Mit Autos. Ganze Tag. Immer.

EMMI: Und abends gehen Sie dann hierher?

SALEM: Ja, hat schön Musik. Viele Kollega Arabisch, weiß nikt andere Platz. Deutsch mit Arabisch nikt gut.

EMMI: Warum?

SALEM: Weiß nikt. Deutsch mit Arabisch nikt gleiche Mensch.

EMMI: Aber am Arbeitsplatz?

SALEM: Nicht gleich. Deutscher – Herr. Arabisch – Hund.

EMMI: Aber das . . .

SALEM: Egal. Nix viel denken – gut. Viel denken – viel weinen.

[*Salem geht mit Emmi zu ihrem Tisch, setzt sich zu ihr an den Tisch.*]

BARDAME: [*zu Emmi*] Wollen Sie noch was trinken?

EMMI: Nein, danke. Ich muß ja morgen so früh raus. Ich zahl dann das Cola.

BARDAME: Eine Mark.

SALEM: Ik zahl Cola. Da.

EMMI: Danke vielmals, aber . . .

SALEM: Du gut sprechen mit Ali, Ali zahlt Cola.

EMMI: Sie heißen Ali?

SALEM: Nikt Ali, aber alle sagt Ali, jetzt ik bin Ali.

EMMI: Wie heißen Sie denn wirklich?

SALEM: El Hedi ben Salem M'Barek Mohammed Mustafa.

EMMI: Oh – der ist aber sehr lang, der Name!

SALEM: Ja, alles in Tismit hat eine lange Name.

EMMI: So. Jetzt muß ich aber gehn. Wiedersehn.

SALEM: Nix wiedersehn. Ik muß gehen mit dir bis zu Hause. Du nix allein, besser.

EMMI: Wenn Sie wollen.

(Töteberg 1990: 54–7)

■■ Analyse the language of the two texts in terms of the features you identified in sentences 1 to 11 above. Which features in the texts are not covered by your original list? Your enhanced list should now include aspects of syntax, morphology, vocabulary and forms of address.

- How would you describe the similarities and differences between the two texts?

- On the basis of these passages, where would you place Thanassis and Ali respectively on the basilect ↔ acrolect scale?

- Ali's speech contains what appear to be conflicting examples of utterances representing quite different levels of competence (e.g. 'Du nix Mann?' vs 'Ik soll mit alte Frau tanzen.'): would you attribute this to ignorance on the part of the script writer or might there be another explanation?

As well as constructing their own particular forms of the foreign language, it is common for non-native speakers to develop new speech patterns involving the use of both languages. **Code-mixing** differs from code-switching (see Chapter 2) in that it entails a blend of the two codes in one stretch of speech, rather than an abrupt and identifiable switch from one to the other at a particular point. At its simplest, this can mean merely inserting individual words from the second language into an utterance that is basically in the first language: 'I went to the *Bahnhof* to get a *Fahrkarte* for my trip to Munich.' But when the 'base' language is an **inflecting** or an **agglutinative** language (i.e. it marks grammatical features like case or number morphologically), it is interesting to observe the extent to which the forms 'imported' from the second language are adapted to the morphological patterns of the first. The following passages (from Tekinay 1984) show what may happen when German words are 'mixed' into Turkish:

12 Yedinci ayda *urlauba* gittik. Antalya'da *urlaup* yaptık. Benim *famılı* orda, *versteyn? Kinderler* gelmedi.
    [We went *on holiday* in July. We spent *the holiday* in Antalya. My *family* is there, *you see*. The children didn't come.]

13 Sonra kocam *betiribe* gidiyor. Yolu da cok uzak. Hem *ubanla* hem *esbanla* gidiyor, iki durakta *busla* gider.
    [Then my husband goes *to the factory*. It's a very long way. He goes not only *by U-Bahn* but also *by S-Bahn*, and then he goes two stops *on the bus*.]

14 *Avuslantsamt'a* gittim, *anmelduk* yaptırdım. *Arbayserlaupnisim* var, *Gott zay dank*.
    [I went *to the foreigners' registration office*, and *registered*. I have *a work permit, thank God*.]

■ In what ways have the German words and phrases in italics been adapted phonetically and morphologically to fit the Turkish context?

The acquisition process

One of the most remarkable things about the forms of German produced by the non-native speakers studied in many research projects since the early 1970s is the fact that speakers of typologically different languages (mainly Turkish, Greek, Serbo-Croat[1] and several Romance languages) develop varieties of German that are very similar to each other: many of the features identified in the previous section occur in the speech of, say, Spanish-speakers just as much as in that of Greek-speakers. Why? In this section, we shall examine three hypotheses that have been advanced as possible explanations for this phenomenon.

The transfer hypothesis

We saw in the previous section how learners of a foreign language (L2) often import items from that language into their own (L1) and, whether consciously or not, frequently manipulate these foreign forms to make them 'fit' the new context. It seems intuitively obvious that they will also use this ability to transfer features from L1 to L2, as a temporary strategy for expressing themselves in the foreign language until they acquire the means of doing so 'authentically'. On the other hand, if this were the case here, we would expect learner varieties of German to differ according to the learners' L1.

The best way to resolve this is to examine some data. In the following examples (from Keim 1984), the original (deviant) German utterance is followed by an equivalent (but non-deviant) sentence in the speaker's first language and then a literal translation of this sentence into English. Only those examples where the relevant grammatical pattern is the same in all three sentences may provide support for the transfer hypothesis (although

---

1 Serbian and Croatian are referred to here as one language (Serbo-Croat) as this was a common practice at the time when the studies referred to here were carried out. However, it has always been controversial, and since the war in the former Yugoslavia in the early 1990s it has become the norm to identify two separate languages.

this could still be no more than a coincidence). The examples illustrate three common deviant grammatical constructions: deletion of subject pronoun ('bleibe hier' instead of 'ich bleibe hier'), location of finite verb in final position in main clause ('er auf dem Boden sitzt'), and deletion of preposition in prepositional phrases ('wir fahren England').

1 Deletion of subject pronoun

ORIGINAL: Im Polizei jetzt gesagt
(Bei der Polizei hat man gesagt)
SERBO-CROAT: Na policiji su sada rekli
TRANSLATION: At police station have now said

ORIGINAL: Aber nix weiß wie diese Klinik
(Aber ich weiß nicht, wie diese Klinik heißt)
ITALIAN: Ma non so, com'e il nome di questa clinica
TRANSLATION: But don't know what the name of the clinic is

ORIGINAL: Wann komme, vielleicht fünf Jahre hierbleibe
(Wenn sie kommen, bleiben sie vielleicht fünf Jahre hier)
SPANISH: Quando vengan, se quederan possiblemente cinco anos aqui
TRANSLATION: When come, stay perhaps five years here

ORIGINAL: Und dann gehen Kur
(Und dann ging er zur Kur)
GREEK: και μετά πήγε σε κούρσα
TRANSLATION: And after that went to a health resort

ORIGINAL: Alles uffschreibe und hole Chef
(Ich schreibe alles auf und hole den Chef)
TURKISH: Hepsini yazıyorum ve şefi getiyorum
TRANSLATION: Write everything down and fetch boss

2 Placing finite verb in final position in main clause

ORIGINAL: Ich auch bißchen mehr trinken
(Ich trinke auch ein bißchen mehr)
SERBO-CROAT: (ja) isto malo vise pijem
TRANSLATION: (I) also little bit more drink

ORIGINAL: Ich nur in Deutschland gehe
                            (Ich bin nur nach Deutschland gegangen)
ITALIAN: Sono andato soltanto in Germania
TRANSLATION: Have gone only to Germany

ORIGINAL: Deine Sohn Espania wieder bleibe
                            (Dein Sohn ist wieder in Spanien geblieben)
SPANISH: Tu hijo se ha quevado nuevamente en Espana
TRANSLATION: Your son has stayed again in Spain.

ORIGINAL: (Er) jetzt Wohnung schaffe
                            (Er arbeitet jetzt zu Hause)
GREEK: Τωρα δουλευει στο σπιτι
TRANSLATION: Now is working he at home

ORIGINAL: Ich drei Jahre hier arbeite
                            (Ich arbeite hier seit drei Jahren)
TURKISH: (Ben) üç senedir burada çalışıyorum
TRANSLATION: (I) three years here work

3 Deletion of preposition in prepositional phrase

ORIGINAL: Ich nit große Schule
                            (Ich ging nicht in die höhere Schule)
SERBO-CROAT: Ja nisam isao na visu skolu
TRANSLATION: I didn't go to higher school

ORIGINAL: Ich Rathaus nix gut sprechen
                            (Im Rathaus kann ich nicht gut reden)
ITALIAN: Nel municipio non posso parlare bene
TRANSLATION: At the Town Hall I cannot speak well

ORIGINAL: Ich fahre Espania zwei Wochen
                            (Ich fahre zwei Wochen nach Spanien)
SPANISH: Voy a Espana por dos semanas
TRANSLATION: I'm going to Spain for two weeks

ORIGINAL: Nur Ausländer kommen die Maschine
                            (Nur Ausländer kommen an die Maschine)
GREEK: μόνο ξένοι δουλευουν στη μηχανή
TRANSLATION: Only foreigners work on the machine

ORIGINAL: Ich jetzt herkommen Deutschland
                   (Ich bin nach Deutschland gekommen)
TURKISH: Almanya 'ya geldim
TRANSLATION: I came to Germany

(Klein 1984)

■■   Consider the evidence in each case and decide how much potential support the data provides for the transfer hypothesis.

The pidgin hypothesis

One of the earliest studies of the language acquisition of migrant workers was entitled 'Zum Pidgin-Deutsch der Gastarbeiter' (Clyne 1968) and many of the studies that followed it (e.g. Heidelberger Forschungsprojekt 'Pidgin-Deutsch' 1975) were based on the same conception of so-called *Gastarbeiterdeutsch* as a **pidgin**. The term pidgin is often used in a colloquial sense to mean simply 'bad, broken, imperfect form of a language': 'When we were on holiday in Brittany we tried to get by with our pidgin French.' However, as a technical term in linguistics it has a very specific meaning. The following definition is typical:

> A pidgin is a reduced language that results from extended contact between groups of people with no language in common; it evolves when they need some means of verbal communication, perhaps for trade, but no group learns the native language of any other group for social reasons that may include lack of trust or of close contact.
> (Holm 1988: 4–5; cited in Wardhaugh 1992: 58)

■   Taking this definition item by item, would you say that there may be some justification for calling the phenomenon we are dealing with here a pidgin?

■■   Look at any introductory account of linguistic patterns that are characteristic of pidgins: are they the same kinds of pattern that we have seen in the German material above?

Even if the linguistic evidence looks promising, the fact remains that pidgins are normally associated with parts of the world very far from Central Europe: typically, the Caribbean and the Pacific regions. Map 9.1 shows the global distribution of pidgins. One of the important differences

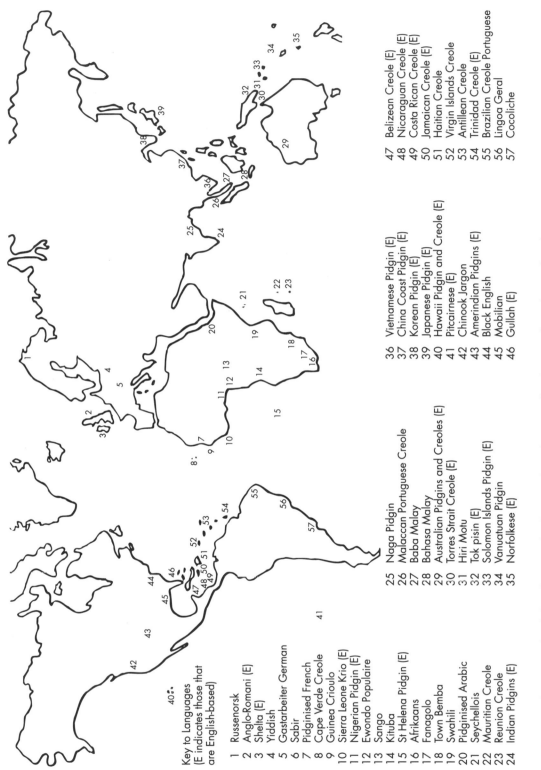

Key to Languages
(E indicates those that
are English-based)

1 Russenorsk
2 Anglo-Romani (E)
3 Shelta (E)
4 Yiddish
5 Gastarbeiter German
6 Sabir
7 Pidginised French
8 Cape Verde Creole
9 Guinea Crioulo
10 Sierra Leone Krio (E)
11 Nigerian Pidgin (E)
12 Ewondo Populaire
13 Sango
14 Kituba
15 St Helena Pidgin (E)
16 Afrikaans
17 Fanagolo
18 Town Bemba
19 Swahili
20 Pidginised Arabic
21 Seychellois
22 Mauritian Creole
23 Reunion Creole
24 Indian Pidgins (E)

25 Naga Pidgin
26 Malaccan Portuguese Creole
27 Baba Malay
28 Bahasa Malay
29 Australian Pidgins and Creoles (E)
30 Torres Strait Creole (E)
31 Hiri Motu
32 Tok pisin (E)
33 Solomon Islands Pidgin (E)
34 Vanuatuan Pidgin
35 Norfolkese (E)

36 Vietnamese Pidgin (E)
37 China Coast Pidgin (E)
38 Korean Pidgin (E)
39 Japanese Pidgin (E)
40 Hawaii Pidgin and Creole (E)
41 Pitcairnese (E)
42 Chinook Jargon
43 Amerindian Pidgins (E)
44 Black English
45 Mobilian
46 Gullah (E)

47 Belizean Creole (E)
48 Nicaraguan Creole (E)
49 Costa Rican Creole (E)
50 Jamaican Creole (E)
51 Haitian Creole
52 Virgin Islands Creole
53 Antillean Creole
54 Trinidad Creole (E)
55 Brazilian Creole Portuguese
56 Lingoa Geral
57 Cocoliche

MAP 9.1 The geographical distribution of pidgins and creoles (not all pidgins and creoles are listed)

Source: Todd 1990

between these situations and the one we are dealing with here is that in the former it was the 'base' languages (e.g. English, French, Dutch, Portuguese) that were 'exported' into locations where they came into contact with other languages, whereas in the German situation the converse is the case.

■■ In pidgin studies a distinction is sometimes drawn between pidgins 'in the broad sense' (which arise from 'secondary hybridisation') and pidgins 'in the narrow sense' (which arise from 'tertiary hybridisation'). Find out what is meant by these terms and try to decide which of them applies to the German context.

■■ Wardhaugh (1992: 59) refers to 'the pidgin German of the *Gastarbeiters* [sic]' as an 'ephemeral' phenomenon: what does he mean by this? Is he right to see it in this way? Why might it be less likely to persist over time than established pidgins in other parts of the world?

■■ What is the relationship between pidgins and **creoles**? Under what circumstances do creoles develop? Why might the emergence of a German-based creole in Germany be unlikely?

■■ Some commentators take the view that we should distinguish between 'product' and 'process': it may be inappropriate to talk of *Pidgin-Deutsch*, but the development of these learner varieties has much in common with pidginisation. What do you think?

The foreigner talk hypothesis

As Figure 9.1 clearly shows, simplified varieties of a language are not produced exclusively by non-native speakers. The Turkish man in this cartoon has native-speaker competence in German; it is the German man who speaks a 'broken' form of the language. The context leaves no doubt that the German is speaking in this way in order to reinforce the contempt towards the 'foreigner' that the content of his utterances makes explicit. However, in other contexts native speakers deliberately simplify their own language in an attempt to communicate with a foreigner whose knowledge of the language is (taken to be) insufficient to permit communication in a 'normal', unsimplified manner (see 'Intercultural encounters', pp. 176–81). Whatever the intention, it is clear that native speakers (perhaps of

FIGURE 9.1 Foreigner talk

Source: Jobst Müller in *Titanic* 8, 1982

all languages) know that their language can be simplified in certain ways, and they can frequently be observed doing this in interaction with foreigners. Furthermore, this **foreigner talk** (FT) often seems to bear a striking resemblance to the language produced by foreigners.

■ Consider the following examples of FT (from Hinnenkamp 1982) and compare them with utterances 1 to 11 on pp. 163–4:

15 Hast du Arbeitserlaubnis?
16 Nee, ich nix Ruski.
17 Finito, jetzt finito (said to a Turk).
18 Ich heute viel kaputt.
19 Gestern du immer Schnaps trinken, Schnaps trinken, ja?
20 Du Läuse? Du jetzt juckjuck kratzkratz!
21 Was's los, Ali? Du boxbox mit deiner Frau?
22 Vater Kapitalist?
23 Naja, Bibel sagt auch: eine Frau genug.
24 Das ist weil alles kommt weite Wege.

This similarity between FT and non-native forms of German raises a number of interesting questions. For example, we have seen that learner varieties are often somehow systematic in the ways in which they deviate from the norms of native-speaker German: do the similarities between these speech forms and FT result from native speakers' accurate observation of the way foreigners speak? Or, conversely, do foreign learners speak the way they do, not because they have failed to absorb and analyse the grammar and vocabulary of the 'real' German they encounter in everyday life, but because the German they encounter is actually FT? Is foreigners' German the model for German FT or vice versa – or is there another explanation altogether for the similarity?

If German FT is an imitation of learner varieties, we are no nearer to explaining why these varieties have the particular form they do. On the other hand, if the learner varieties are based on FT, we need to show why the foreign learners choose FT as their model rather than other forms of German: except in very few cases, it is unlikely that FT is the most frequently encountered form, and given its frequently negative connotations it seems implausible that it would be considered a desirable model. However, this does not mean that there is no link between the two speech forms. One possible connection lies in the notion of simplification, with which we began our deliberations on p. 164.

■ Comparisons of FT forms of different languages (e.g. German, English, French, Finnish and Turkish) have revealed considerable similarities in terms of the ways in which the languages are simplified, which suggests that common (perhaps even universal) 'simplification strategies' may be part of our knowledge about language. If native speakers of German and of, say, Turkish and Spanish adopt similar procedures for simplifying their own language, does this suggest to you a further possible (partial) explanation for the common features found in learner varieties of German, regardless of the learners' first language?

■ ■ ■ Having now considered several possible ways of accounting for the acquisition process, what conclusions would you draw? What benefits might the investigation of this particular phenomenon have for the general study of how languages develop?

Intercultural encounters

Successful communication does not depend entirely on the degree of linguistic competence of the participants in a conversation. As we have seen (Chapter 7), even when both speakers have native-speaker competence a lack of sociolinguistic knowledge can seriously impede mutual comprehension, and this can be exacerbated when the two parties do not share the same set of (often culture-specific) assumptions and expectations about particular situations and contexts. Conversely, speakers can overcome communicative difficulties arising from inadequate knowledge of linguistic *forms* by using a range of linguistic and paralinguistic *techniques*. The successful outcome of an intercultural encounter may therefore depend on different types of knowledge (linguistic forms, sociolinguistic conventions, cultural expectations) and on the willingness of both parties to exploit the various means at their disposal to negotiate an understanding. In this section, we shall look at a number of episodes which illustrate some of the problems that can arise and some of the ways in which people respond to them. They will be divided into two general types: 'everyday' and 'institutional'.

Everyday encounter 1: buying a washing machine

A Turkish customer (C) talks to a German sales assistant (SA) about which washing machine he should buy.

C: Hallo.

SA: Bitte?

C: Ich will eine Waschmaschine kaufe. Ich weiß nicht, welche sind.

SA: Eine Waschmaschine suchen Sie?

C: Aha.

SA: Ein Markengerät?

C: Waschmaschine, ich weiß nicht.

SA: Hier hab ich gute Waschmaschine. Da. Siemens.

C: Siemens.

SA: Ja? 800 Schleudertouren, Umdrehungen zum Schleudern, net? Also kommt die Wäsche schon schön trocken raus, gell? Also, nicht trocken, aber nicht mehr so, daß se naß is, net?

C: Is das automatik, oder?

SA: Automatisch. Gut, ja?

C: Aber etwas klein. Haben Sie noch billiger?

SA: Ja, billiger aber nix gut. Die könn' Sie nicht vergleichen mit dem, qualitätsmäßig, ne? Das is unbekannte Marke un nur fünfhundert Drehungen, gell? Wäsche noch naß, wann sie rauskommt, ne? [...] Vierzig Grad heiß, sechzig, funfundneunzig is Koche, gell? Also, fünfundneunzig Kochwäsche mit Vorwäsche A, ja? Hier, immer rechts rumdrehen, ja? Und dann Start, und schon laufen, automatisch ja? Spar heißt, wenn nur ein paar Pullover oder Hemde, also für kleine Wäsche, ne?

C: Mmm, ich will, ich will nach Türkei mitbringen. [...]

SA: Sie müssen eine gute Maschine mitnehmen, Türkei ja, wo Ihnen fünfzehn zwanzig Jahre hält, ja? Und das ist die da. Die hat im Test sehr gut abgschnitten, sehr gut, verstehn Sie? Test? Deutsche Spezialisten ham die Maschine getestet ja? Und habe festgestellt, das ist die beste Maschine.

(based on Roche 1989: 50–1)

■■ How does the sales assistant (SA) try to accommodate his speech to the (Turkish) customer? How consistent is he in his approach?

Everyday encounter 2: telephoning work

Nejmi (N, a Turkish worker) rings his (German) foreman (F) at work to tell him that he is going to be off sick.

N: Ja Willi.

F: Ja.

N: Ich bin Nejmi.

F: Bitte?

N: Ich bin Nejmi.   5

F: (emphatisch) Nejmi!

N: Ja, Willi ich bin jeden Tag Arzt gehen, ne.

F: Was bist du?

N: Ja, jeden Tag ich bin Arzt gehen. Meine Augen ganz dicke und rot.

F: Die Augen dick.   10

N: Ja heute wieder ich Arzt gehen, Arzt wieder krank schreiben.

F: Hat dir die Frau einen aufs Auge gegeben?

N: (unsicher) Ja, hier das is Augen Frau .. Doktor.

F: Ach der Doktor, ich dachte, deine Frau hat dir welche aufs Auge
      gegeben.

N: Jaja, das Doktor gehen, ne.   15

F: Mhm.

N: Heute auch wieder gehen, Kontroll gemacht, eh wieder krank

F: Mhm

N: schreiben und Mittwoch wieder gehen, ne.

F: Ja.   20

F: Hm, hast du irgendwo hingeguckt, wo du nich hingucken darfst?

N: Ja eh . .

F: Ins Schweiß- eh Schweißgerät oder was? nein.

N: Eh . . .

F: Schweißflamme, nein, haste nicht.   25

N: Ja, das Tivoli das direkt am Markt, das zweite, ne.

F: Bitte?

N: Eh das andere Seite.

F: Aha.

N: Hauptstraße.   30

F: Aha. Na, is gut Nejmi, nich?

(based on Hinnenkamp 1989: 77–8)

- Telephone conversations generally follow highly structured patterns,
  especially at the beginning and end: in what way is Nejmi's opening,
  in particular, unconventional in terms of the norms of German phone
  calls? What impact might this have on the rest of the conversation?
  How would *you* approach this situation?

- How clear does Nejmi make his situation? (Put yourself in the foreman's
  position on the phone.) How does the foreman react to the account?

- Comment on the possible reasons for the failure of the foreman's joke (ll. 12–15).

- What seems to be happening in ll. 21–31? How does the foreman register and respond to Nejmi's misunderstanding?

Institutional encounter 1: train information

A (a Turkish man) rings up the train information service and speaks to B (a German).

A: Grüß Gott. Ich Türkei fahren, was machen?
B: (Verstört) Was?
A: Türkei fahren. Was machen?
B: Ah, nix Plan.
A: Bitte?
B: Hier is nix Türkei fahren.
A: Und was machen?
B: Was machen?
A: Bitte?
B: Ach geh!

- This is an extreme (but probably not uncommon) example of communication breakdown. What would you say is the reason for the breakdown and how might it have been avoided?

Institutional encounter 2: employment office

A (a Turkish youth) goes to see B (a German official) to seek help in resolving a problem that has arisen as a result of a change in employment law: he had previously been entitled to work and had had a job but then lost it and under the new legislation is required to attend school. However, the school is unable to cater for him and so he falls between two stools.

B: Setz dich Junge. Jetz muß ich dir dasselbe erzählen, was ich dir neulich schon mal erzählt hab. [. . .]
A: Und jeden Tach keine Schule.
B: Ja, das spielt keine Rolle.
A: Ja, was soll ich die andere Tach machen?

B: Eh mm, das weiß ich nicht. Das is Sache von der Schule.

A: Ja ich hab in die Schule gegangen . . .

B: Das weiß ich, das is aber Sache von der Schule. Du mußt dahin, da da beißt die Maus keinen Faden ab.

A: (Pause) (Erstaunt:) Wie?

B: da da hilft, da gibts keine Möglichkeit, is Gesetz, du mußt hin zur Schule.

A: Ja, Gesetz hab ich auch schon, aber ich hatte Arbeiterlaubnis gemacht.

B: Bitte?

A: Ich hatte Arbeiterlaubnis gemacht.

B: Ja, aber jetzt so bald, du darfst jetzt nicht arbeiten, du darfst jetzt nicht arbeiten.

A: (schnell und vorwurfsvoll) Ja was soll ich die andere Tach machen in die Schule wenn wenn keine Plätze gekommen sind?

B: (deutlich und heftig) Das is Sache der Schule. Die Schule muß dafür sorgen, daß ihr Klassen bekommt und die sind auch dabei, das einzurichten. [. . .]

A: Jaja, gibst du mir eine Papier, sach der: die Junge muß jeden Tach in Schule gehn, dann kann ich jeden Tach in die Schule gehn.

B: Ja das brauch ich nicht, das is Gesetz, das is ein Gesetz, das hat die Schule da . . .

A: (etwas verächtlich) Ja, Gesetz, aber vor die Gesetz hab ich schon gearbeiten.

B: Vor dem Gesetz hast du gearbeitet?

A: Ja.

B: Und anschließend wieder rausgekommen und da heißt es . . .

A: (hastig und schnell) Ich hab ich hab ich hab nich genuch Geld gekricht und dahinter hat mir rausgeschmissen.

B: Hier steht in einem, aus einem Arbeitsverhältnis ausscheidet, werden in die Klassen der Berufsvorbereitungsjahre eingeschult, damit Schluß, damit darfst du nicht arbeiten. Da is nix zu machen, is nich möglich.

A: (leise und entmutigt) Ja.

B: Du kannst folgendes machen, du gehst mal hin, meinetwegen, Breite Straße [Ausländerberatungszentrum] . . .

A: (laut) Davon hab ich schon gewesen zwei drei mal, was . . .

B: Die solln mich anrufen.

A: Ja.

B: Dann erklär ich denen das in Türkisch, nee in Deutsch und die übersetzen dir das genau in Türkisch.

A: (beleidigt) ja, ich verstehs, was hast du alles gesacht, hab schon verstanden.

B: Ja, da kann ich dir nicht weiter helfen, Junge.

A: Ja.

B: (schnell und schnodderig) Wenn ich helfen kann, tu ich das, wenn ich aber nich helfen kann, dann kann ich nich helfen. Hierbei kann ich nich helfen. Ja, komm.

A: (verläßt den Raum)

(adapted from Hinnenkamp 1989: 148–9)

■■ This is another unsuccessful episode, despite the fact that B at least appears to be prepared to engage with A and take his request seriously and there do not seem to be any problems of understanding (at the linguistic level at any rate). It is also perfectly conceivable that a German youth with a similar request/problem would have left the room 'empty-handed'. However, not only does A not get what he wants in this sense, but his evidently quite good command of German ultimately fails to prevent his being treated as 'a foreigner' rather than as an individual. What approaches does B adopt in response to A's situation: can you identify distinct 'phases' in the interaction? In what ways do you think he might have responded differently had A been German?

Further reading

Arends et al. (1995), for a general introduction to pidgins and creoles.

Barbour and Stevenson (1990), Chapter 7, sections 7.2–7.4 for a discussion of competing hypotheses concerning the acquisition of German as a second language.

Blackshire-Belay (1991), for a good analysis in English of the forms of learner varieties, with many examples.

Clahsen et al. (1983), for a detailed report on research into the acquisition of German by Spanish- and Italian-speakers in the Ruhrgebiet.

Hinnenkamp (1982), for a lively account of the role of foreigner talk, with many examples.

Keim (1984), for a study of Turkish-speaking learners of German, again with many examples.

Romaine (1988), for a good survey of pidgin and creole languages.

Rost-Roth (1995), for a concise overview in English of studies on inter-cultural communication relating to German in contact with other languages.
Todd (1990), for a basic introduction to pidgins and creoles.

•   •   •

Part three

Current issues: language and 'Germanness'

Chapter 10

Sprachkultur
Preserving the
cultural heritage

Language and national culture

In Chapter 1, we saw how peculiarly important the German language is for the self-definition and self-image of the German people (but also for the Austrians and some of the Swiss). We are now returning to this theme in the final three chapters, in order to explore in more detail some of the manifestations of the relationship between language and Germanness, and the ways in which this relationship is debated in the public domain in Germany. To this end, much of the discussion will be based on (sometimes quite lengthy) extracts from recent writings taken from the press as well as academic sources. The central question will be: what can 'the state of the language' tell us about 'the state of the nation'?

In this chapter, we shall consider some aspects of what is referred to as *Sprachkultur*. This term has an interesting history in itself: for example, *Sprachkultur* was considered an important concept in both German states between 1949 and 1990, but it was understood in quite different ways (see, for example, Bickes and Trabold 1994). For our purposes, we can take it as meaning the conscious attempt to cultivate the knowledge and use of the language as the embodiment of the German cultural tradition. In this sense, it is primarily concerned with fostering and protecting *the* national asset: 'Die Muttersprache ist wie die Landschaft, in die man hineingeboren wird, etwas Angestammtes, eine Heimat, aus der niemand vertrieben werden darf. Wir haben sie ererbt, wir müssen sie heil weitergeben' (Günther Gillesen, 'Recht auf Rechtschreibung', *Frankfurter Allgemeine Zeitung*, 12 August 1988: 8; cited in Glück and Sauer 1990: 192). In particular, this chapter will focus on 'institutionalised' *Sprachkultur*, by looking first at the powerful cultural role of a series of reference books known collectively as 'the *Duden*' and, then, as an illustration of how sensitive a public issue the very form of the German language can be, at the strange case of the reform of German orthography: why should such a dry, academic topic become the subject of furious public debates stretching over decades, and why was it considered so important an issue that its resolution required the unanimous agreement of the *Ministerpräsidenten* of the sixteen German *Länder*?

Authority in language: the *Duden* as a national institution

Dictionaries serve many purposes: they resolve disputes in games of Scrabble, they are indispensable in compiling and solving crossword puzzles, they act as wise advisers or expert consultants for letter-, essay- or book-writers, and by virtue of their solidity they can even come in useful for propping up desks. Admittedly, they come in different sizes, but small ones are no more than handy *aides-mémoire*, something you can carry around with you in case you get caught short in mid-sentence. They have to be reasonably big if we are to take them seriously, for we need to feel confident that they will indeed supply the answer to any query to do with the vocabulary of the language concerned (spelling, meaning, usage, etymology, idioms, etc.). They have to be seen to be definitive: we want to be sure that we are consulting the ultimate arbiter, that the entries in the dictionary bear the stamp of authority.

Yet there are many dictionaries of English and German, and the entry under a particular headword in one may contain information that in some way conflicts with what is to be found in the corresponding entry in another. For this reason, serious Scrabble players have to agree in advance to accept a particular dictionary as definitive for the purposes of their game and prize crosswords often explicitly state the reference work on which the puzzle is based. While these procedures are practical, they imply a relativity in the nature of dictionaries that seems to undermine our desire for a book that provides 'the last word' on linguistic issues. It is therefore felt that there is a need for a linguistic equivalent to the official measure that defines precisely how long a 'yard' or a 'metre' is: individual dictionaries, like individual rulers or tape measures, may be perfectly adequate for our everyday requirements, but there may be occasions (for example, in the interpretation of legal documents) when it is necessary to settle disputes by reference to a universally acknowledged yardstick.

For British English, this role is played by *The Oxford English Dictionary* (OED), for American English by *Webster's American Dictionary of the English Language*, and for German by what is popularly known as simply *Der Duden*. The latter is an ambiguous term, as it can be used to refer generically to a whole series of reference works produced by the same publisher, but in particular to the dictionary whose full title is *Duden. Die deutsche Rechtschreibung*. What distinguishes this German dictionary from its English counterparts is, first, its history, and, second, its status among the German population (its position in Austria and Switzerland is more problematic: see Ammon 1995c). The following passages are taken from an account of the origin and development of the *Duden*, published in 1988 (i.e. two years before unification in 1990):

„Duden" steht nicht im Duden, jedenfalls nicht in der neuen Mannheimer Ausgabe der „Rechtschreibung". Dabei hätte das Wort einen Eintrag im populärsten deutschen Wörterbuch schon deshalb verdient, weil es mehrdeutig ist. Würde es im Stichwörterverzeichnis angeführt werden, müßte der Eintrag folgende Form haben:

[1]Du/den, Konrad (dt. Rechtschreibreformer)
[2]Du/den, der, -s, auch -, Pl. – (Wörterbuch d. Rechtschreibung)
[3]Du/den, $\boxed{wz}$ der (Markenname für Bücher aller Art aus dem Bibliographischen Institut)

Die erste Angabe der fiktiven Notierung nennt den Mann, dessen Name heute für die Institution steht, die er vor mehr als einhundert Jahren geschaffen hat. Bald nach der Reichsgründung von 1871 gab der Gymnasialdirektor Dr. Konrad Duden den „Ur-Duden" heraus, aus dem sich das erfolgreiche deutsche Wörterbuch entwickelte. Vierzig Jahre lang arbeitete Konrad Duden an der Form dieses Buches, acht Auflagen gab er selbst heraus. [. . .]
    In seiner praktischen Tätigkeit als Lehrer sind [auch] die Gründe zu suchen, die ihn veranlaßten, Bücher zu schreiben. Sein Thema war die deutsche Orthographie, ihr Zustand an den Schulen seiner Zeit bewegte ihn, publizistisch tätig zu werden. [. . .] Zu den beiden staatlichen orthographischen Konferenzen (1876 und 1901) wurde er vom Kultusminister zum Vertreter Preußens berufen. An der Herausbildung der deutschen Schulorthographie, die zum Vorbild für die heutige Rechtschreibung wurde, hatte Konrad Duden mit seinen Wörterbüchern entscheidenden Anteil. [. . .]
    Die zweite Bedeutung, mit der das Wort „Duden" verbunden ist, lautet [daher] auch „Wörterbuch der Rechtschreibung". Wenige Wörter des Deutschen werden in solchem Maße als Synonym für die bezeichnete Sache verstanden, wie es beim Begriff „Duden" der Fall ist. Er steht für Rechtschreib-Wörterbücher schlechthin, ist vergleichbar mit Bezeichnungen wie „Tempo" für Papiertaschentücher, „Uhu" für Alleskleber, „Maggi" für flüssige Speisewürze. Harald Weinrich fragte vor einigen Jahren [. . .]:

Aber wo gibt es denn das Wörterbuch, dessen Typus für dieses Jahrhundert repräsentativ sein könntc? [. . .] Der Duden vielleicht? [. . .] Der Duden [. . .] ist ein eigenartiger Sonderfall. In Deutschland verkörpert der Duden die sprachliche Autorität schlechthin. (Weinrich 1976: 352)

Der letztgenannte Satz enthält das Schlüsselwort, das die Ursache für dcn ungebrochenen Erfolg des Dudens seit mehr als hundert Jahren sein durfte: Autorität. Wer auch immer wissen will, wie man ein Wort schreibt, er wird im Duden nachschlagen. [. . .] Und Autorität gilt etwas in Deutschland, auch in der DDR heißt der Duden „Duden". [. . .] Sicher ist der Duden nicht das ideale einbändige Wörterbuch des Deutschen für Deutsche, [. . .] aber von der Wirkung her, ja, von der Liebe her, die die Sprachgemeinschaft dem Duden entgegenbringt, ist er *das* Wörterbuch der deutschen Sprache des zwanzigsten Jahrhunderts. [. . .]

Die dritte Bedeutungsvariante des fiktiven Eintrags ist die öffentlich am geringsten beachtete [. . .]: Der Name "Duden" ist zu einem eingetragenen und damit geschützten Warenzeichen geworden. [. . .] Allerdings erstreckt sich der Musterschutz des Warenzeichens nicht auf die DDR. Die Aktiengesellschaft (AG) „Bibliographisches Institut" kann nicht verhindern, daß der Volkseigene Betrieb (VEB) „Bibliographisches Institut" in Leipzig denselben Namen beibehalten hat. [. . .] So erscheinen heute uneinträchtig nebeneinander zwei Duden, in Mannheim (BRD) und Leipzig (DDR). [. . .]

[Man möchte] dem fiktiven Stichworteintrag „Duden" noch eine weitere Bedeutung hinzufügen, nämlich

⁴Du/den (deutsche Institution)

Spiegelt das Buch doch kaum wie eine andere Einrichtung kontinuierlich deutsche Geschichte wider. Kurz nach dem Vollzug der preußischen Variante nationaler Einigung aus der Taufe gehoben, überlebte der Duden das Kaiserreich, die erste deutsche Republik, die Zeit der politischen Herrschaft des Nationalsozialismus, die wirren Jahre der alliierten Zonenregierungen, wurde gespalten in eine östliche und eine westliche Variante bald nach der Gründung zweier deutscher Staaten, diente in vielfältiger Weise als Beleg für die Spaltung der Nation, wurde deshalb politisch ausgeschlachtet und bildet eigentlich doch nur aktuelle deutsche Zustände ab.

(Sauer 1988: 1–5)

To bring the story up to date, we need only add that the final chapter in the parallel histories of the *Duden* and the German people came a few months after unification, in May 1991:

Duden West kann Duden Ost übernehmen

Deutsche Einheit erzwingt Aktualisierung der Lexika

Von der Berliner Treuhandanstalt traf in Mannheim die mündliche Zusage ein, daß das Mannheimer Verlagshaus alle Geschäftsanteile der Bibliographisches Institut und Verlag Enzyklopädie GmbH, Leipzig, wie auch der Brockhaus GmbH, Leipzig, erwerben kann. Die Zusammenarbeit mit dem Leipziger Bibliographischen Institut werde bereits „erfolgreich eingeübt", heißt es in Mannheim. Die Dudenredaktion Mannheim und die Leipziger Redaktion Deutsch arbeiten gemeinsam mit Hochdruck am ersten gesamtdeutschen „Duden – die deutsche Rechtschreibung", dessen Erscheinen ursprünglich für 1992 angekündigt war [it actually appeared even earlier, in August 1991].

(Frankfurter Allgemeine Zeitung 24 May 1991;
cited in Augst and Sauer 1992: 92)

■ Summarise briefly the four 'meanings' of the word *Duden* as outlined by Sauer.

■ In what respects does the *Duden* occupy a different position in the everyday lives of Germans to that of, say, the *OED* in the lives of English-speakers? Why do you think it appears to be so revered? (Consider why it has been called a 'Volkswörterbuch'.)

■■ Find out as much as you can about the origin and development of the *Duden* through the different phases of German history since 1871.

■■ Try to get hold of copies of the Mannheim and the Leipzig versions of the *Duden* published between 1950 and 1989, and compare the entries under particular headwords (e.g. *Krieg, Demokratie, Nation*).

The *Rechtschreibreform* saga

Most people in anglophone countries would probably consider the study of orthography as a pastime for language 'anoraks' or 'nerds' and consign it to their list of 'least desirable activities'. Nevertheless, it is taken to be of sufficiently wide interest even in the English-speaking world for letters and leading articles about spelling and related issues to be published in serious newspapers. Given what we have already seen about the importance attached to the tradition of the German language as the repository, not merely of German culture, but (some would say) of the very essence of Germanness, it may not be so surprising to find that such apparently dry and esoteric matters as whether 'to cycle' should be written as one word (*radfahren*) or as two (*Rad fahren*), or where words should be divided at the end of a line (*Mu-ster* or *Mus-ter*), are potentially explosive: public attitudes towards the German language are highly volatile, and attempting to 'rationalise' it (or 'rational*ize*' it) is strictly not for the faint-hearted. As long as changes in each new edition of the *Duden* are perceived as merely 'reflecting' accepted steps in the evolution of the language they are tolerated, but attempts to introduce changes, to 'tamper' with the birthright of the Germans and apparently impose change on to the *Duden*, are met at best with suspicion ('if it ain't bust, don't fix it') and at worst with outright hostility ('how dare you interfere with our heritage').

But *is* German orthography 'bust'? *Does* it need 'fixing'? Your response to these questions will depend in part on your views on the need for widely shared norms and in part also on your knowledge of (and confidence in using) existing norms. A typically 'neutral' academic position on the first point is this:

> Der Gebrauch der Sprache – sei es mündlich, sei es schriftlich – unterliegt bestimmten Normen wie andere menschliche Tätigkeiten auch. Diese Normen dienen der Sicherung einer reibungslosen Kommunikation; ihre Einhaltung liegt daher im Interesse eines jeden Sprechenden und Schreibenden wie auch Hörenden und Lesenden.
>
> (Heller 1996: 2)

By contrast, an extreme representation of what the linguist Hans Jürgen Heringer calls the 'Normen? Ja – aber meine!' position is attributed to Bismarck, the Chancellor of the German Reich, on hearing of the new spelling system proposed by an 'orthographical conference' in Berlin in 1876. His views were reported by a colleague:

> Er sprach mit wahrem Ingrimm über die Versuche, eine neue
> Orthographie einzuführen. Er werde jeden Diplomaten in eine
> Ordnungsstrafe nehmen, welcher sich derselben bediene. Man mute
> den Menschen zu, sich an neue Maße, Gewichte, Münzen zu gewöh-
> nen, verwirre alle gewohnten Begriffe, und nun wolle man auch noch
> eine Sprachkonfusion einführen. Das sei unerträglich. Beim Lesen
> auch noch Zeit zu verlieren, um sich zu besinnen, welchen Begriff das
> Zeichen ausdrücke, sei eine unerhörte Zumutung. Ebenso sei es
> Unsinn, Deutsch mit lateinischen Lettern zu schreiben und zu
> drucken, was er sich in seinen dienstlichen Beziehungen verbitten
> werde, solange er noch etwas zu sagen habe.
>
> (Bismarck 1973: 660; cited in Sauer 1988: 87)

Despite the vehemence of these feelings, a new orthographical system was
eventually agreed at the 2. Orthographische Konferenz in Berlin in 1901
and was accepted as having official status in Germany, Austria and
Switzerland. The set of rules enshrined in the *Duden* until 1996 was
broadly the same as this package agreed nearly a hundred years earlier,
and it is obvious that a great deal has happened to the German language
since that time. Some of these changes had been incorporated into the rule
system, but many observers argued that this occurred in an unsystematic
manner, with the result that the evolved orthodoxy was needlessly
complex and hard to learn:

> Eine Reform ist aus zwei Gründen zu fordern. Erstens deshalb, weil
> die DUDEN-Regeln an vielen Punkten unlogisch, haarspalterisch
> und übermäßig kompliziert sind und die Regelteile der DUDEN
> insgesamt aufgeblasen und überfrachtet sind. Zweitens deshalb, weil
> der bestehende Zustand undemokratisch ist: es geht nicht an, daß die
> große Mehrheit der Bevölkerung nach neun, zehn und dreizehn
> Jahren Schulausbildung mit der Rechtschreibung chronische
> Probleme hat. In einem demokratischen Staat sollte die Recht-
> schreibung so geregelt sein, daß sie während der Pflichtschulzeit
> erlernbar ist und von der Mehrheit der Erwachsenen ohne Probleme
> beherrscht werden kann. Sie darf kein Selektionsinstrument im beruf-
> lichen und sozialen Leben sein. Aber das ist schon oft gesagt worden.
> Die Pflege des Brauchtums ist offenbar in Deutschland allemal
> wichtiger als eine Reform, das orthographische Fachwerk, das schon
> längst Flickwerk ist, steht unter Denkmalschutz.
>
> (Glück and Sauer 1990: 194)

Of course, English is notorious for laying orthographical obstacles in the path of its learners (both native and non-native): George Bernard Shaw facetiously but not entirely unreasonably suggested that 'fish' could just as well be spelled *ghoti* (*gh* as in 'cough', *o* as in 'women', and *ti* as in 'nation'). But foreign learners of German have always been aware of difficulties in the German orthographical system too, and it might be some comfort to know that native speakers have just as many problems getting to grips with it. Only a few years after the norms were agreed in 1901, a German school teacher complained bitterly:

> Die deutsche Rechtschreibung nämlich ist nichts weiter als ein wahres Schulkreuz; denn wenn man die Zeit, die dafür aufgewendet wird, die Tränen, die um ihretwillen von den Schülern alljährlich vergossen werden, summieren könnte, man würde erschrecken über das Unheil, das dieser Unterrichtsgegenstand Jahr für Jahr anrichtet. [. . .] Eine Rechtschreibung, die selbst von den Gebildetsten im Volke nicht beherrscht wird, hat ihr Daseinsrecht verwirkt, und je eher sie verschwindet, desto besser.
>
> (Kosog 1912: 3, 24; cited in Sauer and Glück 1995: 85)

Even today, many German-speaking schoolchildren (and adults) might well agree with these sentiments!

Throughout virtually the entire twentieth century there have been debates at all levels of society over the need to reform the German spelling and writing system, but until the so-called 3. Wiener Gespräche zur Neuregelung der deutschen Rechtschreibung in 1994 all attempts failed, as a result either of political opposition or of public hostility, or both. Even the very modest reforms that were agreed at the Vienna talks by delegates (government officials and academics) from Germany, Austria and Switzerland nearly failed to clear the final hurdle of legislation when a small number of senior German politicians belatedly raised objections and insisted on further scrutiny of the proposals. However, they were finally ratified in 1996; the 'new' system (which in fact is not very different from the 'old' one) is to be introduced in schools in August 1998, and there will be a transition period lasting until 2005, during which the old system will be considered as 'not wrong, but outdated'. Our concern here is with public attitudes towards proposed changes in the language rather than with the changes themselves, but to put the kinds of reaction these proposals aroused into context it might be useful to look at some examples. (The illustrations here are taken from Heller 1996, which gives a concise overview.)

The guiding principle was to change only what seemed to call for change: in other words, to try to remove inconsistencies and confusing features, although some things that could well have been changed on this basis were left alone following earlier public outcries. The most celebrated of these was the proposal at the second Vienna conference in 1988 to change *Kaiser* to *Keiser*, on the grounds that the sound [ai] was more frequently spelled *ei* than *ai*: this proved to be a very hot potato indeed and was rapidly abandoned. As far as the relationship between sound and spelling was concerned, the basic idea was to try to retain the same spelling for the stem of all words belonging to one word family. For example, [ɔi] can be written either as *eu* (as in *Kreuz*) or as *äu* (as in *Mäuse*), but in order to make the connection with words like *Schnauze* and *großschnäuzig* clear, the previous *schneuzen* has been replaced by *schnäuzen*. Similarly, [ɛ] can be written as *e* or as *ä*, but as *aufwendig* is related to both *aufwenden* and *Aufwand* two alternative spellings are now specified: *aufwendig* and *aufwändig*.

A number of other key changes have been made in the spirit of increasing simplicity and regularity. For example, *ss* is to be used systematically instead of *ß* after a short vowel, *ß* occurs only after a long vowel: *küssen, Kuss, sie küssten sich* vs *Maß, Muße, Straße*. Similarly, the confusion over whether certain complex verb forms should be written as one word or two (e.g *radfahren* but *Auto fahren*) was resolved by declaring that in principle all such forms would be 'getrennt geschrieben'. More flexibility was required with foreign words, however, since it would have been equally problematic to retain all 'original' spellings as to replace them all with 'German' forms. The approach adopted was therefore to extend existing patterns of alternatives (e.g. either *Megaphon* or *Megafon*, by analogy with *Mikrofon*), but not to propose changes where such patterns did not already exist (e.g. *Philosophie, Metapher, Phänomen* remain as they were).

One of the most controversial aspects of earlier reform debates was the issue of *Groß- und Kleinschreibung*. Since capitalisation of nouns in Danish was abandoned in 1948, German has been the only language to retain this practice, but while many arguments were advanced by reformers for its abolition, these proposals provoked frequently hostile reactions. In the face of such opposition, the architects of the new system concentrated on removing anomalies (e.g. *in bezug auf* but *mit Bezug auf*) and, ironically, introduced a slight increase in the number of words to be capitalised. Finally, the use of commas and the division of words at the end of a line, two of the more arcane aspects of German orthography, both for native speakers and for foreign learners, were also revised with an emphasis on simplicity and greater freedom of choice.

Public debates on the *Rechtschreibreform*

What for some observers was no more than 'eine begrenzte Unfugbereinigungsaktion' (a limited exercise in reducing the degree of 'nonsense' in the system; Zimmer 1995), was for others itself 'zu einem großen Teil Unfug' (Zemb 1995). The actual changes are not in dispute, in the sense that they are clearly set out in a whole series of booklets and guides, but the interpretations of what they represent are highly diverse, and objections even include the claim that the manner of introducing them was unconstitutional ('Wesentlicher Eingriff: Interview mit Verfassungsrechtler Erhard Denninger', *Der Spiegel*, 30 October 1995: 19). Many people may well share the ambivalent position expressed by Gerhard Schröder, Ministerpräsident of Lower Saxony: 'Die Argumente für die Reform kann ich im Kopf nachvollziehen, aber nicht im Bauch' ('Neue Regeln', *Der Spiegel*, 23 October 1995: 103).

The most spectacular response came in the form of the so-called 'Frankfurter Erklärung', launched at the Frankfurt Book Fair in October 1996, in which over 300 writers and publishers (including such prominent figures as Hans Magnus Enzensberger, Günter Grass, Siegfried Lenz and Botho Strauß) vehemently declared their opposition to the reforms. Their intervention even brought the issue on to the cover of *Der Spiegel*, which bore the dramatic headline: 'Der Aufstand der Dichter: Rettet die deutsche Sprache!' (*Der Spiegel*, 14 October 1996).

The following passages are taken from a variety of articles and letters that appeared in the press between the first announcement of the reforms in November 1994 and their ratification in 1996. They are arranged in no particular order: read them first, then attempt the tasks at the end.

The first extract is from an interview in *Der Spiegel* with the Bavarian Education Minister Hans Zehetmair (a member of the conservative Christlich-Soziale Union party), whose belated objections to the proposals in September 1995 caused a further delay in the ratification of the reforms.

SPIEGEL: Es soll künftig mehr groß als klein, mehr getrennt als zusammen geschrieben werden und weniger Kommas geben. Wird mit der Reform das Ziel erreicht, die Rechtschreibung vom Ballast überflüssiger und komplizierter Regeln zu befreien?

ZEHETMAIR: Im großen und ganzen schon. Es ist gut, daß mit manchem Unsinn Schluß gemacht wird, etwa mit dem Unterschied zwischen *Auto fahren* und *radfahren*. Man wird auch *Rad fahren*.

SPIEGEL: Werden die Deutschen weniger Fehler machen als früher, wenn die Übergangszeit vorüber ist, in der sie lernen sollen, nach den neuen Regeln zu schreiben?

ZEHETMAIR: Die Häufung der Orthographiefehler erkläre ich mir nicht in erster Linie damit, daß die deutsche Sprache schwierig zu schreiben ist. Die große Zahl von Fehlern ist vielmehr ein Symptom für die Oberflächlichkeit unserer Zeit. Die Orthographie erfordert Genauigkeit und Gewissenhaftigkeit, und daran lassen es viele fehlen.

[. . .]

SPIEGEL: Wie schreiben Sie: *Heiliger Vater*?

ZEHETMAIR: Den Papsttitel?

SPIEGEL: Ja.

ZEHETMAIR: *Heiliger* groß natürlich.

SPIEGEL: Das ist heute richtig und künftig falsch.

ZEHETMAIR: Wo steht denn das?

SPIEGEL: Im Wörterverzeichnis des Regelwerks, kleingedruckt.

ZEHETMAIR: Unmöglich, das halte ich beinahe für einen Eingriff in Glaubensfragen. Für katholische Christen ist klar, daß es einen *Heiligen Vater*, aber viele *heilige Väter* gibt, also Männer, die ein heiligmäßiges Leben geführt haben oder führen. Diesen Unterschied können doch nicht Sprachwissenschaftler mit irgendeiner Regel einebnen.

('Viele werden erschrecken: Interview mit Bayerns Kultusminister
Hans Zehetmair über die Rechtschreibreform', *Der Spiegel*,
11 November 1995: 226–9)

(Perhaps we have *Der Spiegel* to thank for the fact that *heiliger Vater* was one of the proposals that was ultimately withdrawn from the final version of the proposal!)

This outspoken interview prompted a wide range of reactions from readers. For example:

–   one supported Herr Zehetmair, referring to 'diese katastrophale Reform';

–   another criticised his intervention as 'ein Beispiel für die groteske Inkompetenz von Politikern mit politischen Entscheidungen';

- yet another dismissed the reform as excessively timid: 'dieses kosmetische Herumzupfen an der deutschen Sprache';
- another made her views clear in both content and form: she demanded 'eine konsequente rechtschreibreform: kleinschreibung und strikte anpassung an die aussprache'.

The conservative national newspaper *Frankfurter Allgemeine Zeitung* had long been associated with opposition to reforms (see Zabel 1989, 1995a). In the most recent phase of the process, it published both positive and negative views, but again the latter dominated the discussion:

> Der dreißigjährige Krieg um die deutsche Rechtschreibung endet mit einem sanften Säuseln. Hatten die Reformer anfangs die Abschaffung der Großschreibung von Substantiven verlangt, so geben sie sich jetzt mit der vernünftigen Forderung zufrieden, Ungereimtheiten zu vermeiden, Widersprüche zu beseitigen. [...] Der Triumph der Tradition ist nicht nur ein Sieg der Eindeutigkeit, Verständlichkeit und Differenziertheit, sondern auch eine Liebeserklärung an die Sprache.
>
> (Kurt Reumann, 'Der Mai bleibt prall', *Frankfurter Allgemeine Zeitung*, 25 November 1994: 1)

> Wem sollte die Reform überhaupt nützen? Tatsächlich ist sie ein bürokratischer Selbstläufer. Seit den siebziger Jahren haben sich Fachleute mit diesem Werk beschäftigt. Viel ist davon nicht geblieben. Was jetzt noch gebilligt werden soll, ist nur die letzte Schwundstufe eines gewaltigen Unternehmens, in dessen Mitte bis 1989 die „gemäßigte" Kleinschreibung stand. Jetzt stehen nur ein paar Regeln für die Satzzeichen und fünfhundert Veränderungen in der Orthographie zur Debatte. [...]
>
> Wenn von der Rechtschreibreform die Rede ist, wird von Politikern immer wieder betont, daß sie „kostenneutral" verwirklicht werden solle. Gemeint ist damit vor allem, daß die Verlage ihre Bestände weiter verkaufen dürfen. Ob das so sein wird oder nicht doch ein Zwang zur Anpassung an die neuen Regeln entstehen würde, weiß freilich niemand. Und keiner redet davon, was die überflüssige Reform in zwanzig Jahren bereits gekostet hat.
>
> Die Einwände gegen die Reform beschränkten sich bisher aufs Mäkeln: hier ein Wort und dort eines. Und so läuft der ganze Streit mittlerweile auf einen Kompromiß hinaus: Vielleicht ändert

man fünfzig Wörter weniger. Dann aber hätte die Bürokratie ihren letzten Sieg errungen und etwas Unfertiges durchgesetzt. Die in Lübeck, der Geburtsstadt Thomas Manns, versammelten Ministerpräsidenten [see p. 186] sollten dies verhindern. Und die Kommission sollte aus ihrem Scheitern die Konsequenzen ziehen, sollte sich selbst auflösen.

(Thomas Steinfeld, 'Überflüssige Reform', *Frankfurter Allgemeine Zeitung*, 25 October 1995: 1)

In another article in the same newspaper, Friedrich Dieckmann accuses the reformers of having a vested interest. He describes them disparagingly as:

eine Schar über die deutschsprachigen Länder verteilter Spezialisten, deren vorwiegende Beschäftigung die Konstruktion orthographischer Reformen ist; ihr berufliches Dasein hängt wesentlich davon ab, daß die Ergebnisse ihrer Arbeit vom Staat beachtet und in Verordnungen übertragen werden.

(Dieckmann 1995: 36)

He goes on to attribute their efforts to 'Regelfetischismus':

Natürlich kommt man weder in der Schule noch in der Literatur ohne ein umfassendes Maß an Grundverabredungen aus. Aber amtlich anzuordnen, daß man fortan nicht mehr im dunkeln, sondern im Dunkeln tappt, um die Dinge dort nicht mehr durcheinanderzubringen, sondern durcheinander zu bringen, ist das L'art pour l'art einer in ihren eigenen Voraussetzungen kreisenden Zunft.

(ibid.)

However, a reader's letter (Günter Habedank, Wiesbaden, *Frankfurter Allgemeine Zeitung*, 2 November 1995) challenges both of these points, first hinting that journalists in glass houses shouldn't throw stones (don't they earn their living from writing about such matters too?) and, second, arguing:

Daß es eine wichtige Aufgabe ist, die deutsche Sprachgemeinschaft auch über die Staatsgrenzen hinweg als kulturelle Einheit zu wahren und sich schon allein deshalb sorgfältig um die geschriebene (und gelesene) Sprache zu kümmern, kommt ihm nicht in den Sinn. Wie wäre es mit einem Blick nach Frankreich?

Unsere Schriftsprache hat einen so entwickelten Grad erreicht, daß es unserer Sprachkultur entsprechen sollte, diese Sprache zu pflegen, und das bedeutet auch, ihr ein geregeltes und geschütztes „Leben" zu ermöglichen. Ziel ist also nicht die Reglementierung, sondern ein geregelter Weg für einen von allen Teilhabern der Sprachgemeinschaft nutzbaren Bestand.

■■ On the basis of these passages and any other writings you can find on this subject, compile a list of the arguments that have been put forward and arrange them (a) in terms of support for and opposition to the reforms, and (b) according to categories such as academic/ linguistic, historical, political, cultural, economic, moral, educational, practical, legal. If you have access to German-language newspapers on CD-ROM or on the Internet, you will find many articles and a great deal of correspondence on the subject.

■■ Look at the issue from a historical perspective and show how much or how little has changed in the debates over the last 200 years (see Further reading, pp. 199–200, for sources).

■■■ Compare what you have read in relation to German with debates on English spelling. What similarities and differences are there? For example, are senior government ministers actively involved in discussions about the reform of English spelling?

Further reading

Bickes and Trabold (1994), contains several chapters giving different perspectives on *Sprachkultur*, including the GDR tradition.

Clyne (1995), pp. 180–5, for a summary of the debate.

Glück and Sauer (1990), Chapter 13, on the *Duden* and on the spelling reform debate.

Milroy and Milroy (1985), on the idea of 'authority' in language.

'Neue Regeln: Jetzt oder nie', *Der Spiegel*, 23 October 1995, pp. 102–9, an article about the new proposals, written in accordance with the new system.

Russ (1994), Chapter 7, on German spelling and its reform.

Sauer (1988), a 'biography' of the *Duden* from its beginnings until the late 1980s.

Sauer and Glück (1995), for a detailed historical account of orthography as a public issue in Germany.

Stevenson (1995b), includes a section on the traditions of *Sprachkultur* and *Sprachkritik* in Germany.

Straßner (1995), a comprehensive account of the German tradition of *Sprachkultur*, drawing on and reproducing many primary sources.

Wells (1985), Chapter 9, especially pp. 348–53, on the history of attempts to standardise German spelling.

Zabel (1989), a documentation of press reactions to the 1988 reform proposals.

Zabel (1995b), for a full presentation of the new rules.

● ● ●

Chapter 11

Sprachkritik

Public attitudes

towards language use

The good old days

Here is a modern *Märchen*, a fable for our times:

Es war einmal ein alter Mann, der fand sich in der Welt nicht mehr zurecht. Wenn er durch die Fachwerkgassen seiner kleinen deutschen Stadt schlurfte, sah man ihn gelegentlich innehalten und die Schilder an den feinen Geschäften lesen. Dabei seufzte er dann, schüttelte nach schrulliger Greisenart resigniert den Kopf und fuchtelte manches Mal auch ärgerlich mit seinem Gehstock. Die Passanten betrachteten ihn mitleidig-amüsiert und suchten mit einem schnellen Blick den Grund seines unwilligen Brabbelns. „Monika's Trachtenlook" stand da etwa zu lesen oder „Elisabeth's Kinder-Boutique", auch „Holger's Hosenladen" oder „Lena's Teestübchen". Sie konnten nichts dabei finden, zuckten die Schultern und eilten weiter.

[. . .] Mit einem boshaften Glanz in den Augen konnte man ihn sehen, wenn er sich mit zahnlos mümmelnden Altersgenossen am Rentnerbrunnen traf. Dann zogen sie los und zeigten einander feixend und heimlichtuend ihre neuesten Funde, etwa das Pappschild an einer Bankfiliale: „Heute wegen Umbau's geschlossen" oder den Hinweis einer Bäckerei: „Sonntag nachmittag's von 14 bis 16 Uhr geöffnet". „Das ist ja nicht einmal ein Genitiv", kicherten sie dann, „und trotzdem das lustige Häkchen vor dem -s." Als sie aber eines Tages sich vor Heiterkeit kaum zu lassen wissend – vor einem Sex-Shop standen und mit ihren Stöcken einander prustend das Schild „Erotika's" wiesen, da traf sie der Zorn der Passanten. „Das ist der deutschlateinische Superpluralis, mit Apostroph!" konnte der Alte noch unter Lachtränen keuchen, als Stimmen der Empörung laut wurden. Das sei ja das Letzte, sich in dem Alter schon am Morgen zu besaufen, voll abgedreht, diese Verwesis. [. . .]

Eines schönen Sommerabend's [. . .] machte er sich auf den Heimweg, und weil die Lüfte so lau waren, wählte er die längere Strecke durch eine entlegene Gasse, die er sonst nie betrat. Als er einmal aufblickte, sah er das Schild an einem Geschäft: „Leonoras

Kleider". Es durchzuckte ihn wie ein Blitz. „Ohne Apostroph, ohne Apostroph", flüsterte er, seine Lippen zitterten, die goldenen Tage seiner Jugend stiegen vor ihm auf, und er konnte sich des Tränen's der Rührung nicht erwehren.

(Axel Wermelskirchen, 'Genitivu's cum apo'stropho', *Frankfurter Allgemeine Zeitung*, 29 June 1995: 9)

It is not difficult to trace the origin of this intrusive apostrophe, that causes the old men in this story so much pain: it is one of many (for some people unwelcome) borrowings from English that increasingly characterise contemporary German usage. Indeed, the absence of the possessive apostrophe in many English texts (as in 'We always have our customers interests at heart') might lead us to conclude that it had been exported into German. In fact, of course, it has simply been assigned to other duties, principally to mark the so-called 'greengrocer's plural': 'Lovely red apple's', or 'new potatoe's'. This in turn has enraged the old men's anglophone counterparts, as frequent letters to newspapers testify: one reader of the *Guardian* newspaper recently suggested that 'the public display of incorrect written English be punishable by law'.

It is easy to dismiss such complaints as trivial and pedantic: on the one hand, some would argue, the apostrophe is communicatively redundant, as neither its presence in the 'wrong' place nor its absence in places where it is 'required' is likely to impede understanding; on the other hand, 'educated' people are still perfectly well aware of how and when it should be used. But the evaluation of language use is an important part of active membership in a speech community, and neither professional linguists nor 'educated' people in general (whatever this term means) have a monopoly on the right to express opinions on the subject:

Linguisten neigen dazu, solche Meinungen [i.e. views expressed by 'ordinary people'] als unwissenschaftlich, als zu Stereotypen geronnene Vereinfachungen überholter wissenschaftlicher Auffassungen beiseite zu schieben. Aber auch Sprachmeinungen und -einstellungen gehören zur sprachlichen Realität – besonders dann, wenn sie weit verbreitet sind und weiter verbreitet werden, wenn sie das wertende Sprachhandeln von Meinungsmultiplikatoren, von Erziehern im weitesten Sinne bestimmen. Auch Sprachvorurteile sind wirklich und wirksam.

(Stickel 1987: 312)

In Chapter 10 we looked at attempts to 'fix' the *form* of the language and public reactions to them. In this chapter, we shall consider public views on language *use*. Like *Sprachkultur*, *Sprachkritik* is a term that covers many different concerns (see Further reading pp. 217–18), but the focus here will be on the 'complaint tradition' in public debates on the German language, and in particular on the idea of *Sprachverfall* (language decay) as a symptom of *sozialer Verfall*. If, as we have seen, the German language plays a central role in determining Germanness, it would not be surprising to find considerable sensitivity towards its 'condition': from this perspective, an apostrophe is not merely a marker of grammatical relations but potentially an indicator of social cohesion.

■   How do you react (a) to 'errors' in other people's use of language, and (b) to other people's criticism of language use?

Sprachverfall

Underlying all debates on this issue are two complementary contentions: the synchronic claim that 'the language is decaying/degenerating/in decline, etc.', and the diachronic claim that 'the language is not as good today as it used to be'. Of course, each of these claims implies the other, but it is worth stating both, as specific discussions tend to emphasise either one or the other. The common point is an anxiety about change:

> Wer von „Sprachverfall" spricht oder ähnliche abwertende Begriffe benutzt, meint alle sprachlichen Veränderungen, die ihm mißfallen, und vielen Menschen mißfallen nahezu alle Veränderungen, deren sie sich bewußt sind. Abgesehen von Sprachwissenschaftlern registriert tatsächliche oder vermeintliche Veränderungen nur, wer ein gewisses Alter erreicht hat, und daher sind die Klagen über den Sprachverfall auch typisch für die ältere Generation. [. . .] Spätestens vom fünfzigsten Lebensjahr an beginnt man zu klagen, und die Klagenden gehören fast alle der gehobenen Mittelschicht an.
>
> Man weiß natürlich, daß sich die Sprache entwickelt hat, daß das Deutsch zu Zeiten Karls des Großen und auch noch zu Zeiten Goethes anders war als das heutige und daß es auch in hundert Jahren wieder anders sein wird, man ist auch generell gar nicht gegen Veränderungen, im Gegenteil, aber während der eigenen Lebenszeit

sollte die Sprache möglichst konstant bleiben. Diese Haltung muß im Zusammenhang mit der Einstellung zu Veränderungen in anderen Bereichen, zu kulturellen Entwicklungen im allgemeinen gesehen werden. Was die eigene Muttersprache angeht, so wird diese Einstellung durch den schulischen Deutschunterricht mit geprägt, in dem Sprache immer auch als etwas Statisches, Geregeltes, Normiertes erlebt wird.

(Hoberg 1990: 240)

In other words, although most people are aware that languages change over time, many feel uncomfortable when they witness change actually going on. Moreover, while changes in fashion (e.g. in hairstyles or music) may or may not be for the better, there is a tacit assumption that changes in language can only be for the worse.

■■ The following passage is an edited version of an article in the *Frankfurter Allgemeine Zeitung*, a conservative national newspaper which has for a long time sought to uphold 'high standards' of language use. This particular piece focuses on the language use of public figures, specifically politicians and journalists. Read the article carefully and identify the writer's criticisms. (Some words and phrases have been italicised to make certain points clearer.)

Wichtiger ist die Frage, wie diese beiden Personengruppen die Sprache der Bevölkerung beeinflussen. Mag dieser Einfluß nun positiv oder negativ beurteilt werden, auf jeden Fall ist anzunehmen, daß er beträchtlich ist. Nicht zu bestreiten ist ferner, daß beide, Politiker wie Journalisten, dem Kästchen-Denken huldigen und daß auch die Nachrichtenagenturen das tun, deren Einfluß auf die Sprache ebenfalls nicht gering einzuschätzen ist. Wenn die dort beschäftigten Redakteure Meldungen abfassen, so scheinen sich in ihrem Kopf automatisch bestimmte Schubladen zu öffnen, in denen wiederum bestimmte vorgestanzte Formulierungen liegen, die sie als Gerüst für ihre Texte benutzen.

Beispiele gibt es in Hülle und Fülle. Doch wo anfangen und wo aufhören? Vielleicht beim „umsetzen" oder der „Umsetzung"? [...] Früher wurden Pläne oder Vorhaben *in die Tat umgesetzt, ausgeführt* oder *verwirklicht*. Nun heißt es nur noch: „Das muß umgesetzt werden." [...] Na und? entgegnen die Verfechter der These von der „lebendigen Sprache"; so verändert sich eben die Sprache.

Die Frage, ob sie dabei gewinnt oder verliert, interessiert nicht. Sie registrieren solche Veränderungen nur, ohne sie zu beurteilen. [...]

Ein weiteres Beispiel, nicht minder im Schwange wie „umsetzten", ist „auslösen". Das Verb ist auch so ein Bequemlichkeitswort, das die Sprache ärmer macht. Denn was sonst als Bequemlichkeit ist es, wenn statt *hervorrufen, entfesseln, heraufbeschwören, erregen, zustande bringen, einleiten, entfachen, verursachen, verschulden, erzeugen, bewirken* und was es dergleichen mehr gibt, immer nur das langweilige „auslösen" verwendet wird? [...]

Lebendige Sprache? Man zähle einmal nach, wie oft im Jahr in den sogenannten Medien [...] immer wieder dieselben Metaphern verwendet werden, die durch übermäßigen Gebrauch so abgegriffen sind, daß ihre Benutzung eigentlich Ekel erregen müßte. Da wird bis zum Erbrechen immer von neuem „grünes Licht gegeben", „zur Kasse gebeten" und „unter den Teppich gekehrt", da werden pausenlos irgendwo „Weichen gestellt" und „Nägel mit Köpfen gemacht". Was ist daran „lebendig"? Diese Bilder sind längst tot. [...]

Die Rechtschreibreform, über die seit vielen Jahren geredet wird und die nun allmählich Gestalt annimmt, hat einige Aufregung verursacht. Niemand findet aber offenbar etwas dabei, wenn in Büchern selbst namhafter Schriftsteller immer häufiger Grammatikfehler auftauchen. Der Konjunktiv wird kaum noch beherrscht. Es wimmelt nur so von falschen „würde"-Konstruktionen; es steht „wäre", wo es „sei" heißen müßte; die Apposition, die Beifügung, erhält den falschen Kasus; es wird nicht mehr richtig dekliniert und konjugiert. [...]

Frisches Blut, sagt man, tue degenerierten Familien gut. Ist aber das Einströmen von immer mehr Wendungen aus dem Englischen ins Deutsche tatsächlich ein Gewinn für die Muttersprache? Es geht nicht darum, Fremdwörter generell abzulehnen. Manche sind unentbehrlich [...], andere einfach besser als das von Sprachpuristen vorgeschlagene deutsche Wort, und die Erfahrung lehrt, daß der Kampf gegen die „Fremdwörterei" nicht zu gewinnen ist. Allenfalls ist hinhaltender Widerstand möglich, zum Beispiel gegen Floskeln wie „das macht Sinn", [...] gegen *beraten, diskutieren* und *debattieren* ohne das im Deutschen dazugehörende Fürwort „über".

Wenigstens registrieren sollte man auch den offensichtlich unaufhaltbaren Bedeutungswandel solcher Fremdwörter, über deren ursprüngliche Bedeutung ihre Benutzer sich oft nicht im klaren zu sein scheinen. Eine Ortschaft kann man [z.B.] *evakuieren, entleeren,*

aber wenn Menschen evakuiert werden, klingt das für den, der sich der wahren Bedeutung des Wortes noch bewußt ist, schon etwas merkwürdig. [. . .] Ist es erlaubt, wenigstens noch einmal an die alten Sprachwurzeln zu erinnern, oder gilt auch das schon als unziemliche Herumnörgelei an der sich natürlich weiterentwickelnden Sprache?
(Klaus Natorp, 'Unter den Teppich gekehrt', *Frankfurter Allgemeine Zeitung*, 3 June 1995: B2; italics mine)

One of the most frequently vilified trends in modern German (although it is not as 'new' as some of its opponents seem to think) is the so-called *Nominalstil*, stereotypically associated with bureaucratic texts (see also the text 'Rotkäppchen auf Juristendeutsch' in Chapter 6, pp. 109–10). In a practice it has now abandoned, the *Duden Stilwörterbuch* (1963 edition quoted here) was once scathing in its criticism of this style:

Cäsar hat nach dem Sieg bei Zela nach Rom gemeldet: „Ich kam, sah und siegte." Wenn er den Hauptwortstil geschrieben hätte, den wir heute leider bei so vielen schlechten Schreibern finden, so hätte er gesagt: „Nach Erreichung der hiesigen Örtlichkeiten und Besichtigung derselben war mir die Erringung des Sieges möglich." Freilich hätte ein Mann, der in diesem Stil schreibt, die Schlacht nie gewonnen.

Das Zeitwort ist die Seele des Satzes. Es ist eine schlechte Gewohnheit, die Handlungen in Hauptwörtern auszudrücken und als Zeitwörter die farblosen allgemeinen Verben wie „sein", „erfolgen" usw. zu verwenden. Der Satz wird dadurch blaß und unbestimmt.
(Duden Stilwörterbuch 1963)

The reverse process has been identified in English: the use of nouns as verbs. In an editorial headlined 'Noun but the Brave', the *Guardian* attacked this trend (again, italics have been added):

[. . .] Let us – as an official from the Severn-Trent Water Authority put it on the Today programme the other day – '*example* that for you.' The BBC's admirable radio programme The World This Weekend, which used merely to be produced, is now said to be 'studio-produced' by someone or other. Who invented this word? Since the BBC has managed without it for more than 60 years, why is it needed now? [. . .] Business and industry are even guiltier. 'We are *exiting* the old year', the chairman of ICI informs his employees, while the chairman of the Chrysalis group declares that: 'Profits were lower than the record levels achieved in 1989 after *expensing* a significant investment in new talent.' [. . .] Everywhere (newspapers not excluded) people are *faxing*, *tandying*, *modeming* and even *messaging*. Take refuge in a restaurant and you may be told that your wine is delayed because it is being 'room-temperatured.' It is time that this business was stopped: or, to put it another way, that action to halt it was urgently *prioritised*.

('Noun but the Brave, *Guardian*, 29 December 1990; italics mine)

This is one of the responses this piece provoked:

> To park, to pinpoint, to contact, to service (as in service a car), to tape (as in tape an interview), to featherbed, to steamroller, to audition [. . .] anything wrong with these verbs? All were produced by the process of conversion – switching to a different word-class – stigmatised in your leader.
>
> Conversion is centuries old, and Shakespeare was particularly adept at it ('Wouldst thou be windowed in great Rome?' Anthony and Cleopatra). It is sad to see the Guardian playing the part of a linguistic King Canute, a role better suited to newspapers with more experience in it. The time to start worrying is when the English language becomes so arthritic that it no longer permits such mobility.

One of the interesting points about this reply is that it supports its case by referring to Shakespeare, with the implicit message: 'if it was good enough for him, it should be good enough for us.' Calling 'dead poets' as witnesses in linguistic debates is a common tactic, used in place of rational argument to back up all shades of opinion. At the same time, these cultural authorities are often called upon for the opposite reason, to demonstrate the inevitability of change: 'Shakespeare may have written "Let's be no stoics nor no stocks" (*Taming of the Shrew*), but that doesn't mean it's all right to use double negatives in modern English.'

■■ In the light of these discussions, and recalling the distinction we have made between the terms synchronic and diachronic, consider why debates about alleged *Sprachverfall* or language decay may be problematic.

■■ Compare the views expressed by Klaus Natorp and others like him with these passages from an article by the writer and cultural critic Hans Magnus Enzensberger in *Die Zeit*:

Diese Verwahrlosung! Dieser Amerikanismus! Diese rüden Stummelsätze aus der Diskothek! Diese unglaublichen Patzer im Schulaufsatz! Und so weiter. Das kennt man. Man kennt den müden Stumpfsinn der alternativen *scene*, man kennt die berüchtigten Zwanzigjährigen, deren Wortschatz kaum über achthundert Vokabeln hinausgeht und deren Grammatik die Struktur eines Kaugummis hat; allerdings auch die Klagen darüber kennt man, ja sie hängen einem möglicherweise schon zum Hals heraus.

Denn die Herren, die unserer Sprache da so eilfertig beispringen, als wäre sie eine altersschwache Patientin: diese muskulösen Pfleger machen sich ja nicht erst seit gestern an ihrem Rocksaum zu schaffen. Und heute wie damals bleiben ihnen nachhaltige Erfolge versagt – glücklicherweise, möchte ich meinen, wenn ich bedenke, was diese Apostel des guten, wahren und richtigen Deutsch sich schon alles geleistet haben an Dünkel, Verbohrtheit und Besserwisserei. [. . .]

Die Sprache ist nämlich immer lebendiger und jünger als ihre arthritischen Leibwächter. Sie pfeift darauf, von ihnen reingehalten und beschützt zu werden. [. . .] Hinter dem Rücken ihrer Aufseher aber läßt sich die Sprache munter mit den Vandalen ein, vor denen jene sie zu bewahren suchen. Großmütig wie eh und je gibt sie sich hin dem frechen, penetranten, falschen, chaotischen, gepfefferten, gemeinen, obszönen Gequassel der Fußballer, Schuler, Knastbrüder, Börsianer, Soldaten, Zuhälter, Flippies, Penner und Huren. Der reinste Horror-Trip, müßten die Herren vom zuständigen Sprachdezernat da ausrufen, wenn ihnen diese vulgäre Wendung nicht fremd wäre.

(Hans Magnus Enzensberger, 'Unsere Landessprache und ihre Leibwächter', *Die Zeit*, 24 August 1979: 29)

Vox pop: *Sprachverfall* and public opinion

The views of intellectuals and journalists are one thing, but what do 'ordinary people' think? Every year since 1991, the Gesellschaft für deutsche Sprache in Wiesbaden has invited nominees for the 'Unwort des Jahres' (to complement its longer-standing search for the 'Wort des Jahres'), the aim being to identify 'welche Sprachschöpfung den Erfordernissen sachlicher Angemessenheit und der Menschenwürde am wenigsten gerecht gewesen [ist]' (Schlosser 1993: 43): proposals have included *Gebührenanpassung* (meaning a fee increase), *Stellenabbau* (similar to the English 'downsizing', meaning redundancies) and *Dunkeldeutschland* (a pejorative term for the new Bundesländer). Everyone has opinions on language, even if they are not often consciously formed and articulated. One of the problems in finding out what individuals actually think is that when they are asked to express an opinion they often seem to resort to precisely the kinds of formulation we encounter all the time in media debates. For example, in the survey we shall look at in this section (see Stickel 1987), typical responses were: 'daß die deutsche Sprache . . . mißbraucht, mißhandelt, manipuliert, vergewaltigt, verhunzt oder mit Füßen getreten wird, daß sie verfällt, verdorrt, verarmt, verkommt, verwildert, verludert (wird) oder in der Gosse landet'. Interestingly, these comments too seem to refer sometimes to the language itself and sometimes to language use but, either way, language is viewed as a living thing, and is often even personified.

Another problem with this particular survey is that it was conducted through newspapers: readers were invited to fill in a questionnaire and return it to the Institut für deutsche Sprache in Mannheim, which then processed the results. This means that the responses were not representative of a cross-section of the community, but came overwhelmingly from people who were in the habit of reading these newspapers and who felt sufficiently strongly about the issues to go to the trouble of completing and posting the questionnaire; furthermore, about a quarter of the respondents were teachers and the average age was 53. It is therefore not surprising that 84 per cent answered 'zum Schlechten' to question 1, and that the 'ja' answers to all parts of question 2 ranged from 75 per cent to 94 per cent.

Meinungsumfrage: Was halten Sie vom heutigen Deutsch?

1   Manche Mitbürger meinen, daß sich die deutsche Sprache in besorgniserregender Weise zum Schlechten verändert oder schon verändert hat. Andere sind dagegen der Auffassung, daß sich das Deutsche lediglich nach den sich verändernden Lebensumständen und Bedürfnissen der Menschen weiterentwickelt. Welcher der beiden Auffassungen neigen Sie zu?

(a)   Die Sprache verändert sich zum Schlechten   [ ]
(b)   Die Entwicklung der Sprache bietet (derzeit)   keinen Anlaß zur Sorge   [ ]

2 Einige Sprachkritiker bemängeln bestimmte Erscheinungen des derzeitigen Sprachgebrauchs. Stimmen Sie kritischen Auffassungen wie den folgenden zu oder nicht?

(a) Die Fähigkeit zu angemessener mündlicher und schriftlicher Ausdrucksweise hat stark abgenommen, vor allem bei Jugendlichen. Ja [ ] Nein [ ]

(b) Viele Mitbürger haben keinen Sinn mehr für sprachliche Umgangsformen. Ja [ ] Nein [ ]

(c) Bestimmte Sprachregelungen (z.B. für den Konjunktiv in Redewiedergaben, für den Gebrauch des Genitivs oder anderer grammatischer Formen) werden von vielen Menschen nicht mehr beachtet. Ja [ ] Nein [ ]

(d) Fachleute drücken sich oft dann unverständlich aus, wenn sie sich an Laien wenden. Ja [ ] Nein [ ]

(e) Es werden insgesamt zu viele Fremdwörter gebraucht. Ja [ ] Nein [ ]

(f) Vor allem im öffentlichen Sprachgebrauch wird über unangenehme oder gefährliche Dinge und Vorgänge oft mit verharmlosenden oder irreführenden Wörtern und Wendungen gesprochen. Ja [ ] Nein [ ]

(Stickel 1987)

■■ If you have access to a reasonable number of native speakers, ask them to respond to these questions and compare your findings with those of the original survey. If you are unable to do this, you could consider whether the questionnaire might be applicable to English (and if so, try it out!).

Perhaps more significant for our purposes than the quantitative results were the comments given in support of the responses. Consider, for example, the most common explanations given for the 'decline of the German language':

– die negative Entwicklung der Gesellschaft: „Die Sprache entwickelt sich zum Schlechten wie die Gesellschaft";
– die zunehmende „Amerikanisierung" der Bundesrepublik: „der Sog der amerikanischen Führungsmacht";

- der „Mangel an staatlichem Bewußtsein" seit dem Kriegsende;
- die sprachliche Beherrschung der Alltagswelt durch die „visuellen Medien";
- das „Sprachunvermögen der Jugend", unter anderem bedingt durch „schlechten Deutschunterricht";
- die allgemeine „Vernachlässigung der Rechtschreibung";
- der Mangel an guten sprachlichen Vorbildern bzw. die Orientierung des Sprachgebrauchs „an falschen Vorbildern".

(for further examples, see Stickel 1987: 292–301)

■■ Again, ask your informants whether they agree with any of these comments and ask them to elaborate.

Engleutsch

The most obvious manifestation of sociolinguistic insecurity in German-speaking societies is the concern over the so-called *Überfremdung* of the German language through the constant 'infiltration' of English words (look again at Klaus Natorp's article on pp. 205–7). Once again, neither the phenomenon of English influence nor the public and academic debates about it is new (see Wells 1985), but as recently as 1994 the Institut für deutsche Sprache invited readers of its journal (*Sprachreport* 4/1994) to send in their views on the reasons why anglicisms are used and/or resisted, and the topic simply will not go away. For example, in the *Spiegel* interview referred to in Chapter 10 (pp. 195–6), Bavarian Education Minister Hans Zehetmair expressed his views on the matter like this:

ZEHETMAIR: Mich beschäftigt sehr stark die Frage, welche Folgen sich für die deutsche Sprache und Rechtschreibung aus der Entwicklung der Europäischen Union ergeben. Meine Antwort ist: Die Deutschen dürfen sich weder überheblich abschotten, noch dürfen sie sich all dem, was von draußen auf sie einströmt, unkritisch anpassen oder gar unterwerfen.

SPIEGEL: Was bedeutet das für die Praxis?

ZEHETMAIR: Wir dürfen nicht einfach Anglizismen oder andere fremde Wörter übernehmen, sondern müssen uns darüber klarwerden, was sie bedeuten, und dann überlegen, ob es deutsche Ausdrücke dafür gibt.

SPIEGEL: Also doch die deutsche Sprache abschotten?

ZEHETMAIR: Nein. Man soll sich um deutsche Ausdrücke bemühen, oft wird man sie nicht finden. Aber heutzutage bemüht man sich gar nicht darum. Viele, die im öffentlichen Leben stehen, geben ein schlechtes Beispiel. Da wird recycelt und gekidnappt, angeturnt und gestylt. Es gibt noch viel schrecklichere Wörter als diese, die mir gerade einfallen. Auf diese Weise machen wir die eigene Sprache den Deutschen fremd. Das muß nicht sein, vieles läßt sich ohne Krampf verdeutschen.

(*Der Spiegel*, 11 November 1995)

Concerns such as these are explored in an article in the weekly newspaper *Die Zeit* (23 June 1995, p. 42) by Dieter E. Zimmer, a seasoned observer of this and other linguistic issues. The article appeared under the alarming headline 'Sonst stirbt die deutsche Sprache' and is based on the following thesis:

Das Verhältnis der Deutschen zu den ausländischen Wörtern in ihrer Sprache: es spiegelt wohl ihr Verhältnis zu den „Fremden" überhaupt. Die Wellen deutschtümelnder Sprachreinigung, die vom siebzehnten Jahrhundert bis zum Zweiten Weltkrieg immer wieder über das Land hinweggingen, müssen sich den Verdacht gefallen lassen, Ausdruck einer allgemeineren Abneigung gegen alles Nichtdeutsche gewesen zu sein, geboren aus jener Mischung aus Unterlegenheitsgefühl und Überheblichkeit, die sich in der deutschen Geschichte so fatal gegenseitig bedingt und hochgeschaukelt haben.

Unsere heutigen Schwierigkeiten, ein angemessenes Verhältnis zu den in unsere Sprache zahlreicher denn je einströmenden ausländischen Wörtern zu finden, ist ein Reflex auf eben diese unglückselige Geschichte xenophobischer Fremdworthetze.

(Zimmer 1995b: 42)

The dilemma for the Germans, Zimmer argues, is that promoting 'verbal hygiene' (see the section on *(Sprach)kulturpessimismus*, pp. 216–17) by protecting the German language from foreign incursions sounds suspiciously like 'ethnic cleansing':

In Deutschland [jedenfalls] existiert heute keinerlei des nationalistischen Ressentiments unverdächtige Kraft, die dafür einträte, das Deutsche an der deutschen Sprache zu bewahren. Es ist uns nahezu unvorstellbar geworden, daß es durchaus eine Zustimmung zur eigenen kulturellen „Identität" (die von der Sprache mehr als von

allem anderen konstitutiert wird) ohne Hybris und Chauvinismus
geben könnte.

(ibid.)

However, he believes that some kind of action is necessary: 'Die
Sprachentwicklung erreicht nämlich den Punkt, an dem der Fortbestand des
Deutschen [. . .] überhaupt in Frage steht.' The reason for this apocalyptic
vision lies in his view that the behaviour of foreign words has changed:

> In der Vergangenheit war der Einstrom fremder Wörter und
> Wendungen jeweils zeitlich begrenzt und auf bestimmte, relativ
> isolierte Sprecherkreise beschränkt. [. . .] Der heutige Zustrom aber
> wird nicht eines baldigen Tages versiegen; im Gegenteil, mit der
> wachsenden weltweiten Verflechtung aller Lebensbereiche wird er
> weiter anschwellen.

(ibid.)

Although Zimmer does not explicitly make this analogy, his discussion of
foreign words (we could call them *Gastwörter*) is very similar to the way
in which foreign people in Germany are often discussed: 'they came for a
particular purpose on the assumption that they would not stay for long,
but now it appears they are here for good, in which case they should be
"naturalised", adapted to fit the German pattern'.

> Sobald sich ein fremdes Wort diesem Regelsystem [i.e. the grammar
> of a language], diesem Code einfügt, so daß es ohne allzu große
> Regelsprünge frei verwendet werden kann, gefährdet es die
> autochthone Sprache genausowenig wie jedes Wort germanischer
> Herkunft. Dann fragt sich nur, was sich auch bei jedem neuen Wort
> germanischer Herkunft fragt, ob es einen Zugewinn an Ausdrucks-
> kraft darstellt; tut es das, bereichert es die Sprache.
>
> Es ist nämlich nicht damit getan, einem Wort die bloße Einreise
> zu gestatten. Wie die Menschen müßten auch Wörter in eine
> zivilisierte Beziehung zu ihrer neuen Umwelt treten können, der
> sprachlichen.

(ibid.)

He claims that while in the past foreign words that did not simply disappear
again were 'phonetisch und orthographisch eingebürgert' (e.g. *Schock,
Bluse, Keks*), this no longer happens.

Sie sollen Ausländer und unter sich bleiben. Die Folge ist, daß wir im neudeutschen Makkaronisch sprechend und schreibend ständig von Code zu Code springen müssen.

Was liegt da vor? Welche kollektive Schrulle hindert uns? Ist es die alte nationale Arroganz, die uns einflüstert, ausländische Wörter verdienten es nicht, mit den Attributen deutscher Sprachangehörigkeit ausgestattet zu werden? Ist es im Gegenteil das alte Minderwertigkeitsgefühl, das uns sagt, jede Verdeutschung tue den fremden Wörtern einen Tort an? Nach meinen Erfahrungen ist es etwas anderes, Profaneres: die deutsche Oberlehrerhaftigkeit. Eindeutschen hieße nämlich auch: sich dem Verdacht auszusetzen, man wüßte nicht, wie ein Wort an seinem Herkunftsort gesprochen und geschrieben wird.

(ibid.)

The problem, then, is that in order to show how erudite and cosmopolitan they are, German-speakers are allowing the English vocabulary to behave like a cuckoo, taking over the nest in which it has been deposited. The result is a kind of hybrid language, in which 'nahezu alle sinntragenden Wörter englisch sind. Das ergibt dann solche Sätze: [. . .] „Miles & More führt ein flexibles Upgrade-Verfahren ein: Mit dem neuen Standby oneway Upgrade-Voucher kann direkt beim Check-in das Ticket aufgewertet werden" (Lufthansa). [. . .] Die deutsche Sprache liefert solchen Sätzen nur noch das Füllmaterial' (Zimmer 1995b). Although Zimmer concedes that this currently occurs mainly in particular registers, he suggests that it is spreading. To see how German compares with other European languages in this respect, he looked at how sixty of the most common English computing terms had been 'accommodated' in seven languages. The percentage figures given in the following list indicate the proportion of these terms that have been adapted to the linguistic structures of the respective languages: French 82 per cent, Swedish and Spanish 80 per cent, Dutch 64 per cent, Danish 59 per cent, Italian 58 per cent, and German 50 per cent. From this he concludes: 'Französisch, Schwedisch und Spanisch sind danach also die intaktesten europäischen Sprachen, Deutsch und Italienisch die kaputtesten. Vielleicht ist es doch kein Zufall, daß Italien und Deutschland auch das gebrochenste Identitätsbewußtsein haben.' Finally, he prophesies that the outcome of this development will be that the emerging 'Trümmersprache' will establish itself as the orthodox form: 'Aber die Brücke zum Deutsch der Vergangenheit wird dann abgebrochen sein. Das ist dann eine tote Sprache, eine von vielen.'

■■ Zimmer's article is clearly very provocative and at least some of the arguments are (presumably deliberately) highly exaggerated. What do you think his intention in writing the article was? How logical are his arguments, both internally and in relation to each other? How persuasive is the evidence he adduces to support his arguments? (The article is too long to include in its entirety here, but you should be able to answer these questions on the basis of the extracts.)

■■ Debate the sociolinguistic and political issues raised in this section under the heading: 'Deutsch ist keine Einwanderungssprache'.

(Sprach)kulturpessimismus

Complaints about the standard or quality of language knowledge and language use have not changed a great deal over the centuries, and the list of scapegoats is simply extended as and when new ones (television and television presenters, computers, etc.) present themselves. It is also part of the tradition to associate *Sprachverfall* with *Kulturverfall*: the state of the language (language use) is taken to be indicative of the state of the culture it articulates. This can apply not just to specific features of language use, such as those discussed earlier in this chapter, but also to 'linguistic capabilities' in general. For example, a study of aggressive behaviour in German schools concluded amongst other things:

> „Der Einfluß von Medien wird im Zusammenhang mit Konzentrationsschwächen ebenso deutlich, wie die sprachliche Verrohung auf den nachlassenden Erziehungseinfluß in der Familie hinweist", stellt Frau Schultz-Hector [Kultusministerin von Baden-Württemberg] fest. Notwendig sei eine Kultur des Redens und Zuhörens sowie der einfühlsamen Aufmerksamkeit für andere. [. . .] Immerhin tragen 38 von 10 000 Schülern eine Waffe, die zwar nicht unbedingt zum Einsatz kommen muß, die Gewaltbereitschaft jedoch stärkt, wenn die verbalen Formen der Auseinandersetzung frühzeitig versagen. [. . .] Schüler müssen offenbar nicht nur lernen, überzeugend und logisch zu argumentieren, sondern ebenso, ihre Gefühle in angemessener Weise sprachlich zum Ausdruck zu bringen.
>
> (Heike Schmoll, 'Gemeinsinn, soziale Verantwortung, Sprachkultur',
> *Frankfurter Allgemeine Zeitung*, 31 January 1995: 3)

However, this kind of educational programme is very different from policies and practices advocated by some in the context of what Deborah Cameron calls 'verbal hygiene', which appear to be based on the belief that:

> Ignorance or defiance of grammatical rules is equated with anti-social or criminal behaviour. Grammar needs to be taught, we gather, less to inculcate the norms of polite usage than to encourage respect for persons and property, to keep people clean and law-abiding, to build 'character' and discourage indiscipline and 'sloppiness'.
>
> (Cameron 1995: 94)

■■■ To pull the various strands of the debates discussed in this chapter together, write an essay in which you discuss, in relation to German, the following proposition: 'Verbal hygiene and social or moral hygiene are interconnected; to argue about language is indirectly to argue about extra-linguistic values' (Cameron 1995: 114).

Further reading

Cameron (1995), especially Chapter 3; an excellent and lively discussion of debates about language and an alternative perspective on prescriptivism.

Clyne (1995), Chapter 8, on the nature of English influence on German.

Drosdowski (1988), on *Sprachverfall* and the state of the German language, by the (then) head of the Dudenredaktion.

Gesellschaft für deutsche Sprache (1993), a collection of essays on the public use and evaluation of language.

Glück and Sauer (1995), on various linguistic trends, including the 'absorption' of foreign words.

Klein (1986), critical essays on *Sprachverfall*.

Milroy and Milroy (1985), on prescriptivism and the 'complaint tradition' in English.

Polenz (1994), on the history of linguistic purism and debates about the 'quality' of the German language.

Sieber (1994), on a Swiss research project on language knowledge and language use of school students.

Townson (1992), Chapters 5 and 6, on the recent academic and political orientation of *Sprachkritik*.

Trabold (1993), especially Chapter 5, on *Sprachverfall*.

Wells (1985), Chapter 10, on the history of linguistic purism and debates about the 'quality' of the German language.

Zimmer (1986), a lively and thought-provoking collection of journalistic essays on trends in contemporary German usage.

•   •   •

Chapter 12

Sprachwende

Language change
as social change

East meets West

Travellers passing through the railway station in Bautzen (a small town in Saxony) in the summer of 1995 were greeted by the following friendly notice:

Werte Reisende!

Für Ihre Auskünfte und Informationen steht Ihnen die Service-Leistung der Fahrkartenschalter zu jeder Zeit zur Verfügung.

At first sight there may seem to be nothing remarkable about this: it is the kind of notice you would expect to find in any station or airport. However, on closer inspection this brief text reveals itself as a curious sociolinguistic hybrid, the product of a presumably unintentional amalgamation of two distinct discourses (or manners of speaking). On the one hand, we are addressed by what, five years earlier, would still have been the normal form of public address in this East German town (complete with formal exclamation mark); on the other hand, we are then politely offered a service, and the offer is couched in terms that belong firmly in the culture of Western-style 'customer care' (complete with obligatory anglicisms). These few words encapsulate the essence of the most far-reaching, most closely observed and scrutinised and most rapid processes of sociolinguistic change in the history of German, a process that began in the autumn of 1989 and in some respects at least has already been completed.

In this short space of time, virtually every aspect of the former GDR has been dismantled: not only the political and economic structures, but also the public institutions and the social practices that made life in the East German state distinct from that in its Western neighbour. As all of these things are in some respect dependent on language, it is obvious that social and political change on this scale could not take place without having an impact on the language: indeed, as we shall see, some of the social and political changes were actually brought about through linguistic change. The key issue, then, is the way in which changes in the conditions of people's daily lives are experienced, enacted, articulated and come to terms with linguistically. The emergence and subsequent disappearance of words and expressions that were characteristic of life in the GDR may be interesting in themselves, but what is more significant both socially and linguistically is the role that language in general played before, during and after the so-called *Wende* of 1989–90: in what ways was this political turning point also a '*Sprachwende*'?

The following questions about the effects of change on the now supposedly unified speech community of Berlin, posed by an East German linguist, could equally well apply to Germany as a whole:

> Zu untersuchen ist, welche abweichenden sprachlichen Elemente den Berlinern bekannt sind, ob der Berliner den Bewohner des jeweils anderen Stadtteils an seiner Sprache erkennt und wieweit er sich mit dem eigenen Sprachverhalten identifiziert. Wieweit sind die verschiedenen Gruppen der Berliner willens und in der Lage, sprachlich-kommunikative Unterschiede zu überwinden? Von welchen Gruppen wird die Ausbildung gemeinsamer sprachlicher Normen bestimmt, wie verläuft die Entwicklung dahin, welche Rolle spielen dabei politische, wirtschaftliche sowie soziale Faktoren und Erfolge des Zusammenwachsens? Welchen Einfluß haben bei den einzelnen Personen psychische Faktoren und ihre Biographie? Von besonderer Bedeutung sind sprachlich bedingte Verständigungsschwierigkeiten und soziale Probleme, die sich aus dem unterschiedlichen Sprachgebrauch ergeben oder dadurch ausgelöst werden. Dabei ist festzustellen, ob die sich aus der Vereinigung Deutschlands ergebenden sprachlichen Prozesse ein Ost-West-Problem oder nur ein Ost-Problem sind, welche Entwicklungsetappe beim Beitritt Ostberlins zum Sprachgebiet Westberlin bzw. Westdeutschland jetzt erreicht worden ist.
>
> (Schönfeld 1993: 189)

A West German linguist, expressing a similar view, warns against misleading generalisations and adds a crucial historical dimension:

> Es gab keine „westdeutsche Sprache" und keine „Sprache der DDR", es gibt heute kein „Westdeutsch" und kein „Ostdeutsch". Nicht um *die* Sprache geht es, sondern um den Sprach*gebrauch*, um die spezifischen Redeweisen, um bestimmte sprachliche Wendungen, um den besonderen Gebrauch einzelner Wörter, um sprachliche Gewohnheiten und Einstellungen, um das unterschiedliche sprachliche

221

Verhalten der Deutschen in Ost und West, ja schließlich auch um die unterschiedlichen Erfahrungen, die wir Deutsche in den letzten Jahrzehnten gemacht haben.

(Müller 1994: 119)

For many years, virtually throughout the lifetime of the GDR, a debate was conducted (with greater or less intensity depending on the general political climate and the temperature of relations between the two German states) in academic journals and newspapers of all kinds on the question: 'Gibt es zwei deutsche Sprachen?' In answering this question with a firm 'no', Gerhard Müller is representing what by the late 1980s had finally become the consensus among all serious observers. The general view was that beyond a limited set of lexical items and certain semantic contrasts, the substance of the German language had not been affected by the political division of Germany, and that as most of the differences that could be identified were generally confined to formal, official contexts (politics, economics, state institutions, etc.), they had little impact on everyday language. The logical conclusion from this argument was that these differences would evaporate, should the 'need' for them disappear. It was therefore ironic that just as the debate had virtually been laid to rest, the opportunity to test this conclusion arose and the real differences were revealed: not so much in the structure of the language as in the ways in which it was used (ways of speaking, of interacting, of interpreting others) and in the unexpectedly profound imprint of 'official' language on everyday usage.

■■ The rest of this chapter will be devoted to differences in everyday language use, but to understand them fully it is important to have some idea of the nature of the so-called 'Sprachspaltung debate'. You can look at this in two ways:

(a) What concrete lexical and semantic differences can be identified between the forms of standard German that developed in the FRG and the GDR between 1949 and 1989? (See Clyne 1995, Chapter 3.)

(b) In what sense was the language debate in fact a pretext or a vehicle for conducting an ideological debate? (See Townson 1992, Chapters 5 and 6; Stevenson 1993.)

Ritual communication: official language and everyday life in the GDR

Reflecting on the sociolinguistic conditions under which GDR citizens had lived, East German academic and politician Wolfgang Thierse commented that they did not speak a different language from their Western neighbours, but they had 'ein anderes Verhältnis zur Sprache' (Thierse 1993: 116). What did he mean by this?

It is probably the case in all speech communities that there are different styles or registers (see Chapter 6) which are considered appropriate in particular contexts, and that some kind of social sanction is imposed on anyone who flouts such conventions. What made the GDR as a speech community different in this respect from the Federal Republic or other Western states was the rigorously prescribed use of the official discourse in a very wide range of contexts: not just in political speeches or in articles in the state-run newspaper *Neues Deutschland*, for example, but in all texts (spoken and written) that were intended for public consumption. Furthermore, this 'ritualised' language consisted of more than just individual words: it had to do with the way whole texts were composed. It can be seen in its extreme form in official political texts, such as this almost impenetrable extract from a speech by Kurt Hager, the principal ideologist of the SED (Sozialistische Einheitspartei Deutschlands, i.e. the former East German Communist Party):

> Der in Vorbereitung des IX. Parteitages ausgearbeitete Forschungsplan der Gesellschaftswissenschaften ist Bestandteil unserer einheitlichen Wissenschaftpolitik. Durch die Arbeit der Wissenschaftlerkollektive, der Einrichtungen und Wissenschaftlichen Räte muß vor allem gesichert werden, daß die gesamte Forschungsarbeit inhaltlich auf das Niveau der politischen, ideologischen und theoretischen Anforderungen gehoben wird, wie sie in den Parteitagsbeschlüssen fixiert sind, und daß die Arbeit nach den vom Parteitag gesetzten Maßstäben organisiert wird.
>
> (cited in Teichmann 1991: 255)

Everyone in the GDR was familiar with this kind of language and one of the essential components of communicative competence in their speech community was the ability to 'decode' texts such as this (i.e. what is he really saying?) and to switch in their own speech between this variety and the normal form of everyday speech. However, the extent to which the official discourse penetrated people's experience of everyday life should not be underestimated, and there was an important intermediate level of (especially, but not exclusively, written) communication that tends to be overlooked:

> Nun darf man aber nicht übersehen, daß auch nichtoffizielle Bereiche des Lebens sprachlich von der Wirklichkeit des autoritären Staates geprägt waren, so z.B. Familienfeiern mit ihren Ritualen wie sozialistische Namensgebung, Jugendweihe, sozialistische Eheschließung u.a. (Fix 1992), so auch Alltagsgespräche. Politisierte Sprache gebrauchte man z.B., wenn im privaten Kreis über das Arbeits- und Schulleben gesprochen wurde. Erscheinungen des Arbeits- und Schulalltags mußten mit den einmal vorhandenen Bezeichnungen fachlichen Charakters wie *Kollektiv, Wettbewerb, Plan, Parteiversammlung, Pionierversammlung, FDJ-Sekretär, Unterrichtstag in der sozialistischen Produktion* benannt werden, wollte man sich verständigen. Selbst in Alltagsgespräche, die sich nicht auf Institutionen wie Arbeit oder Schule bezogen, drang spezifischer Wortschatz ein, den man zwar nicht politisiert nennen kann, den man aber als DDR-typisch zu bezeichnen hat und der Sprecher aus den neuen Bundesländern sicher am längsten von Sprechern aus den alten Ländern unterscheiden wird.
>
> (Fix 1994: 131)

Consider the area of social activity that at some stage impinges on everyone's life: education. The school played a central role in the construction of the socialist society of the GDR, a comprehensive social process in which pupils, teachers and parents were (at least theoretically) constantly involved. The various forms of 'collective', groups in which all members of the community had clearly specified roles, show the scale and complexity of the internal organisation of individual institutions and the educational process as a whole. Some measure of the pervasive influence of official linguistic patterns throughout a given domain can be gleaned from the mass of texts that were generated routinely within schools and related institutions. Look at the following extracts from longer texts, and then address the questions below. (Unless otherwise indicated, all the texts are taken from unpublished sources. They are discussed in detail in Stevenson 1995c.)

Text 1a   Konzeption zum 35. Jahrestag der DDR

In der Vorbereitung des 35. Jahrestages der DDR geht es vor allem darum, das Wissen der Schüler über die 35jährige Entwicklung ihres Heimatlandes zu erweitern und zu vertiefen, sowie Stolz auf die Errungenschaften der Werktätigen zu wecken. Sie sollen erkennen, daß die erreichten Erfolge das Ergebnis großer Anstrengungen und Leistungen der von der SED geführten Werktätigen sind und daß auch in Zukunft der Kurs der Hauptaufgabe in ihrer Einheit von Wirtschafts- und Sozialpolitik konsequent fortgesetzt wird.

gez. XXX (Parteisekretär) YYY (Direktor)
(instructions to teachers in a particular school)

Text 1b   Lehrpläne

Der polytechnische Unterricht hat einen wesentlichen Teil daran, daß den Schülern sozialistische Arbeitsgewohnheiten anerzogen und sie an gesellschaftlich nützliche Arbeiten herangeführt werden. [. . .] Sie lernen verstehen, daß die Arbeit des Werktätigen in den sozialistischen Betrieben die Grundlage für das Leben aller Menschen in unserer Republik ist.
(Lehrpläne 1, central government documentation on the national curriculum
published in 1980; cited in Schlosser 1990: 98)

Text 2   Arbeitsplan des Fachzirkels Deutsch

Mit der Einführung neuer Lehrpläne im Fach Deutsche Sprache und Literatur erhöhen sich die Anforderungen, die an jede Unterrichtsstunde gestellt werden. Es gilt, die Qualität des Literaturunterrichts zu verbessern und – wie Margot Honecker [the then Education Minister, whose husband Erich Honecker was the General Secretary of the SED] auf der zentralen Direktorenkonferenz formulierte – „die dem literarischen Kunstwerk innewohnenden Möglichkeiten für die Persönlichkeitsentwicklung" zu nutzen. Der Literaturunterricht soll stärker als bisher einen wirkungsvollen Beitrag zur kommunistischen Erziehung der Schüler leisten. Daher sind im Rahmen der Arbeit des Fachzirkels Deutsch alle Möglichkeiten auszuschöpfen, die einen erziehungswirksamen und bildungseffektiven Unterricht fördern. [. . .] Daher stehen sich alle Kollegen mit Rat und Tat zur Seite.
(paper outlining aims and objectives of the year's work in the
German department of a school, written by the head of department and
circulated to her colleagues)

Text 3   Rechenschaftsbericht der Klasse 10b

Im vergangenen Schuljahr erfüllten wir unseren Arbeitsplan nur teilweise. Wir veranstalteten zwar einen Kuchenbasar, dessen Erlös wir für die Solidarität spendeten, und eine Weihnachtsfeier, welche wohl bei allen Begeisterung fand, aber es kamen z.B. ein gemeinsamer Kinobesuch sowie eine Radtour zu kurz, auch mit einer Einladung eines Arbeiterveterans klappte es nicht ganz. [...] Man darf natürlich auch die politischen Gespräche, welche unser Agitator P.S. leitete, nicht vergessen. Den Lehrgang für Zivilverteidigung schlossen wir mit guten Ergebnissen ab. Einige Schüler erhielten wegen ihrer Einsatzbereitschaft eine Auszeichnung. [...] In der 10. Klasse muß noch mehr darauf geachtet werden, daß es nicht dazu kommt, daß ständig dieselben FDJ-ler an freiwilligen Einsätzen teilnehmen. Der Arbeitsplan der 10. Klasse müßte also noch konkreter die Arbeit der einzelnen Schüler kennzeichnen.

(annual report on a class's activities, written by pupils under supervision of the teacher)

Text 4   Zeugnis

Auch in diesem Schuljahr wies Sabine gute Leistungen auf. Als 1. Sekretär der GOL [Grundorganisationsleitung: organising committee of the Freie Deutsche Jugend within the school] leistet Sabine an unserer Schule eine vorbildliche gesellschaftliche Arbeit. Auch im Klassenkollektiv nimmt Sabine eine führende Rolle ein. In Auseinandersetzungen und Diskussionen mit Klassenkameraden und Schülern unserer Schule bezieht sie einen festen Klassenstandpunkt. Im Ensemble unserer Schule arbeitet sie aktiv mit.

(report on individual pupil)

Text 5   Mit Pioniertreffen-Schwung ins neue Jahr

[...] Natürlich ist für alle Schüler eine fleißige und gewissenhafte Lernhaltung das ganze Jahr über das Wichtigste. Im Unterricht und in der Pionier- [Party organisation for younger children] und FDJ-Arbeit [Freie Deutsche Jugend = Party youth organisation] wollen wir uns mit den neuesten Erkenntnissen von Wissenschaft und Technik vertraut machen, denn wir sind die Erbauer und Gestalter unserer Zukunft.

(article written by a team of 'young reporters' from a school and published in the regional newspaper *Lausitzer Rundschau*)

Text 6   Lehrvertrag

Das Lehrziel ist die Erziehung und Bildung eines Facharbeiters, der sich bewußt für den Sieg des Sozialismus einsetzt, den die Fäfigkeit zu hoher Qualitätsarbeit sowie die Entwicklung solcher Eigenschaften wie Liebe zur Arbeit, Fleiß, Gewissenhaftigkeit, Exaktheit, Pünktlichkeit und Disziplin, Ordnungssinn, beharrliches Eintreten für das Neue, Unduldsamkeit gegenüber Mängeln in der eigenen Arbeit und in der Arbeit anderer auszeichnet.

(standard contract for trainee)

■■   Try to answer these questions in relation to the texts:
   –   For what purpose were the texts written?
   –   Who was the intended readership?
   –   What specific features of the texts (e.g. particular words and phrases, ways of referring to people and activities) contribute to the impression of a 'ritualised' form of communication?
   –   Comment on Text 2 in the light of the following remarks:

Richtlinien für den Unterricht

„Schließlich setzte sich die Meinung durch, daß die Ausbildung der Lesefertigkeiten *noch konsequenter* in den Mittelpunkt des Lesenlernens zu stellen ist." (M. Honecker in Deutsche Lehrerzeitung 25, 1989) Für den Geübten lautete der Untertext: Die Schüler können generell sehr schlecht lesen. Es ist etwas versäumt worden. Deshalb muß mehr geübt werden. „Es muß *weiter* im Mittelpunkt der Aufmerksamkeit bleiben, die Sicherheit aller Schüler in den Grundrechenarten zu erhöhen. [...] Die Schlüsselfrage – und das ist die Meinung vieler Lehrer – besteht *weiter* darin, an der *noch solideren* Ausprägung des grundlegenden mathematischen Wissens und Könnens zu arbeiten." (ibid.) Der Untertext beider Aussagen lautet: Das Kopfrechnen und die Rechentechniken überhaupt wurden vernachlässigt. Das hat sich als falsch erwiesen. Es muß also geübt werden.

Diese Formen erfüllen die Funktion des Beschönigens (es wird unterstellt, daß etwas schon gut ist, aber noch verbessert werden kann), des Verschleierns (vieles von dem Gesagten ist eigentlich schlecht) und der Lückenhaftigkeit (Probleme werden nicht genannt).

(adapted from Fix 1992: 56–7)

■ What similarities can you identify between individual texts (e.g. 1a and 1b; 5 and 6)? In what ways might texts with a similar purpose produced in a West German (or British or American) context differ from these?

Texts such as these indicate how much had to be 'unlearned' under the new system post-1990. However, another form of ritual communication was much more in the spotlight during the *Wende* period of 1989–90, and played an important part in the very process of socio-political change: the *Losung*, or political slogan. Anyone who has seen photographs or film recordings of the demonstrations in cities like Berlin and Leipzig at that time will have seen the marchers carrying banners with short, pithy slogans, typically stating demands or commenting on the regime. But the real significance of these mini-texts may not be immediately apparent to the foreign observer, who may well be accustomed to seeing demonstrators bearing banners. This was a very common sight in the GDR too, especially on ceremonial occasions such as May Day, but part of the highly orchestrated nature of those events was the fact that the slogans were prescribed by the authorities. They always referred to the same recurring themes and had the transparent purpose of affirming the status quo and stressing the 'common endeavour'. For example, these are some of the slogans drawn up by the Central Committee of the SED for what turned out to be the last May Day celebration of its kind, in 1989:

Vierzig Jahre DDR – Alles mit dem Volk, alles durch das Volk, alles für das Volk!

Gruß und Dank allen Werktätigen für ihren Beitrag zum Werden und Wachsen unserer Deutschen Demokratischen Republik!

Weiter voran auf dem bewährten Kurs der Einheit von Wirtschafts- und Sozialpolitik!

Unser Gruß den Bruderparteien, den Werktätigen aller sozialistischen Länder!

Gemeinsam für Frieden und Sozialismus!

Forscher, Konstrukteure und Technologen! Mit kühnen Ideen und Tatkraft zu neuen wissenschaftlich-technischen Spitzenleistungen!

Jung- und Thälmannpioniere! Mit guten Ergebnissen bei der Erfüllung des Pionierauftrages „Meine Liebe, meine Tat meiner Heimat DDR"! Vorwärts zum 40. Jahrestag der DDR!

Feste Solidarität mit dem Volk von Nikaragua!

Weiter voran unter dem Banner von Marx, Engels und Lenin!

The very act of appearing on the streets with your own slogans, particularly if they were critical of the regime, was therefore risky to say the least. But the defiance articulated in the non-official slogans at the demonstrations during the *Wende* period was not merely in their content, but in the appropriation of a tool previously used by the Party to address and instruct the people and in the originality, creativeness and playfulness of the new slogans. This was a symbolic act of 'de-ritualisation' of a traditional means of public communication. Here are some examples (from Fix 1994 and Lang 1990):

Ein Vorschlag für den ersten Mai: Die Führung zieht am Volk vorbei.

Reformer müssen an der Spitze steh'n, sonst sagen wir auf Wiederseh'n.

SED, das tut weh!

Logen sie gestern, lügen sie heute, es sind immer die gleichen Leute.

Mit dem Fahrrad durch Europa, aber nicht als alter Opa.

Wir lieben unsere Heimat – grenzenlos!

Es geht nicht mehr um Bananen, jetzt geht's um die Wurst!

■■ Consider these and other examples of *Demo-Sprüche*, and try to identify the various ways in which the traditional *Losung* was transformed (e.g. use of rhyme, puns, modifying familiar expressions such as proverbs or nursery rhymes, literary references).

■■ East German linguist Reinhard Hopfer has pointed to the crucial role of language in the demise of the GDR:

> Die Revolution in der DDR zeigte sich nicht zuletzt in dem massiven Protest gegen die Orwellschen Verhältnisse in der Sphäre der gesellschaftlichen Kommunikation. In früheren Zeiten mag es so etwas wie Hungerrevolten gegeben haben. In der DDR revoltierte auch die Sprache.
>
> (Hopfer 1992: 11)

■ Referring to this passage, West German linguist Peter von Polenz (1993: 128) proposes the term *Sprachrevolte* to represent the effects of changes in public language use in the GDR in the autumn of 1989. Investigate the validity of this idea by looking at texts from that time, e.g. public speeches made by Party leaders and by speakers (both 'ordinary people' and 'celebrities') at demonstrations in Leipzig and Berlin, slogans on banners at the demonstrations.

Kultur des Mißverständnisses

For most people (especially, but not only, from the East) the first opportunity to see for themselves whether and to what extent differences between lifestyles and living conditions in East and West actually existed came only with the opening of the Wall in 1989. In fact, real differences were not hard to find, but it is often the perception of differences (whether verifiable or not) that affects attitudes and relationships in such situations. Stereotypical images of the 'other' Germans were in many cases deeply rooted, but could you actually tell whether someone was from the East or the West just by hearing them speak or talking to them? Of course, a pronounced regional accent could give the speaker's origins away, but were there differences in 'manners of speaking' (*Sprechweisen, Kommunikationsstile*)? Many people, in both East and West, certainly thought so. For example, the following remarks by school students in Brandenburg are typical of views expressed by young East Germans:

> diese Sprücheklopfer, die in Westdeutschland in der Szene sind und hier in Ostdeutschland genau so cool wirken wollen wie die *da drüben*.

> Die Westdeutschen sprechen viel mehr, sie wissen genau, wie sie sich geben sollen, gestisch und mimisch, und das schüchtert dann die Ostdeutschen ein bißchen ein.

Die Westler erzählen mehr, was sie gehört haben und was sie erfahrcn haben, während die Ostler mehr so Gefühle äußern.

A study carried out during the *Wende* period itself showed that many people felt they could identify whether particular radio programmes had been broadcast from the GDR or from West Berlin, basing their judgements on the speakers' speech styles (Liebe Reséndiz 1992). The same applies to written texts. For example, the participants (from West and East) in another study were asked to say which of a series of *Partnerschaftsanzeigen* had been taken from West German magazines or newspapers and which from East German ones.

The first one was taken from the West Berlin magazine *Tip*:

Eine Frau, Anfang 40, häßlich, gefühllos, uninteressant und -beweglich, mit Neigungen zu Abhängigkeit, Langeweile und Verdruß begegnet dem sinnlichen, an vielem interessierten, humorigen, selbständigen Mann. Nur wo?

The second text was taken from the East Berlin paper *Berliner Zeitung*:

Bin 31/1,86, schlk., suche ehrl., aufgeschl., jg. Frau f. dauerh. Partnersch. Int.: Musik, Reisen, Kino u. all. Schöne. Halte viel v. Treue, Geborgenh. u. Liebe. Bin Optimist, um mit Dir ein gemeins. Leben aufzubauen. Jede ernstgem. Zuschrift (mit Bild bevorz., n. Bed.). w. beantw.

Most of the 'judges' rightly guessed that the first advertisement was a 'Western' text, but for quite different reasons. East Germans said, for example, 'Unsere Frauen haben sich nicht so erniedrigt' and 'So'n Quatsch wurde in unseren Anzeigen nicht gedruckt'. West Germans, on the other hand, made comments such as 'Meiner Meinung nach haben Ost-Bürger Schwierigkeiten mit Ironie' and remarked on the author's 'Selbstbewußt-sein zu ihrer Person', her 'Selbstironie'. In other words, the same text was interpreted as an expression of self-abasement and of self-confidence or self-assurance. The same contrasts emerged in the analyses of the other advertisements:

Ost- und Westinformanten haben ein deutliches und weitgehend identisches Profil von Ost- und Westanzeigen vor Augen. Als negativ wird an der westlichen Selbstpräsentation empfunden, daß sie oberflächlich, künstlich, übertrieben und unnatürlich sei. Ostdeutsche fragen sich, warum Wessis sich in Anzeigen so verstellen. Tendenziell überwiegen negative Urteile in den Begründungen der Ost-informanten. „Blödsinnige Übertreibung", „oberflächliche Ironie", „entspricht der allgemeinen aufgesetzten Lockerheit (coolness)". Die gleichen Merkmale können auch positiv gewertet werden, vor-wiegend von Westinformanten, nämlich als phantasievoll, ironisch, witzig, selbstbewußt, interessant, locker. „Respektlosigkeit" wird dem Westen zugeschrieben und offenbar unterschiedlich bewertet.

Dagegen erkennen Ost- wie Westinformanten Ostanzeigen an der „normalen, nicht übertriebenen Ausdrucksweise", an Sach-lichkeit, Korrektheit, Ernsthaftigkeit: als typisch empfinden sie die genaue Aufzählung „vielfältiger" Interessen; die wird manchmal im Westen als „Obergenauigkeit", als „reine, relativ stupide Aufzählung der Qualifikation" empfunden.

(Weydt 1993: 215–18)

■■ Sum up the views expressed here and by the young people quoted above about perceived differences in East/West communicative styles.

The potential sociolinguistic significance of real or perceived differences in communicative behaviour becomes clear if you look at interaction between speakers rather than merely at individual texts, particularly in contexts which were previously relatively unfamiliar to East German speakers. For example, one of the biggest hurdles for many of those engaged in trade and commerce to overcome was how to 'talk business' in the context of the market economy. This was not just a matter of vocabulary, but involved a whole range of communicative practices: forms of address, manner of speaking, non-verbal behaviour. Sabine Ylönen observed negotiations at the Leipzig Trade Fair in September 1990 between the West German representative of a Finnish construction company and an East German businessman who wanted to build houses in the Dresden area (Ylönen 1992). Although the West German is the one with something to sell and the East German is the customer, it is the former who dominates the discussion. For example, after the customer (C) has explained what he wants to do (build detached family houses), the sales representative (SR) launches into a lengthy and fluent sales pitch:

SR: Wir ham jetz hier nur ein' Teil da und äh, es kommt ja immer darauf an, wir könn' ja keine maßgeschneidertn Lösung' anbietn für das, was Sie jetz hier konkret in der DDR brauchen. In der DDR sind Sie vor eine neue Situation gestellt und wir bzw. unsre Mandanten aus Finnland auch, so daß Sie uns im Prinzip sagn müßten, welche Leistung' Sie erbring' könn', wie Sie den Markt beurteiln – soweit Ihn' das jetz schon möglich ist – und dann müßtn wir'n Weg findn, unter unsren Mandantn jetz die richtign mit Ihn' zusamm'zubring' und vor alln Ding' auch das richtige Produkt zu entwickln. Äh smuß ja nich immer das gleiche sein, was den Finn'

C: Nein

SR: gefällt und was den Deutschn gefällt, ja? Vielfach sind Änderung' nötig, aber der Markt is da.

C: 's klar.

SR: Grade im Gewerbebereich. Wir ham hier diese Holzhäuser als Kiosk oder Imbißstand, stelln

C: Ja

SR: sich 'n Naherholungsgebiet vor, was entwickelt werdn soll. Wir könn' also ohne weiteres in jeder Größe 'n Golfklub oder irgndwas baun und die ganzn Einfamilienhausbebauung', die jetz komm'.

C: Das is das, äh wo wir die Hauptintresse hätten, was hier ganz aktuell wird äh, was bisher ja

SR: Ja

C: ouch anders gelaufn is, wo jeder sein Haus irgendwie selber baun mußte [*lachend*]

SR: Ja

C: äh, wo doch off die Baufirm' jetz äh ouch diese Markt . . . dieser Marktbereich zukommt.

(Ylönen 1992)

■   How does the West German (SR) place himself in a dominant position in this exchange?

Another aspect of the world of work that reveals the difference in experience between East and West Germans is the job interview. Consider the following extracts from role-played interviews, recorded during an employment training course for East Germans:

A *(Interviewer asks East German interviewee whether, as he has claimed on his application form to know Russian, he would be prepared to develop a service network in the Baltic states)*

Da kann ich Ihnen erst mal ein grundsätzliches „Ja" auf Ihre Frage entgegenhalten, natürlich, ich habe Russischkenntnisse, die aber vervollständigt werden müssen, weil ich momentan meines Erachtens nicht in der Lage bin, mich fließend in Russisch zu verständigen, aber wenn Ihre Firma angedacht hat, das Servicenetz in Richtung Osten auszubauen, dann darf ich vielleicht mal fragen, . . . ob dort angedacht ist von Ihrer Firma, einen Fortbildungslehrgang in Russisch anzubieten, wo ich meine Bereitschaft natürlich sofort signalisiere, um dort ein gutes funktionierendes Service- und Vertriebsnetz auszubauen.

B *(Interviewer asks West German interviewee about his knowledge of foreign languages)*

Ja, also, Englisch: würd ich behaupten ist sehr gut in Wort und Schrift, ja? Also, weil ich eben zwei Jahre auch ne Schule [in den USA] besucht habe. Französisch ist sicherlich ausbaufähig, ich hab fünf Jahre lang an der Schule Französisch gehabt, mir fehlts eigentlich an Praxis, aber ich bin überzeugt davon, wenn ich öfters mal die Gelegenheit hätte, zum Beispiel in Frankreich mich aufzuhalten, daß das sicherlich ausbaufähig ist.

(Auer 1994)

■ What differences can you identify in terms of the formality of style, self-presentation, attitude towards interviewer, etc.?

What these two examples have in common is that they illustrate what has been called the 'Kultur des Mißverständnisses' (see Good 1993): the outcome of forty years of separation was not the emergence of two partially distinct linguistic systems, but of two partially distinct *Kommunikationsgemeinschaften* characterised by different sets of communicative norms. As an East German linguist, now working in the 'West German' Institut für deutsche Sprache, remarked: 'Die innere Spaltung des staatlich vereinten Landes drückt sich spürbar darin aus, daß Menschen, die die gleiche Muttersprache sprechen, ständig das Gefühl haben, aneinander vorbeizureden' (Fraas 1993: 260). This 'Aneinandervorbeireden' shows graphically how the way we experience life conditions the way we talk. As Jens Reich, the physicist and leading figure in the reform movement in the GDR, put it on receiving the Goethe Medal in 1991:

Es ist durchaus möglich, daß in einem Land zwei Gesellschaftsstrukturen nebeneinander bestehen [. . .] mit zwei Gesellschaften kann man auch zwei Kulturen und zwei Sprachen haben. Ich meine „Sprachen" in einem gehobenen Sinne, nicht die erbsenzählende Untersuchung darüber, ob in einem Gebiet Brathendl heißt, was sie im anderen Broiler nennen. Ich meine Sprachmuster, Denkschablonen, ja sogar die verfeinerten Elemente der Körpersprache, an denen man die Herkunft eines Sprechers ausmachen kann. [...] Ist es wirklich ein Unglück, wenn Deutschland aus zwei Teilen besteht, von denen der eine ein halbes Jahrhundert atlantische und der andere osteuropäische Orientierung hatte? Die unsere [...] hat zwei Generationen so tief geprägt, daß wir uns jetzt mit einem Tschechen oder Polen über existentielle Probleme leichter verständigen können als mit vielen Westdeutschen. Wenn zu uns Besuch aus Moskau oder Prag kommt, dann finden wir sofort die gemeinsame Sprache, die das Verständnis anzeigt.

(Reich 1991: 7; cited in Ylönen 1992: 20)

■■ If you have access to Germans from both the former GDR and Western Germany, ask them to comment on Reich's views (or indeed on any of the other texts in this section).

Prospects

In one sense, there is no denying that East/West differences exist: that is, in the sense that they have always existed, just as have North/South differences (see Chapter 4). However, the forty years of relative lack of contact have given these contrasts a new perspective (for the 'ordinary person', if not for the linguist). Despite its tongue-in-cheek nature, the following article is based on an assumption that the story is newsworthy, while it would not have been if it had featured, say, a Bavarian judge in a court in Schleswig-Holstein:

So kommt die innere Einheit nicht voran. [...] Ein Schöffe aus der schönen sächsichen Stadt Meißen hat sich in Dresden geweigert, seiner Bürgerpflicht nachzukommen, weil – so ließ er das hohe Gericht wissen – er den Dialekt des Richters nicht mehr ertragen konnte. Der Betroffene, Vorsitzender Richter der Jugendkammer beim Landgericht Dresden, kommt aus Baden-Württemberg. Damit scheint der Fall klar. „Sie sprechen kein richtiges Deutsch", ließ der Schöffe den Richter wissen, verweigerte die Mitarbeit, und schon war

> der Prozeß gegen eine Diebesbande geplatzt. Die Rechtsordnung sieht für eine Verweigerung dieser Art den Rechtsweg vor: Der Schöffe bekam erstmal ein Bußgeld von zweihundertfünfzig Mark aufgebrummt. Doch kann eine solche erzwungene Mitarbeit der Demokratie wegweisend für das Recht im einigen Vaterland werden, in dem es offenbar unterschiedliche Muttersprachen gibt? Haben Sachsen einen Rechtsanspruch, ausschließlich auf Sächsisch abgeurteilt zu werden? Müssen schwäbelnde Richter in den neuen Bundesländern Deutschkurse belegen? Kommen jugendliche Diebesbande im Osten fortan straflos davon, weil es an Dolmetschern aus den westlichen Dialekten mangelt? Müssen der sächsische und der schwäbische Dialekt als rettungslos inkompatibel betrachtet werden, so daß diese beiden Stämme nicht zusammengehören, also mitnichten zusammenwachsen können?
>
> (Dirk Schümer, 'Dialektik der Einheit', *Frankfurter Allgemeine Zeitung* 11 March 1995: 29)

However, the real issue here has to do neither with regional dialects nor with the question of whether there were two (partially) distinct national standard varieties of German. From what we have seen, it may be that Western critiques of language in the GDR largely missed the point: on the one hand, the supposedly restricted and specialised official discourse actually penetrated quite deeply into everyday life and everyday language and, on the other hand, while most people probably had few regrets at the passing of either the political system or the associated language, many retained an attachment to familiar terms precisely because they related to mundane aspects of life in the GDR. For them, the systematic displacement of 'East German' terms by 'West German' ones was a form of 'linguistic imperialism' and part of the socio-political process of 'internal colonisation' that masqueraded as 'unification'. This resentment was manifested in the apparently disproportionate hostility towards ostensibly trivial changes:

> Das trifft zum Beispiel für *Kita* [*Kindertagesstätte*] und *Tram* zu. Eine Ostberlinerin schrieb in der „Berliner Zeitung": „Mein Enkel, stolz darauf, dem Krippenalter entwachsen zu sein, weigert sich störrisch, in die „Kita" zu gehen. Bei dem Wort „Kindergarten" strahlende Augen, bei „Kita" Protest und Widerwillen. Da werden sich einige Kitarinnen noch auf einiges gefaßt machen müssen. Ich will alles dafür tun, daß dem Kleinen die schöne altdeutsche Bezeichnung

„Kindergarten" nicht abhanden kommt." Ähnlich heftig ablehnend reagierten im Sommer 1991 mehrere Ostberliner Leser der „Berliner Zeitung", als das Kürzel *Tram* statt *Straßenbahn* für das Verkehrsmittel Straßenbahn, das in Westberlin nicht vorhanden ist, vom Senat in Ostberlin eingeführt und in den Medien verwendet wurde, auch in den Zusammensetzungen *Trambahn*, *Tramschienen*. In einem Leserbrief behauptet ein Ostberliner, daß der Senat die Bezeichnung *Tram* mit ähnlichen Methoden durchsetzen wolle, wie es die Oberen der DDR mit *Telespargel* für den Fernsehturm getan haben.

(Schönfeld 1993: 201)

Reactions such as this are good examples of sociolinguistic insecurity or hypersensitivity, and they show very clearly how linguistic change is often not merely a consequence of social change but also a part of it. However, they are also characteristic of the early stages of change, and it is already clear that in spite of occasional attempts to revert to older, GDR-typical terms, the changes are becoming established and people are adapting to them quite rapidly. At the same time, it is likely to take a generation or so for the underlying differences to fade:

Ebenso undenkbar für Westdeutsche ist die in einer Ostberliner Zeitung erschienene Todesanzeige: „Nach einem arbeits- und entbehrungsreichen Leben, geprägt von Krieg und Faschismus sowie unermüdlichem Engagement für Frieden und soziale Gerechtigkeit, verstarb meine liebe Mutter, unsere Omi, Genossin . . . ". W. Lepenies, der diesen Text zitiert, kommentiert ihn wie folgt [. . .]: „Dieser Text – der in der kommunistenfreien Bundesrepublik nie hätte erscheinen können – verrät das politische Ressentiment der ostdeutschen Hinterbliebenen; die Überheblichkeit des westdeutschen Lesers aber liegt in seinem Unwillen, zu erkennen, daß sich hinter diesen parteikonformen, ihm fremden und unverständlichen Abschiedsworten ein Lebenslauf verbirgt, der eine eigene Würde und Legitimität beansprucht: Noch im Tode zeigt sich, wie anders die Deutschen in Ost und West in den letzten vierzig Jahren gelebt haben."

(Fraas 1993: 261)

■■■ Explore the problems of sameness and difference raised in this chapter, showing the significance in the context of contemporary Germany of the relationship between social and linguistic change.

Further reading

Burkhardt and Fritzsche (1992), a collection of essays on different aspects of language use during and after the *Wende*.

Clyne (1995), Chapter 3, for a good overview of East/West language debate with many examples.

Good (1993), for a discussion of the term in the title with many illustrations; the other articles in this special issue of the journal *Muttersprache* are also worth consulting.

Lerchner (1992), an interesting collection of essays by East German linguists.

Polenz (1993), a review of articles and books on the subject published between 1990 and 1993.

Schlosser (1990), probably the best account of the forms and functions of language in the GDR.

Schönfeld and Schlobinski (1995), for a clear, concise discussion of socio-linguistic change in Berlin after the *Wende*, with many examples.

Stevenson (1993), for a historical analysis of the relationship between language and national identity in Germany, including a discussion of the East/West debate.

Stevenson (1995c), for a discussion of the reasons for communicative and adaptive problems confronting East Germans after unification.

Welke et al. (1992), special issue of a journal, containing a number of articles dealing with different aspects of the topic.

•   •   •

Index of terms

(Note: The index is intended only as a brief guide to the ways selected concepts are used in this book. In many cases, the terms are open to a wide range of definitions and interpretations.)

239

sound on an adjacent one, e.g. *geben* pronounced as [ge:bm̩].

autochthonous 21
Resident in a particular place from earliest known times.

basilect 162
The most rudimentary variety of a pidgin language.

code-mixing 167
Blending two speech varieties (languages, dialects, etc.) together within a single utterance.

code-switching 20
Changing from one speech variety (language, dialect, etc.) to another during a conversation.

colloquial speech 62
A general term for speech forms that differ less markedly from standard German than dialects and are used over a wider geographical area.

communicative competence 38
The knowledge of the norms or conventions governing the use of different forms of language according to the social situation in a given speech community.

complementary distribution 37
(In this context) a relationship between two language varieties in which each is used exclusively for one set of functions (or in one set of domains).

copula 164
A verb like 'be' or 'seem' that links a subject with a comple-ment both of which refer to the same thing or person, e.g. 'she is a doctor'.

creole 172
A pidgin that has developed into

a fully fledged language and become the mother tongue of a speech community.

diachronic 5
Referring to the historical development of a phenomenon (such as language).

dialect 62
Definitions vary, but the term is used here to mean any non-standard speech form that differs significantly from standard German at all linguistic levels and is associated with a particular geographical (usually rural) location.

diglossia 37
A particular form of societal multilingualism in which the two languages or language varieties are said to be in complementary distribution.

diphthong 67
A vowel sound in which there is an audible change during its production, e.g. [ai], [au].

domain 37
A social setting such as school, home, church or workplace.

elision 80
The omission of sounds or syllables in connected speech, e.g. *sie ist 'ne alte Bekannte von mir.*

empirical 130
Based on experiment and observation rather than theory.

etymology 5
The study of (or an account of) the origin and history of a word.

foreigner talk 175
A simplified form of a language

used by native speakers in communication with non-native speakers who are (presumed to be) not fully proficient in the language.

fricative 67
A consonant produced by forcing air through a narrow gap in the vocal tract, causing audible friction, e.g. [f], [s].

front vowel 67
Vowel produced with the tongue at or near the front of the mouth, e.g. [i:].

generic 148
Refers to a class of word that denotes a class of items, e.g. 'bird', which subsumes eagle, sparrow, etc., or 'the reader of this book', meaning 'all readers of this book'.

hyponymy 151
A semantic relationship between two words, in which the more specific term is included in the more general, e.g. 'cat' and 'dog' are both hyponyms of 'animal'; in this example, animal is said to be the 'superordinate' term.

hypotactic 120
Refers to sentence structures in which one component is dependent on, or subordinate to, another, e.g. *Wir sind alle in die Kneipe gegangen, nachdem wir unsere Aufsätze eingereicht hatten.*

individual multilingualism 22
The ability of an individual to use more than one language with some degree of proficiency.

inflecting 167
Refers to a language (e.g. Latin)

in which words often contain more than one grammatical component, but where each component cannot necessarily be identified as a separate item, e.g. in 'in den Wolken', *den* contains the elements 'definite article', 'plural', and 'dative'.

isogloss 72
A line on a map indicating the boundary of an area in which a particular linguistic feature is used.

language maintenance 34
An outcome of situations in which two or more languages are in contact, whereby both (or all) of the languages continue to co-exist.

language shift 34
An outcome of language contact situations whereby one of the languages displaces the other(s).

lenition 67
Process by which a sound becomes less strongly articulated, e.g. when 'writer' is pronounced like 'rider'.

lexis 68
Vocabulary.

lingua franca 45
Any language used to permit communication between speakers of different native languages.

linguistic relatedness 10
A principle used in determining whether two or more linguistic 'varieties' may be considered forms of the same language: do they share certain grammatical structures and vocabulary?

speech community 34
Used here in the very loose sense of a group of people sharing a linguistic repertoire (see Hudson 1996: 25–30 for a discussion of various definitions).

speech event 126
A communicative exchange which can be analysed in terms of identifiable, culture-specific structural patterns, e.g. greetings, ordering a drink, telling a joke.

standard 10
A form or variety of a language that has been standardised through the writing of grammars, compiling of dictionaries, etc.

stop 67
See plosive.

style 111
Has many different definitions; here, it is used in reference to those aspects of a text over which the writer/speaker has considerable control, and it is characterised in terms such as formal/informal, personal/impersonal, serious/humorous.

synchronic 5
Referring to a particular point in time.

tag question 80
A question attached to a statement inviting either

a positive or negative response, e.g. it's boiling, isn't it?

talk 127
A term used to refer to speech as a form of patterned social behaviour.

territorial principle 32
(In this context) the principle that a particular language (or languages) has official status within a given territory and must be used in all dealings with official authorities, etc.

text type 94
A means of classifying individual texts (whether written or spoken) for the purpose of description and analysis, e.g. letter, interview, newspaper article.

Überdachung 10
The idea that a single 'standard' language variety has an 'umbrella' effect enabling two or more non-standard varieties to be classified as belonging to the same language.

variable 79
A linguistic feature that is subject to social or stylistic variation and can therefore be realised in two or more ways.

variant 79
One of the possible realisations of a sociolinguistic variable.

• • •

Bibliography

Ammer, Andreas and Elke Link (eds) (1989) *München zwischen Sekt und Selters*, Cadolzburg: ars vivendi verlag.

Ammon, Ulrich (1972) 'Zur sozialen Funktion der pronominalen Anrede im Deutschen', *Zeitschrift für Literaturwissenschaft und Linguistik* 7: 73–88.

—— (1991a) *Die internationale Stellung der deutschen Sprache*, Berlin, New York: de Gruyter.

—— (1991b) 'Die Stellung der deutschen Sprache in Europa und in der Welt im Verhältnis zu ihrer Stellung in den EG-Gremien', *Sociolinguistica* 5: 70–84.

—— (1995a) 'To what extent is German an international language?', in Stevenson (1995a), pp. 25–53.

—— (1995b) *Die deutsche Sprache in Deutschland, Österreich und der Schweiz*, Berlin, New York: de Gruyter.

—— (1995c) 'Kloss, Knödel oder Klumpen im Hals? Über Teutonismen und die nationale Einseitigkeit der Dudenbände', *Sprachreport* 4/95: 1–4.

—— Ulrich Knoop and Ingulf Radtke (eds) (1977) *Grundlagen einer dialektorientierten Sprachdidaktik*, Weinheim: Beltz.

Appel, René and Pieter Muysken (1987) *Language Contact and Bilingualism*, London: Edward Arnold.

Arends, Jacques, Pieter Muysken and Norval Smith (eds) (1995) *Pidgins and Creoles*, Amsterdam: Benjamins.

Auer, Peter (1994) 'Broken discourses: cultural and intercultural aspects of East German job interviews', paper presented

at the 10th Sociolinguistics Symposium, University of Lancaster, March 1994.

Augst, Gerhard (1977) *Sprachnorm und Sprachwandel*, Wiesbaden: Athenaion.

——— (ed.) (1992) *Deutsche Sprache – Einheit und Vielfalt* (= *Der Deutschunterricht*, 44/6), Velber: Friedrich.

——— and Wolfgang Werner Sauer (1992) 'Der Duden – Konsequenzen aus der Wende?' in Welke et al. (1992), pp. 71–92.

Barbour, Stephen and Patrick Stevenson (1990) *Variation in German*, Cambridge: Cambridge University Press.

Barsch, J. (1966) *Deutscher Alltag. Ein Gesprächsbuch für Ausländer*, Munich.

Bayer, Klaus (1979) 'Die Anredepronomina Du und Sie', *Deutsche Sprache* 3: 212–19.

BBC (1992–4) *Deutschland heute*, Series 1/2/3, London: BBC Select.

Beneke, Jürgen (1993) '„Am Anfang wollten wir zueinander . . ." – Was wollen wir heute? Sprachlich-kommunikative Reflexionen Jugendlicher aus dem Ost- und Westteil Berlins zu einem bewegenden Zeitthema', in Reiher and Läzer (1993), pp. 210–38.

Benz, Wolfgang (ed.) (1983) *Die Bundesrepublik Deutschland, Band 2: Gesellschaft*, Frankfurt am Main: Fischer Taschenbuch Verlag.

Berg, Imke, Manfred Maier, Artur Ruppert, Erhard Schultz, Irmgard Schmidt-Sommer and Heinrich Wacker (1978) *Situationen*, Stuttgart: Klett.

Biber, Douglas (1991) *Variation Across Speech and Writing*, Cambridge: Cambridge University Press.

Bickel, Hans and Robert Schläpfer (eds) (1994) *Mehrsprachigkeit: Eine Herausforderung*, Aarau: Sauerländer.

Bickes, Hans and Annette Trabold (eds) (1994) *Förderung der sprachlichen Kultur in der Bundesrepublik Deutschland*, Stuttgart: Bleicher Verlag.

Bismarck, Otto von (1973) *Werke in Auswahl. Band 5: Reichsgestaltung und europäische Friedensbewahrung* (edited by Alfred Milatz), Darmstadt.

Blackshire-Belay, Carol (1991) *Language Contact: Verb Morphology in German of Foreign Workers*, Tübingen: Narr.

Born, Joachim and Gerhard Stickel (eds) (1993) *Deutsch als Verkehrssprache in Europa* (= Institut für deutsche Sprache Jahrbuch 1992), Düsseldorf: Schwann.

Braun, Peter (1987) *Tendenzen in der deutschen Gegenwartssprache*, Stuttgart: Kohlhammer.

BRD Report (1991) *Maskuline und feminine Personenbezeichnungen in der Rechtssprache. Bericht der Arbeitsgruppe Rechtssprache vom 17. Januar 1990*, Deutscher Bundestag. Drucksache 12/1041.

Brunhöber, Hannelore (1983) 'Wohnen', in Benz (1983), pp. 183–208.

Büchner, Georg (1971) *Dantons Tod and Woyzeck* (edited by Margaret Jacobs), Manchester: Manchester University Press.

Burkert, Michael (1993) 'Deutsch als Amts- und Arbeitssprache in der Europäischen Gemeinschaft', in Born and Stickel (1993), pp. 44–63.

Burkhardt, Armin and K. Peter Fritzsche (eds) (1992) *Sprache im Umbruch*, Berlin, New York: de Gruyter.

Cameron, Deborah (1995) *Verbal Hygiene*, London: Routledge.

Chambers, Jack and Peter Trudgill (1980) *Dialectology*, Cambridge: Cambridge University Press.

Clahsen, Harald, Jürgen Meisel and Manfred Pienemann (1983) *Deutsch als Zweitsprache*, Tübingen: Narr.

Clyne, Michael (1968) 'Zum Pidgin-Deutsch der Gastarbeiter', *Zeitschrift für Mundartforschung* 35: 130–9.

—— (1995) *The German Language in a Changing Europe*, Cambridge: Cambridge University Press.

Comrie, Bernard (ed.) (1987) *The World's Major Languages*, London, Sydney: Croom Helm.

Coulmas, Florian (ed.) (1981) *Conversational Routine*, The Hague: Mouton.

—— (1985) 'Reden ist Silber, Schreiben ist Gold', *Zeitschrift für Literaturwissenschaft und Linguistik* 15: 94–112.

—— (ed.) (1991a) *A Language Policy for the European Community*, Berlin: de Gruyter.

—— (1991b) 'Die Sprachenregelung in den Organen der EG als Teil einer europäischen Sprachenpolitik', *Sociolinguistica* 5: 24–36.

—— (1992) *Die Wirtschaft mit der Sprache*, Frankfurt: Suhrkamp.

—— (1993) 'Was ist die deutsche Sprache wert?', in Born and Stickel (1993), pp. 9–25.

—— (1995) 'Germanness: Language and nation', in Stevenson (1995a), pp 55–68.

Crystal, David (1987) *The Cambridge Encyclopaedia of Language*, Cambridge: Cambridge University Press.

—— (1992) *An Encyclopaedic Dictionary of Language and Languages*, Oxford: Blackwell.

Deutscher Bundestag (1993) *Plenarprotokoll* 12/140, 11 February 1993, Stenographischer Bericht.

Dieckmann, Friedrich (1995) 'Auf deutsch ins Reine', *Frankfurter Allgemeine Zeitung*, 12 October.

Dittmar, Norbert, Peter Schlobinski, and Inge Wachs (1986) *Berlinisch*, Berlin: Verlag Arno Spitz.

Drosdowski, Günther (1988) *Ist unsere Sprache noch zu retten?*, Mannheim, Vienna.

Durrell, Martin (1992) *Using German*, Cambridge: Cambridge University Press.

Edwards, John (1994) *Multilingualism*, Oxford: Blackwell.

Eggerer, Wilhelm and Hans Rötzer (1978) *Manz Großer Analysenband I*, Munich: Manz.

Eichheim, Hubert (1993) 'Deutsch in einem zusammenwachsenden Europa – aus der Sicht des Goethe-Instituts', in Born and Stickel (1993), pp. 262–72.

Eurydice (1989) *Teaching of Languages in the European Community: Statistics*, Brussels: Eurydice.

Fasold, Ralph (1984) *The Sociolinguistics of Society*, Oxford: Blackwell.

Felix, Sascha (ed.) (1980) *Second Language Development*, Tübingen: Narr.

Ferguson, Charles (1976) 'The structure and use of politeness formulas', *Language in Society* 5: 137–51.

Finkenstaedt, Thomas and Konrad Schröder (1990) *Sprachschranken statt Zollschranken? Grundlegung einer Fremdsprachenpolitik für das Europa von morgen*, Essen: Stifterverband für die Deutsche Wissenschaft.

Fischer, Hardi and Uri Trier (1962) *Das Verhältnis zwischen Deutschschweizer und Westschweizer*, Berne, Stuttgart: Huber.

Fix, Ulla (1992) 'Rituelle Kommunikation im öffentlichen Sprachgebrauch der DDR und ihre Begleitumstände', in Lerchner (1992), pp. 3–99.

—— (1994) 'Sprache vor und nach der „Wende": „Gewendete" Texte – „gewendete" Textsorten', in Heringer et al. (1994), pp. 131–46.

Flood, John, Paul Salmon, Olive Sayce and Christopher Wells (eds) (1993) *Das unsichtbare Band der Sprache*, Stuttgart: Akademischer Verlag.

Fraas, Claudia (1993) 'Verständigungsschwierigkeiten der Deutschen', *Muttersprache* 103: 260–3.

—— (1995) 'Die Deutschen nach der Vereinigung', *Sprachreport* 4/95: 7–11.

Gesellschaft für deutsche Sprache (ed.) (1993) *Wörter und Unwörter*, Niedernhausen: Falken-Verlag.

Gloy, Klaus (1977) 'Ökologische Aspekte der Dialekt-Verwendung', in Ammon et al. (1977), pp. 73–91.

Glück, Helmut (1992a) 'Die internationale Stellung des Deutschen auf dem europäischen Arbeitsmarkt', in Kramer and Weiß (1992), pp. 47–75.

—— (1992b) 'Aktuelle Beobachtungen zum Namen Deutsch', in Welke et al. (1992), pp. 141–71.

—— and Wolfgang Werner Sauer (1990) *Gegenwartsdeutsch*, Stuttgart: Metzler.

—— (1992) 'Man spricht Deutsch. German spoken. On parle allemand. Die deutsche Spracheinheit, von außen gesehen durch die inländische Brille', in Augst (1992), pp. 16–27.

—— (1995) 'Directions of change in contemporary German', in Stevenson (1995a), pp. 95–116.

Good, Colin (1993) 'Über die „Kultur des Mißverständnisses" im vereinten Deutschland', *Muttersprache* 103: 249–59.

Gorny, Hildegard (1995) 'Feministische Sprachkritik', in Stötzel and Wengeler (1995), pp. 517–62.

Grimes, Barbara (ed.) (1984) *Languages of the World: Ethnologue*, Dallas: Wycliffe Bible Translation.

Grimm, Jacob (1870/1976) *Deutsche Grammatik* Band I, Hildesheim: Olms.

Groom, Winston (1986/1994) *Forrest Gump* (German translation), Munich: Heyne.

Haas, Walter (1982) 'Die deutschsprachige Schweiz', in Schläpfer (1982), pp. 77–160.

Haefs, Hanswilhelm (ed.) (1989) *Der Fischer Weltalmanach*, Frankfurt am Main: Fischer Taschenbuch Verlag.

Halliday, Michael (1989) *Spoken and Written Language*, 2nd edn, Oxford: Blackwell.

Handelskammer Hamburg (ed.) (1989) *Konsulats- und Mustervorschriften*, 28th edn, Hamburg: Carl H. Dieckmann.

Heidelberger Forschungsprojekt 'Pidgin-Deutsch' (1975) *Sprache und Kommunikation ausländischer Arbeiter*, Kronberg: Scriptor.

Heller, Klaus (1996) *Rechtschreibreform* (= *Sprachreport, Extra-Ausgabe*) Mannheim: Institut für deutsche Sprache.

Hellinger, Marlis (1990) *Kontrastive feministische Linguistik*, Munich: Hueber.

—— (1995) 'Language and Gender', in Stevenson (1995a), pp. 279–314.

——, Marion Kremer and Beate Schräpel (1985) *Empfehlungen zur Vermeidung von sexistischem Sprachgebrauch in öffentlicher Sprache*, Hannover: University of Hannover English Department.

Heringer, Hans Jürgen, Gunhild Samson, Michel Kauffmann and Wolfgang Bader (eds) (1994) *Tendenzen der deutschen Gegenwartssprache*, Tübingen: Niemeyer.

Hess-Lüttich, Ernest W. B. (ed.) (1992) *Medienkultur – Kulturkonflikt. Massenmedien in der interkulturellen und internationalen Kommunikation*, Opladen: Westdeutscher Verlag.

Hinnenkamp, Volker (1982) *Foreigner Talk und Tarzanisch*, Hamburg: Buske.

—— (1989) *Interaktionale Soziolinguistik und interkulturelle Kommunikation*, Tübingen: Niemeyer.

Hoberg, Rudolf (1990) 'Sprachverfall? Wie sieht es mit den sprachlichen Fähigkeiten der Deutschen aus?', *Muttersprache* 2–3/90: 233–43.

Hoffmann, Charlotte (1991) *An Introduction to Bilingualism*, London: Longman.

Hoffmann, Fernand (1979) *Sprachen in Luxemburg: sprachwissenschaftliche und literaturhistorische Beschreibung der Triglossie-Situation*, Wiesbaden: Steiner.

Holly, Werner (1995) 'Language and television', in Stevenson (1995a), pp. 339–73.

Holm, John (1988) *Pidgins and Creoles*, Cambridge: Cambridge University Press.

Holmes, Janet (1992) *An Introduction to Sociolinguistics*, London: Longman.

Hopfer, Reinhard (1992) 'Christa Wolfs Streit mit dem „großen Bruder". Politische Diskurse der DDR im Herbst 1989', in Burkhardt and Fritzsche (1992), pp. 111–33.

House, Juliane and Gabriele Kasper (1981) 'Politeness markers in English and German', in Coulmas (1981), pp. 157–85.

Hudson, Richard (1996) *Sociolinguistics*, 2nd edn, Cambridge: Cambridge University Press.

Jacobson, Howard (1983) *Coming from Behind*, London: Chatto & Windus.

Keim, Inken (1984) *Untersuchungen zum Deutsch türkischer Arbeiter*, Tübingen: Narr.

Klein, Wolf Peter and Ingwer Paul (eds) (1993) *Sprachliche Aufmerksamkeit. Glossen und Marginalien zur Sprache der Gegenwart*, Heidelberg: Universitätsverlag C. Winter.

Klein, Wolfgang (ed.) (1986) *Der Wahn vom Sprachverfall und andere Mythen* (= *Zeitschrift für Literaturwissenschaft und Linguistik* 62), Göttingen: Vandenhoeck und Rupprecht.

Kloss, Heinz (1978) *Die Entwicklung neuer germanischer Kultursprachen seit 1800*, 2nd edn, Düsseldorf: Schwann.

König, Werner (1978) *dtv-Atlas zur deutschen Sprache*, Munich: dtv.

Kosog, O. (1912) *Unsere Rechtschreibung und die Notwendigkeit ihrer gründlichen Reform*, Leipzig.

Kramer, Wolfgang and Reinhold Weiß (eds) (1992) *Fremdsprachen in der Wirtschaft*, Cologne: Deutscher Instituts-Verlag.

Kretzenbacher, Heinz (1991) 'Vom *Sie* zum *Du* – und retour?', in Kretzenbacher and Segebrecht (1991), pp. 9–77.

Kretzenbacher, Heinz and Wulf Segebrecht (1991) *Vom Sie zum Du – mehr als eine neue Konvention?*, Hamburg: Luchterhand.

Lang, Ewald (1990) *Wendehals und Stasi-Laus. Demo-Sprüche aus der DDR*, Munich: Heyne.

Lansburgh, Werner (1977) *Dear Doosie. Eine Liebesgeschichte in Briefen*, Frankfurt am Main: Fischer Taschenbuch Verlag.

Lerchner, Gotthard (ed.) (1992) *Sprachgebrauch im Wandel*, Frankfurt am Main: Lang.

Liebe Reséndiz, Julia (1992) 'Woran erkennen sich Ost- und Westdeutsche? Eine Spracheinstellungsstudie am Beispiel von Rundfunksendungen', in Welke et al. (1992), pp. 127–40.

Macpherson, A. S. (1931) *Deutsches Leben*, London: Ginn.

McRae, Kenneth (1983) *Conflict and Compromise in Multilingual Societies*, vol. 1, Switzerland, Ontario: Wilfred Laurier University Press.

Mattheier, Klaus (1980) *Pragmatik und Soziologie der Dialekte*, Heidelberg: Quelle und Meyer.

Meisel, Jürgen (1980) 'Linguistic simplification', in Felix (1980), pp. 13–46.

Milroy, James and Lesley Milroy (1985) *Authority in Language*, London: Routledge.

Möhn, Dieter and Roland Pelka (1984) *Fachsprachen*, Tübingen: Niemeyer.

Mohr, Annette and Ulrike Schneider (1994) 'Die Situation der deutschen Sprache in internationalen Organisationen', *Info DaF (Informationen Deutsch als Fremdsprache)* 6/1994: 612–31.

Moosmüller, Sylvia (1995) 'Evaluation of language use in public discourse: language attitudes in Austria', in Stevenson (1995a), pp. 257–78.

—— and Ralf Vollmann (in press) 'Das Phänomen „Standardsprache" am Beispiel Österreichs', *Sociolinguistika Slovaka*.

Muckenhaupt, Manfred (1994) 'Von der Tagesschau zur Infoshow. Sprachliche und journalistische Tendenzen in der Geschichte der Fernsehnachrichten', in Heringer et al. (1994), pp. 81–120.

Muhr, Rudolf (ed.) (1993) *Internationale Arbeiten zum österreichischen Deutsch und seinen nachbarsprachlichen Bezügen*, Vienna: Verlag Hölder-Pichler-Tempsky.

Müller, Gerhard (1994) 'Der „Besserwessi" und die „innere Mauer". Anmerkungen zum Sprachgebrauch im vereinigten Deutschland', *Muttersprache* 2/94: 118–36.

Müller, Martin and Lukas Wertenschlag (1985) *Los emol. Schweizerdeutsch verstehen*, Zurich: Langenscheidt.

Müller-Thurau, Claus Peter (1983) *Lass uns mal 'ne Schnecke angraben. Sprache und Sprüche der Jugendszene*, Düsseldorf: Econ Verlag.

'Neue Regeln: Jetzt oder nie', in *Der Spiegel* 23 October 1995, pp. 102–9.

Neuner, Gerhard, Reiner Schmidt, Heinz Wilms and Manfred Zirkel (1986) *Deutsch aktiv*, Berlin, Munich: Langenscheidt.

Newton, Gerald (ed.) (1996) *Luxembourg and Letzebuergesch: Language and Communication at the Crossroads of Europe*, Oxford: Clarendon Press.

Polenz, Peter von (1993) 'Die Sprachrevolte in der DDR im Herbst 1989', *Zeitschrift für germanistische Linguistik* 21: 127–49.

—— (1994) *Deutsche Sprachgeschichte*, Band II, Berlin, New York: de Gruyter.

Pusch, Luise (1984) *Das Deutsche als Männersprache*, Frankfurt: Suhrkamp.

—— (1990) *Alle Menschen werden Schwestern*, Frankfurt: Suhrkamp.

Püschel, Ulrich (1992) 'Von der Pyramide zum Cluster. Textsorten und Textsortenmischung in Fernsehnachrichten', in Hess-Lüttich (1992), pp. 233–58.

Reich, Jens (1991) 'Ost ist Ost und West ist West. Über die kulturellen und seelischen Konflikte in Deutschland', *Frankfurter Rundschau* (23 March).

Reiher, Ruth (ed.) (1994) *Sprache im Konflikt*, Berlin: de Gruyter.

—— and Rüdiger Läzer (eds) (1993) *Wer spricht das wahre Deutsch?*, Berlin: Aufbau Taschenbuch Verlag.

Roche, Jörg (1989) *Deutsche Xenolekte. Struktur und Variation der Äußerungen deutscher Muttersprachler in der Kommunikation mit Ausländern*, Berlin: de Gruyter.

Romaine, Suzanne (1988) *Pidgin and Creole Languages*, London: Longman.

—— (1994) *Language in Society*, Oxford: Oxford University Press.

Rost-Roth, Martina (1995) 'Language in intercultural communication', in Stevenson (1995a), pp. 169–204.

Runge, Erika (1968) *Bottroper Protokolle*, Frankfurt am Main: Suhrkamp.

Russ, Charles (ed.) (1990) *The Dialects of Modern German*, London: Routledge.

—— (1994) *The German Language Today*, London: Routledge.

Samel, Ingrid (1995) *Einführung in die feministische Sprachwissenschaft*, Berlin: Erich Schmidt.

Sauer, Wolfgang Werner (1988) *Der «Duden». Geschichte und Aktualität eines „Volkswörterbuchs"*, Stuttgart: Metzler.

—— and Helmut Glück (1995) 'Norms and reforms: fixing the form of the language', in Stevenson (1995a), pp. 69–93.

Saville-Troike, Muriel (1989) *The Ethnography of Communication*, Oxford: Blackwell.

Schank, Gerd and Gisela Schoenthal (1983) *Gesprochene Sprache*, Tübingen: Niemeyer.

Scharschik, Walter (1973) *Herrschaft durch Sprache. Politische Reden*, Stuttgart: Reclam.

Scheuringer, Hermann (1992) 'Deutsches Volk und deutsche Sprache', *Muttersprache* 102: 218–29.

Schläpfer, Robert (ed.) (1982) *Die viersprachige Schweiz*, Zürich, Cologne: Benziger.

Schlobinski, Peter (1984) *Berlinisch für Berliner*, Berlin: arani.

—— (1987) *Stadtsprache Berlin*, Berlin, New York: de Gruyter.

—— (1995) '*Jugendsprachen*: Speech Styles of Youth Subcultures', in Stevenson (1995a), pp. 315–37.

Schlosser, Horst Dieter (1990) *Die deutsche Sprache in der DDR*, Cologne: Verlag Wissenschaft und Politik.

—— (ed.) (1991a) *Kommunikationsbedingungen und Alltagssprache in der ehemaligen DDR*, Hamburg: Buske.

—— (1991b) 'Notwendige Rückblicke auf eine historisch gewordene Kommunikationsgemeinschaft', in Schlosser (1991a), pp. 7–17.

—— (1993) 'Das Unwort des Jahres', in Gesellschaft für deutsche Sprache (1993), pp. 43–50.

Schmid, Carol (1981) *Conflict and Consensus in Switzerland*, Berkeley: University of California Press.

Schoenthal, Gisela (1989) 'Personenbezeichnungen im Deutschen als Gegenstand feministischer Sprachkritik', *Zeitschrift für germanistische Linguistik* 17: 296–314.

Schönfeld, Helmut (1993) 'Auch sprachlich beigetreten? Sprachliche Entwicklungen im zusammenwachsenden Berlin', in Reiher and Läzer (1993), pp. 187–209.

—— and Peter Schlobinski (1995) 'After the Wall: social change and linguistic variation in Berlin', in Stevenson (1995a), pp. 117–34.

Sempé, Jean-Jacques (1962) '*Women and Children First*', London: Perpetua Books.

Sieber, Peter (ed.) (1994) *Sprachfähigkeiten – Besser als ihr Ruf und nötiger denn je!*, Aarau, Frankfurt am Main, Salzburg: Sauerländer.

statec (1993) *Luxembourg in Figures*, Luxembourg: Service Central de la Statistique et des Etudes Economiques.

Stedje, Astrid (1989) *Deutsche Sprache gestern und heute*, Munich: Wilhelm Fink Verlag.

Stein, Bernd (1995) *Hamburg City Blues*, Hamburg: Screen Line.

Steinberg, Jonathan (1976) *Why Switzerland?*, Cambridge: Cambridge University Press.

Stevenson, Patrick (1993) 'The German language and the construction of national identities', in Flood et al. (1993), pp. 333–56.

—— (ed.) (1995a) *The German Language and the Real World*, Oxford: Clarendon Press.

—— (1995b) 'The study of real language: observing the observers', in Stevenson (1995a), pp. 1–23.

—— (1995c) '*Gegenwartsbewältigung*: Coming to Terms with the Present in Germany', *Multilingua* 14/1: 39–59.

Stickel, Gerhard (1987) 'Was halten Sie vom heutigen Deutsch? Ergebnisse einer Zeitungsumfrage', in Wimmer (1987), pp. 280–313.

—— (1988) 'Beantragte staatliche Regelungen zur „sprachlichen Gleichbehandlung": Darstellung und Kritik', *Zeitschrift für germanistische Linguistik* 16: 330–55.

Stötzel, Georg and Martin Wengeler (eds) (1995) *Kontroverse Begriffe*, Berlin, New York: de Gruyter.

Straßner, Erich (1995) *Deutsche Sprachkultur. Von der Barbarensprache zur Weltsprache*, Tübingen: Niemeyer.

Swiss Report (1991) *Sprachliche Gleichbehandlung von Frau und Mann in der Gesetzes- und Verwaltungssprache. Bericht einer interdepartementalen Arbeitsgruppe der Bundesverwaltung*, Schweizerische Bundeskanzlei.

Teichmann, Christine (1991) 'Von der „langue de bois" zur „Sprache der Wende"', *Muttersprache* 3/91: 252–65.

Tekinay, Alev (1984) 'Wie eine „Mischsprache" entsteht', *Muttersprache* 5/6: 396–403.

Teubert, Wolfgang (1992) 'Die Deutschen und ihre Identität', in Burkhardt and Fritzsche (1992), pp. 233–52.

Thierse, Wolfgang (1993) '„Sprich, damit ich dich sehe". Beobachtungen zum Verhältnis von Sprache und Politik in der DDR-Vergangenheit', in Born and Stickel (1993), pp. 114–26.

Thimm, Caja (1993) '„Ja, liebe Zeit – das war doch charmant vorgetragen!" Weibliche Sprachform als Anlaß politischen Konfliktes', in Reiher and Läzer (1993), pp. 161–86.

Todd, Loreto (1990) *Pidgins and Creoles*, 2nd edn, London: Routledge.

Töteberg, Michael (ed.) (1990) *Fassbinders Filme 3*, Frankfurt: Verlag der Autoren.

Townson, Michael (1992) *Mother-tongue and Fatherland*, Manchester: Manchester University Press.

Trabold, Annette (1993) *Sprachpolitik, Sprachkritik und Öffentlichkeit*, Wiesbaden: Deutscher Universitäts-Verlag.

Trömel-Plötz, Senta (1982) *Frauensprache: Sprache der Veränderung*, Frankfurt: Fischer.

Vassberg, Liliane (1993) *Alsatian Acts of Identity*, Clevedon: Multilingual Matters.

Wachau, Susanne (1990) 'Empirische Untersuchung zur Sprache Jugendlicher: Über Sprechstile, Schreibstile und Sprachbewußtheit', unpublished MA thesis, University of Osnabrück.

Walker, Alastair (1980) 'North Frisia and linguistics', *Nottingham Linguistic Circular* 9/1: 18–31.

Wardhaugh, Ronald (1985) *How Conversation Works*, Oxford: Blackwell.

—— (1992) *An Introduction to Sociolinguistics*, Oxford: Blackwell.

Weinrich, Harald (1976) 'Die Wahrheit der Wörterbücher', in *Probleme der Lexikologie und Lexikographie. Jahrbuch 1975 des Instituts für deutsche Sprache*, Düsseldorf: Schwann.

Welke, Klaus, Wolfgang Werner Sauer and Helmut Glück (eds) (1992) *Die deutsche Sprache nach der Wende* (= Germanistische Linguistik 110–111), Hildesheim: Olms.

Wells, Christopher (1985) *German: A Linguistic History to 1945*, Oxford: Oxford University Press.

Weydt, Harald (1993) 'Zärtl. Sie, m. bet. frl. Figur, die (. . .) eine m.-l. WA bes., sucht . . . Partnerschaftsanzeigen in Ost und West', in Klein and Paul (1993), pp. 213–19.

Wie funktioniert das? Die Technik im Leben von heute (1978) Mannheim: Bibliographisches Institut.

Wildermuth, Rosemarie (ed.) (1978) *Heute und die 30 Jahre davor*, Munich: Ellermann.

Wimmer, Rainer (ed.) (1987) *Sprachtheorie. Der Sprachbegriff in Wissenschaft und Alltag* (= *Jahrbuch 1986 des Instituts für deutsche Sprache*), Düsseldorf: Schwann.

Ylönen, Sabine (1992) 'Probleme deutsch-deutscher Kommunikation', *Sprachreport* 2–3/90: 17–20.

Zabel, Hermann (1989) *Der gekippte Keiser*, Bochum: Brockmeyer.

—— (1995a) 'Die 3. Wiener Gespräche zur Neuregelung der deutschen Rechtschreibung im Spiegel der Presse', *Muttersprache* 2/95: 119–40.

—— (1995b) *Die neue deutsche Rechtschreibung*, Niedernhausen: Falken-Verlag.

Zemb, Jean-Marie (1995) 'Alles gleich ist alles anders', *Frankfurter Allgemeine Zeitung*, 2 September.

Zimmer, Dieter E. (1986) *Redens Arten*, Zürich: Haffmans Verlag.

—— (1995a) 'Ein Gräuel . . . doch längst keine Katastrofe', *Die Zeit*, 15 September.

—— (1995b) 'Sonst stirbt die deutsche Sprache', *Die Zeit*, 23 June.

•   •   •